# 21 Questions for 21 Millionaires

## How Ordinary People Create Extraordinary Success

Brandon Pipkin

Cover design by Dzubyan Marva

For more information visit www.21for21.com

© 2011 Brandon Pipkin

ISBN-13: 978-1466432338

ISBN-10: 1466432330

*To all those who seek success, financial or otherwise.*

# Table of Contents

# Chapter 1: The Truth About Success

*"I just worked real hard and the moneymaking came by accident."*

*Millionaire 21 Richard Zuschlag*

The success experts are wrong, dead wrong.

And in their excited frenzy to sell their highly marketed, tightly packaged, hyperbole-filled, *guaranteed* systems for success they are causing others to get it wrong, too.

Take back their books, CDs, and systems and get your money back from the motivational seminar. You don't need to learn "The 15 Surefire Steps to Success," or "The 8 Principles for Financial Freedom," or "The 72 Secrets of Super Wealth Building," to be successful.

You don't need written goals or the advice of a mentor and you should put your subscription to travel and luxury magazines on hold because simply dreaming about it doesn't make you rich either.

These gurus, enlightened ones, business leaders, authors, and consultants each declare that their system is *the* system guaranteed to bring you the happiness and wealth you desire. They claim to have *the* secret. They assert that their book or package holds *the* key to prosperity. They share platitudes and principles that they say are *absolutely essential* for attaining success. And they claim that their techniques are so powerful and the results so imminent that they will revolutionize your life.

Their systems, secrets, keys, platitudes, principles, and techniques are void of one important thing – the truth.

The system that was guaranteed to make you successful turns out to be a bust. The secret was something you already knew. The key unlocked wealth for the author, but not for you. The platitudes were only that and the principles and techniques were ineffective in application.

But not to be denied in your quest and hungry for success you continue your search. You run to the next guru who, unlike the last, surely must have it figured out or must have the answer for your unique situation.

*"The flame of each new theory fades, only to be replaced by another 'new and improved' solution that promises to do what the others before could not."*[1]

How many hundreds of hours and thousands of dollars are needlessly wasted each year searching for wealth and happiness without finding it?

Don't get me wrong, most of the experts believe that what they are saying is true and undoubtedly their advice has worked for some. But their "absolutely-guaranteed, works-for-everyone" systems for success are far from it.

Think about it. If there were *one, guaranteed* success system, why would all of the others be necessary? If one or even all of those systems worked for everyone, why are we not all retired and in Barbados right now?

After years of buying and believing what the experts were selling and only getting further into debt and more and more frustrated, I learned the truth about success by interviewing 21 down-to-earth millionaires about how and why they did what they did.

What I found is that not much of what they did matches what the experts say you have to do.

These millionaires' experiences prove that success isn't about the planning and hoping. It's not about reading the right book or listening to the right person's advice or in working with a mentor.

It's not about following someone else's blueprint and it certainly isn't created by wanting it badly enough. Visualization, goal setting, and thinking alone won't take you there.

It's all about–wait, could it be? A book that is willing to share its message three pages into it instead of baiting you to read forty pages into its self-absorbed, incomprehensible profundity? Yes, now continue reading–WORK.

There is no plan that will compensate for work. There is no success principle that is more powerful than work. There is no desire, visualization, or goal that accomplishes anything until it is coupled with work. There is no advice that replaces action and there is no "system" to it.

*"Work will win when wishy-washy-wishing won't."* [2]

Not only are work and its resultant sense of satisfaction their own rewards, work also creates opportunities.

In this book I share the stories of how work got 21 millionaires where they are and how it compensated for everything else. As you read the interviews with each millionaire you'll see how work is the "secret" to any success, no matter what your definition is. You will also see how hard work brought some of the millionaires even more success than they were thinking they would achieve.

These people created success not by relying on experts, gurus, or supposed enlightened ones, and they certainly didn't read books (not even this one!) to become successful. Instead, they listened to what was guiding them internally and they worked. By working hard, no matter what the circumstances, their unique path to success was created.

These millionaires worked constantly without being fanatical. They put effort into the little things. They put their nose to the grindstone and did so, in most cases, without knowing where it would lead. They were happy just to be doing something productive.

They simply worked.

There are many forgotten virtues in our world today and one of them is good old-fashioned hard work. If I am guilty of selling anything in this book, it is the truth of how 21 ordinary people created extraordinary success through hard work.

Through this book I wish to restore the value of work in the hearts and minds of any who seek happiness – financial or otherwise.

And I'm the guy who would know.

## A Little Background

Having grown up in poor circumstances, I was anxious to be successful in all areas of my adult life, especially the financial realm. I wanted to provide well for my family and repay the many acts of kindness we so frequently received from others in my formative years. For example, I remember one Christmas we received a box of toys from someone who knocked at the door and said that Santa was delayed in Kansas and had asked him to deliver a package to us.

I couldn't wait to do the same kinds of things for other people and I thought success would come easily. But I didn't understand the importance of work.

Aside from my time as a church missionary and some other experiences, I had not really worked. Sure, I would show up and do the job, but I wasn't giving it my all because my expectation was that a little work would go a long way.

I was pompous enough to believe that I was smart enough, talented enough, good looking enough, and charming enough that with only a little effort and lots of belief I would be able to move mountains. I wasn't focused on my various jobs because I was sure the right opportunity was just around the corner and everything else was temporary.

With only that little bit of work things didn't open up and happen for me the way I thought they would and should. Circumstances didn't align to make my path easy. Instead of a life of young fame and fortune, I was working two jobs just to survive.

4

Luckily, while working that second job, I was introduced to a personal development and mentorship group focused on creating success. I caught fire wanting to learn about success, leadership, wealth creation, and personal development. I was excited to learn what I was doing wrong and how I could be successful.

## Learning About Success

For the next several years I spent money on tapes, CDs, books, seminars, and presentations that promised to help me think the right way and be successful. I read websites, e-zines, newsletters, and emails. I got books and audio books from the library.

I digested whatever I could get my hands on. I availed myself of what the success and personal development gurus had to offer and was motivated to implement it.

I believed in myself; set goals; wrote those goals down, kept them where I would see them, and told others what those goals were; consulted with a mentor; envisioned success; dreamed big; did something every day to bring me closer to my dream; maintained a positive attitude; and did all of the other things the experts say are necessary to create success. I thought success, spoke success, and dreamed success. I posted pictures of what I wanted, visualized the desired end state and planned my path working backwards.

It didn't work.

Rather than success untold, I had debt untold. Rather than happiness, I had frustration.

I didn't reach the success I was told I should have been able to and consequently wondered what was wrong with me – after all, it couldn't be the experts who were wrong.

I wondered if it might be my financial circumstances that were preventing me from reaching success; maybe I needed to make more money so I could invest in the experts' complete systems. Maybe the real secrets were in there, not in their free and low cost-information that I was using. (Note the irony here of thinking I needed to make more money before I could find out about how to make more money.)

Then I thought maybe my mindset was the problem and needed to be changed. When I still couldn't create success, I thought maybe it just wasn't the right time. But then I thought about the experts' advice of "you can do anything you set your mind to," and "you're in total control of your life," so again I wondered what I was doing wrong and kept searching for the secret to success that eluded me.

Adding insult to injury, I finally figured out that I was anything but good looking or charming – so much for being able to rely on those qualities to help me on my journey.

The good news, though, is that through trying to figure out what creates success I picked up on one thing: the value of work. I was finally putting in real work and that led to a perfect storm of circumstances.

**Idea for the Book**

While I was seeking answers about how to be successful, I came across an idea by Robert Allen who described how passion and financial compensation are tied together. He said we all have unique gifts, talents, and interests, a passion, with which we have been endowed to bless the world.

He equates the sharing of one's passion to the playing of a unique note in the symphony of life. When we all play our notes, the symphony is rich and wonderful. When one doesn't share their passion, the symphony of life is impoverished of that person's sound.

Allen also asserts that when we share our passion we impact the world in such a unique and powerful way that it can't help but compensate us financially for that contribution.

Wow, what a great thought! I immediately wanted to share it with others to encourage them to share their passion with the world and help them achieve the success that I also so badly wanted.

For years I had wanted to write a book but didn't know what to write about until I came across Allen's idea. The thought came to me to interview 21 ordinary millionaires to learn how they had found their passion and thus found their success. I wanted to use millionaires who were not necessarily well known to demonstrate that you don't have to be a celebrity or athlete to live your passion and that success is closer than we think.

## What is Your Passion?

I ran across one little problem with my grand idea.

On the third interview I found that the connection between passion and success might not be what I thought it was. It was a beautiful Friday morning and I was talking with Matt, a customer-turned-friend who had sold his business for several million dollars. Earlier in the interview I had asked him if he had set goals on his path to becoming a millionaire. He hadn't.

Later I asked, "What is your passion?"

Rather quickly he responded, "I really don't know. I've been asked that question before and I honestly have never sat down and thought about what am I passionate about."

Huh?

Up to that point, based on what I had heard, read, seen, and believed, I thought success was conditioned upon finding something about which you were passionate, setting goals, and creating a plan to accomplish those goals; then pursuing that plan with discipline, focus, and determination.

Matt's answers were contrary to all of that.

Not only did he ruin the perfect subtitle for the book (Find Your Passion, Find Your Success), Matt shattered what I thought was a surefire way to find my own success and inspire others to do the same. More importantly, though, he sent me on a quest for the truth.

From that point on, my focus in the interviews was different. Rather than trying to validate the blueprint of passion creating success and prove my hypothesis right, I wanted to hear in the millionaires' own words, from their own experiences, the how and why they did what they did. I wanted the truth, whatever it was.

I wanted to know if the other millionaires, like Matt, didn't really know what their passion was. I wanted to know if they had had goals and if those goals were written. I wanted to know if they used visualization, had a written business plan, or any plan at all. I wanted to know if there was a formal system they followed, such as an expert's guaranteed system. I wanted to know if they had had mentors and who those mentors were. I wanted to know if they ever had a desire to become a millionaire. I wanted to know about their belief system. I wanted to know what advice they would give to someone looking to be successful. I wanted to know what really creates success.

In seeking the truth, I found it.

****

# Chapter 2: What I Learned
# From Interviewing 21 Millionaires

*"I think at that point in time you need to dispense with everybody's opinion and just go with your own instincts."*

*Millionaire 15 Cynthia McKay*

Millionaire 2 Jeffrey Luftig set out to be a high school shop teacher. He got a bachelor's degree in industrial science, did his student teaching, and had a job lined up. Then one of his professors told him that he should get a master's degree instead.

Jeffrey thought the professor's reasoning for doing so made sense and he trusted him, so he pursued a master's. It was a turning point in his life and ultimately Jeffrey went on and earned his Ph.D.

After graduation, he started teaching as an assistant professor at State University of New York [SUNY] at Oswego and settled in, thinking he would work in higher education for the rest of his life. He quickly took on new roles within education, including Assistant Department Head at the University of Northern Iowa. After a time, the head of that department moved to Eastern Michigan University, and asked Jeffrey to be the technology department head there.

While at Eastern Michigan University, he got a call asking him to teach continuing education classes at General Motors in statistical methods and process control. He found out that he was the only one on his faculty who was able to do it, bringing about what he calls another turning point in his life, since it opened the door to other opportunities.

Jeffrey encountered some resistance, however, when the dean of the college told him that he couldn't be paid for teaching the classes at GM. Jeffrey taught the classes anyway and GM loved it. They asked for more classes and then for an advanced course, which they opened to other companies. A few people from Ford came. They were impressed with Jeffrey and asked him to teach the class in-house for them.

That eventually led to Jeffrey consulting full-time at Ford through an endowed chair at the university and working with renowned quality expert Dr. W. Edwards Deming for two years.

One day Jeffrey thought to himself that the cost of his children's college education might be more than he could handle on a university salary, so he decided to replicate in the private world what he had done at the school: create a consulting practice.

He thought he would consult for a year or two, put some money away, and then go back to higher education. With that he gave up a full professorship, academic tenure, and associate dean status. The university faculty all told him he was out of his mind: "You've hit the epitome of where we all strive to get and you're giving it up."

"I didn't see it quite that way," Jeffrey commented when telling the story.

He started his own consulting company and it soon got out of hand as clients wanted more and more of his services. Fourteen years later he had built an international organization with six locations, 30-35 annual employees, and revenues over those years totaling $100 million.

All from the idea to consult for a year or two.

I asked Jeffrey if he ever expected his business to grow to the level it did.

"It would depend on when you asked me," he responded.

"The day I started it, I didn't see it as a business. I saw it as a way to do some consulting and teaching and make a significant amount of money in a relatively short period of time. But 'significant' changes throughout time."

Like many of the other millionaires I interviewed, it wasn't Jeffrey's intention to become a millionaire or to create a large organization. His original intent was simply to provide enough money for his children to go to whatever college they wanted.

Jeffrey's story perfectly illustrates what I learned from the 21 millionaires I interviewed because he, like most of the rest, could not have planned for the outcomes he achieved. He, like the rest, achieved what he did without a master plan, a formal mentor, or a grand vision. Instead, he and the other millionaires worked hard, took logical steps when the time was right, kept moving forward by finding and doing things that worked, and pursued his unique path to success.

Here it is in a list. The millionaires:

1.     Worked hard.

2.     Went line upon line.

3.     Moved forward by course correcting.

4.     Followed their unique path.

These are the four commonalities the millionaires share. I call them "commonalities" instead of "traits" because "trait" seems to imply something tangible and scientific; something with which you are born or can develop through conscious effort.

"Commonalities" fits better because the millionaires are not necessarily gifted with extraordinary qualities, nor was there concerted effort involved to acquire or develop these. It's just what they did. It is only in looking back on their lives and through the interviews that it comes clear what worked to get them where they are.

These commonalities among the millionaires are so interconnected that it's difficult to speak of one without tying it into one or more of the others, but I'll try.

## Commonalities

### 1. Worked Hard

All of the millionaires worked hard at each stage in his or her life.

Some had paper routes or sold things in their younger years and in their early adulthood they worked hard, as is evidenced in their educational pursuits. Twenty of them have at least a year of education beyond high school. The one who does not served in the military and now teaches at the college level. Nineteen have associate's degrees or above, 17 have bachelor's degrees, and 10 have advanced degrees.

When they started working after college they gave it all they had not knowing where that work would lead. In other words, none of them worked with an eye to the next step. Working hard is just part of who they are.

Concerning work Jeffrey said, "A lot of people probably have (the kind of background that I do, but) I executed on the opportunities that were presented to me." In other words, he put in the effort; he took action where others may not have.

Another part of this commonality is that most of the millionaires weren't concerned with whether something was the right action or wrong action, or whether they were working harder or smarter – they just did something.

In most cases they didn't plan much or theorize either. As Millionaire 11 Mark Sanborn put it, he would "rather be splashing around in the ocean than sitting on the shore doing a strategic plan."

Through the interviews I found an unexpected connection between passion and work. Most of these millionaires worked hard and then found their passion, not vice versa. Millionaire 18 Shawn Kane said, "I fell into the profession that I'm in now and it became my passion."

Something else that was interesting was that instead of trying to manufacture opportunities or exert undue pressure to make things happen, the millionaires went with the flow of where life was taking them and didn't fight against that energy, (see the next commonality). That, however, cannot be mistaken for a lack of hard work or for being lazy.

An analogy might be this: Rather than determining where they wanted to go and then finding the right path, the right vehicle, and the right crew to take them there, they just got in the nearest vehicle and started driving in the direction that looked good at the time. Along the way, great things happened and they ended up somewhere pretty special.

Most of the millionaires didn't work hard so that they could become millionaires. Most worked for the general objective of being successful, or to build something of value, to prove others wrong, to improve something, or to get out of something they didn't like. Similar to Millionaire 21 Richard Zuschlag's experience, they "just worked real hard and the moneymaking came by accident."

These millionaires took consistent action that over time created huge results.

An important note is that because work is ennobling, it naturally improves and enhances self-esteem. As a result, most of the millionaires didn't practice positive speech, positive affirmations, or external motivation techniques. There was no need to manufacture self-worth or convince themselves that they would be successful. They went to work and success followed naturally.

Of the characteristics the millionaires share, the most common is "doing" – not waiting until circumstances were perfect; until someone provided the right tools, the right motivation, or the right help; or until they knew enough. In fact, Millionaire 15 Cynthia McKay and others credit naivety for their success.

At every point, they just started working on what made sense in the moment, which is the connection to the next commonality.

## 2. Line upon Line

"Line upon line…here a little and there a little,"[1] is the most accurate way to describe how these millionaires approached their lives.

"Step by step" might be another way to think of it, but that phrase isn't as accurate since it implies a uniform progression, which is not how the millionaires did things. With the exception of one or two, they did not have concrete plans for their lives and did not start by visualizing the end and working backwards to create it. They didn't force the moment or have a clear path on which they stayed unwaveringly.

Instead, they took life as it came and built their success little by little, piece by piece, without knowing what the finished product, or even the next step, would look like. They were happy just to be productive in the moment.

Think about Jeffrey's story from above. He didn't have a grand vision of what he wanted to accomplish nor did he know where each preceding step would lead. He didn't envision himself as the head of a multinational consulting firm with satellite offices and a private plane – he wanted to be a high school shop teacher for heaven's sake! Then he just wanted to make some money for a year or two. All of the rest of it built line upon line.

Likewise, most of the other millionaires didn't follow a programmed path, nor did they have a vision that guided their decisions. Even those that had a vision, with the exception of one, said it wasn't concrete and that they had to be flexible and take life as it came. Each millionaire was open to opportunities and situations as they presented themselves and weren't locked into something that blinded them to other options.

They followed their intuition and took steps that they said seemed to make sense at the time. Looking back on it, it was in the first interview that I heard the truth about that, but it didn't register.

Millionaire 1 Lee Carlson didn't get into real estate because it was his passion or because he always had a goal to do it and worked backward to get there. He got into it because he learned what real estate agents made, was tired of farming and dairying, and thought real estate was a good way to make some easy money. That's as deep as it went.

As I mentioned, the millionaires didn't try to manufacture opportunities in life or set their own timetable for when things should happen. They didn't dictate to the universe how they wanted things to happen. They were open to how things *were* happening.

The millionaires worked day-by-day and in so doing built a foundation that opened opportunities and put them in a position to capitalize on them. In Jeffrey's case for instance, 20 years after starting on his original journey he was primed and in a position to start a company.

As with Jeffrey, each step for the millionaires built on the last in a way that they couldn't anticipate but in a way that made the next move the logical step. Jeffrey said his education and experiences "all came together in a very serendipitous way. I could not have planned it. But that's the way it came out."

Moving little by little means not having all of the answers at once. Many of the millionaires, Jeffrey included, didn't write a business plan before starting their business. Most of those millionaires who now advise others to write their goals down and have a plan did not have solid goals and plans at the time, if they had any at all.

Line upon line also means not being fanatical. Although the millionaires worked hard and enjoyed building their businesses, most of them struck a very good balance between work and family. A few were even heavily involved in volunteer positions at church or in coaching their children's teams.

Additionally, moving line upon line means that the millionaires were not what you might call "risk-takers." Sure, some of them took risks, and some talk about having to put yourself out there to be successful, but most started their businesses in small and simple ways and moved a little bit at a time so the hazards were minimal.

The millionaires also weren't looking for their big break or the big next step. They "executed on the opportunities" as they were presented without knowing at the time that they were opportunities; it was only in hindsight that they recognized their significance. In the moment, they didn't know where a decision would lead, only that that it made sense to take it.

Even those who were good at planning and goal setting, like Millionaire 9 Theresa Szczurek and Millionaire 20 Rob Emrich, moved line upon line.

Szczurek left a corporate job to start her own business because it was the next logical step, not because she had always planned to do it. And although she had an intention to start a business, she and her partner had to go line upon line to discover what that business would be.

Emrich felt moved to do something and along the way it grew and morphed into many other things. He also talks about the need to be flexible with plans and goals.

None of these 21 ordinary people became a millionaire by doggedly pursuing their original plans.

> *"We must be ready to allow ourselves to be interrupted by God."*[2]

Maybe it was the lack of rigid plans that gave them the freedom to take advantage of opportunities that came up. And when they took advantage of something that didn't turn out so well, they had the next commonality working for them.

### 3. Kept Moving Forward by Course Correcting

These millionaires casually mention that they made a lot of mistakes and found a lot of things that didn't work.

They didn't dwell on them, though. They added that information to their knowledge base and moved forward trying something else.

These are average people. They are not proficient in everything they do. None of them has the Midas touch. For examples refer to Millionaire 1 Lee Carlson's discussion on farming and dairying,

Millionaire 5 Heidi Ganahl's discussion on *The All American Girl Gone Wrong*, Millionaire 6 Steve Rosdal's discussion on scrimshaw, Millionaire 7 Vance Andrus' discussion on failed businesses, Millionaire 14 Doug Krug's discussion on starting from nothing multiple times (you get the point). But they keep doing something and that is what propels them forward. If it's the wrong something, they correct for it or move on to something else.

These millionaires understood that failure is for a moment, not forever. Millionaire 18 Shawn Kane said, "A failure to me is not a failure. It's a challenge to learn a better way to do something." Millionaire 19 Judith Briggs said, "I look at failures as learning experiences." Millionaire 8 Barry Hamilton remarked, "I had failures and successes early on in life. I think it taught me to continue to pursue things that I liked and if I didn't quite get there and failed, it didn't mean I was a failure. It just meant that it wasn't meant to be and I needed to go to the next one."

Also, the millionaires weren't super intelligent people who sensed the shifting winds and made their moves ahead of the market. They weren't opportunists who seized the next big thing. It was much simpler than that; they followed intuition and changed when necessary.

By working hard, moving line upon line, and course correcting, a unique path to success and in life opened up for each millionaire, which is the next commonality.

**4. Unique Path**

Like all of the millionaires, Jeffrey's path was unique. He, like the others, followed his instincts and did what made sense to him, not necessarily what made sense to or had worked for others.

He didn't listen to those who said he was crazy to leave higher education. He didn't have a formal mentor who provided him with a proven path. He didn't consult the experts' advice to avoid mistakes and make the right next move.

No, he just made what seemed to him to be the right move at the time and it worked out. It worked out because he knew better than anyone else what his unique circumstances, needs, interests, skills, and background were – a common story among the millionaires.

These millionaires' experiences are why I say the success experts miss the mark by encouraging a guaranteed pattern for success. Your path is not my path, is not Jeffrey's path, is not anyone else's path.

I'm not saying that others' advice can't be helpful and you shouldn't listen to them at all. Indeed, the millionaires listened to informal mentors–friends and associates whose advice they trusted–but they took that advice for what it was worth and more heavily relied on their gut, intuition, and God. For at least Millionaire 7 Vance Andrus and Millionaire 17 Bryan Willis, it also included listening to their wives.

Interestingly, many of the millionaires are leery about giving advice to others, saying things like Millionaire 17 Bryan Willis did in response to the question, "What should others who want to be successful know?" His answer was, "I'm not qualified to say what anybody else would need to know."

When it comes to success, especially entrepreneurship, I'm not sure there are many experts. By its very nature, entrepreneurship is about the individual and the circumstances. You can't capture that in a bottle and package it.

And even though I'm sharing with you what I learned from these entrepreneurial millionaires, this book does not constitute expert advice. You have to learn for yourself, from your own successes and mistakes, because there's more than one way to skin a cat. There was no right way or wrong way for these millionaires. There was just the way they did it.

Unconsciously, they understood that they were in the best position to make decisions about their own life and career and knew that if they made a wrong decision, it wasn't the end of the world (refer back to commonality #3).

## Bonus Commonality: Right Place, Right Time

Although not consistent across all stories, several of the millionaires also mentioned being fortunate enough to be in the right place at the right time or having benefited from luck.

Adding a layer to that, Millionaire 7 Vance Andrus and Millionaire 21 Richard Zuschlag commented that luck is created through hard work.

## Bottom Line

Each of the millionaires worked hard and took life as it came. They didn't have grand plans or big dreams. By working hard they were in a position to see the next logical transition in their life that in hindsight can be labeled an opportunity.

Most of them weren't very good planners. They were doers. Wherever they were, whatever they were doing, they worked.

These millionaires show you can create success without a dream, a passion, an eye for opportunity, unwavering discipline, written goals, formal mentors, or any of the other things you may have heard are absolutely necessary. After years of studying the advice of the experts and gurus and finding it wanting, I'm excited to share with you how 21 ordinary people created extraordinary success.

****

# Chapter 3: The Methodology Behind the Interviews

*"That is the key to it: being in the flow and trusting and listening."*

*Millionaire 14 Doug Krug*

I think it's helpful for you to understand my methodology of approaching the interviews. As I look back on it, I approached the interviews in somewhat the same manner the millionaires approached their lives and work – I didn't have a concrete plan and was open to where things might lead, even with the first three interviews when I was trying to validate my hypothesis of find your passion, find your success.

## How I Found Them

I started with Lee Carlson, whom I knew through church. After interviewing him I put the project on the shelf for a year because I got a great contract job with some restrictive intellectual property requirements and I didn't want to chance losing the book. When that contract was not renewed due to the economy (I promise, it was not performance related, folks), I went looking for my next gig.

Through a series of circumstances that aligned just right as I was pursuing the next logical step in my progression, I met Gina Schreck[1] and talked with her about how to get started as an independent speaker and trainer. She recommended that I talk to Ashley Andrus.[2]

Though the initial reason for our meeting together had nothing to do with the book, I shared the idea with Ashley. This was completely contrary to what I normally would have done because in the past I wanted to keep my ideas close to the chest for fear of ridicule or theft.

Ashley, however, was quick to provide encouragement for the idea and references to several millionaires, which jumpstarted the interview process.

As the project developed, I contacted other millionaires I had known through personal or professional association, I got referrals to some from friends whom I told about the book, and some I found through Internet searches.

Interestingly, I was not able to force any interviews. At times I tried to find millionaires who fit certain profiles that might provide different insights or appeal to certain audiences, but I came up empty in those attempts. Additionally, I didn't plan to interview all entrepreneurial millionaires; that's just the way it worked out.

Initially I tried to interview only what I call "bank account millionaires," meaning they had made at least a million dollars in cash. Instead, I was led to a few "asset millionaires" whose stories were compelling and I recognized that since they could sell their businesses or assets tomorrow and become bank account millionaires it would be a good idea to use their stories.

When lining up the interviews I went with the flow and followed where it took me. In fact, after writing the book and sending it out for edits, one of the original millionaires had to back out and has since been replaced. Just one more opportunity to go with the flow.

**The Questions & Answers**

I was able to do initial research on some of the millionaires either online or during the call to schedule the interview. I then came to each interview with at least 25, but usually around 40, prepared questions, most of which were the same for each interview. Initially I wondered if each millionaire's answers to the questions would lead to a pattern. I wondered if when all was said and done, if the same 21 questions and their answers across all interviews would prove most pertinent.

The answer was no.

Because the idea was to understand each millionaire's heart-set, mindset, background, desire, and drive–the how and why he or she became a millionaire–I followed the unique flow of each interview to get to those answers. I then selected in hindsight what turned out to be the 21 most pertinent answers from each interview, whether it was a response to a question from the prepared list or one I had asked on the fly. Luckily, there were a few questions that were consistent across all interviews, giving you several points of comparison.

## In Their Words

My goal in interviewing the millionaires, after I figured out that there wasn't a direct correlation between passion and success, was simply to get to the truth. I've therefore tried to share the millionaires' stories in their words, with their honest answers, without editing to prove my point or validate my views.

I've done my best to present the information the way I received it, accounting for the need to break it down into palatable chunks (who really wants to read 500 pages, even if we are talking millionaires), and to improve the clarity. And since the spontaneous spoken word isn't always straightforward and easy to follow, I've cleaned up the text while remaining true to the questions and answers.

I could have rewritten the interviews to follow more of a story pattern, but then you would not get the full value of the millionaires' thoughts and experiences in their own words and it may have been harder to understand how their answers provide direct insight to the questions asked. You may have also accused me, although we hardly know one another, of rigging the information to my liking.

Also, if I had rewritten it, you would have had a nice polished apple, instead of seeing the real deal of the millionaires' personalities, strengths, weaknesses, and challenges. This would have defeated the purpose of the book, which is to give you the unvarnished truth about success, the way I learned it.

As a result of this down-to-earth, unbiased style, you will see that the millionaires' ideas don't always agree with each other (see below) and that some millionaires gave advice on how to be successful that doesn't seem to align with the way they created success. I tried to dig deeper into some of those instances to clarify, which you will see as you read their stories.

## Varying Thoughts

Millionaire 6 Steve Rosdal said the business environment is not as forgiving today as it was when he built his business in the 1970s and 80s. However, Millionaire 3 Matt Given said, "there was a lot of blood in the road on the way there," meaning he made a lot of mistakes while building his successful businesses in the 1990s and 2000s.

Millionaire 2 Jeffrey Luftig said that to be successful you have to figure out a strategy. However, Millionaire 3 Matt Given said he operated by the seat of his pants; Millionaire 6 Steve Rosdal said, "I had no master plan, I was playing volleyball"; and Millionaire 16 Lane Nemeth said her business at first was one big experiment and that she wasn't terribly serious about it.

Millionaire 15 Cynthia McKay encourages people not to share their goals with others who may belittle or ridicule them. Millionaire 8 Barry Hamilton, however, encourages people who want to be successful to communicate to others what they are looking for.

Most of the millionaires said that being successful takes hard work, and some said it takes an incredible amount of work. Millionaire 14 Doug Krug, however, said that if things are too hard, it's time to reevaluate, that too much struggle is an indication of being out of sync with Source (one's definition of God or higher power).

I guess the message in these varied thoughts is that whatever path works for you is the right one.

**Note**: I mentioned previously that Millionaire 2 Jeffrey Luftig didn't have a business plan and that Millionaire 15 Cynthia McKay recommends you not share your goals with others. You won't find those statements within their interviews because although it was discussed during the interview and I thought it was important to share, doing so within the context of the interview hampered the flow and readability.

\*\*\*\*

# Chapter 4: Who Are These Millionaires?

*"...there's no singular path."*

*Millionaire 11 Mark Sanborn*

I hesitate to provide my analysis of each millionaire because it is only fair for you to form your own opinion. Yet, since there is no need to read each millionaire's story or to read from the first interview to the last, here is a little bit of information to help you decide where to start.

**Millionaire 1 Lee Carlson**: Made his money in real estate after trying farming and dairying. A relationship guy, family is very important to him.

**Millionaire 2 Jeffrey Luftig**: Built a successful consulting practice after leaving a career in higher education. His education and experiences came together in a very serendipitous way while his engineering mindset, combined with a penchant for solving problems, served him well.

**Millionaire 3 Matt Given**: Built three successful banking/payroll businesses and is now consulting. A fun-loving, take-life-as-it-comes guy, Matt now gets to do what he really likes – spend time with his family, train for triathlons, and help others grow their businesses.

**Millionaire 4 Jeffrey Hill**: A young star at Proctor and Gamble, Jeffrey had opportunities presented to him that led to running a high-powered consulting firm. He has since become an investor and philanthropist.

**Millionaire 5 Heidi Ganahl**: Had a business plan written when tragedy struck. She put that plan on hold for more than 10 years and came back to it when the timing was right. She built a booming doggy day and overnight camp business, Camp Bow Wow.

**Millionaire 6 Steve Rosdal**: Wanted to get out of New York so he moved to Denver. He started an Indian jewelry business, which then led to creating one of the most successful jewelry stores in Denver, Hyde Park Jewelers.

**Millionaire 7 Vance Andrus**: A lawyer who failed in several businesses then hit it big, but not before making a bold move to become unstuck in life.

**Millionaire 8 Barry Hamilton**: A software engineer turned business owner who also invested in commercial real estate.

**Millionaire 9 Theresa Szczurek**: A disciplined engineer who wanted to start a business so she went looking for the idea. It came, the business grew and was sold, and then she went on a quest to find out how people pursue a passionate purpose in their life.

**Millionaire 10 Jack Odom**: A spine surgeon who grew up on a farm and wanted to have the respect from others in his field.

**Millionaire 11 Mark Sanborn**: A well-renowned leadership author and speaker, Mark knows the value of a disciplined, but unscripted, approach to becoming what you want to.

**Millionaire 12 John Simcox**: Knew he had to provide for his new bride so he got out into the working world as quickly as he could. He always had written goals and after taking little steps here and there, opened a successful jewelry store chain, JC Keepsake.

**Millionaire 13 Bill Begal**: Grew up around entrepreneurs and inherently understood that was the way to make money. Toiled for an unpleasant boss while learning the industry in which he would later make millions.

**Millionaire 14 Doug Krug**: All about being in the flow. He made snap decisions that led to exciting adventures even while working day jobs. He now teaches people to pay attention to the inner voice.

**Millionaire 15 Cynthia McKay**: A former lawyer who credits naivety for her success after jumping feet first into a business about which she knew nothing – gift baskets. She is now a successful franchisor and business coach with yet another college degree.

**Millionaire 16 Lane Nemeth**: Creating Discovery Toys, a multi-million dollar direct sales organization, was just one big experiment to her. She took challenges as they came, worked through them, and continues to do so today as she starts another exciting adventure.

**Millionaire 17 Bryan Willis**: Working 80- to 100-hour weeks in corporate America was Bryan's forte, not only because he loved the challenge and the work, but also as a result of his intense drive to provide for his family. Hard work opened up opportunities, which Bryan made the most of to reach a spot he called a "pipe dream."

**Millionaire 18 Shawn Kane**: Grew up around success in northern California and watched his parents work hard. Fell into the business he's in and it became his passion.

**Millionaire 19 Judith Briggs**: Bought a 1-800-GOT-JUNK franchise after catching the vision and soon thereafter became one of the most successful franchisees in the system. Two things she loves: Her family and the business.

**Millionaire 20 Rob Emrich**: A social entrepreneur turned business owner, he created success at a young age. He now owns several businesses each valued at no less than $1 million.

**Millionaire 21 Richard Zuschlag**: A fitting end cap to the interviews, he summed up what I had learned from the others – you never know what something is going to turn into at the time but if you work hard, make what seems like the logical next decision, and learn from your mistakes, you find yourself years later in the middle of something successful. He runs a large medical transportation company in Louisiana and Texas.

Enjoy the interviews and the millionaires' stories!

A quick guide to the interviews

The 21 questions I asked each millionaire are **bolded** in each interview.

"**B:**" *is short for "Brandon:" and indicates a follow-on or clarification question I asked.*

To see a color picture of each millionaire go to www.21for21.com/about/the-millionaires.

****

# Millionaire 1 Lee Carlson

Founder, Carlson Associates, Inc.

www.carlsonland.net

Married, seven children

Bachelor's, Real Estate Broker's License

*I know Lee from church. He was more than gracious spending time with me and allowed me to fumble my way through the first interview.*

**You said that getting into real estate was the best thing you ever did. Tell me more about that.**

The things that preceded it were wheat and dairy farming.

As a wheat farmer during the mid 1950s you couldn't make a living because crops didn't grow; there was a drought. Then I got into dairying thinking it was going to be a regular income. It was a regular income, but it was a regular job twice a day for 10 years – it took me that long to finally get rid of the cows. Then I did some cattle trading for a year or so.

My brother and I had a farm together and we split it up. He sold his half and I figured out that the real estate agent made $17,000 on the sale. I thought to myself, "That real estate man doesn't know any more than I do. I'm going to get into real estate. That sounds like easy money."

I got a manual, studied it, and passed the test. A few years later, I went to school and got my broker's license so I wouldn't have to work under anybody else.

One of the reasons I thought farming would be good is my kids can be right here; they can work on the farm. I got smarter and said, "I don't want my kids to do this. I don't think they want to do it."

My five sons and two sons-in-law all eventually got their real estate licenses and joined with me. It's been a great business, especially to have my family with me and see them every day. I thought that would never happen when I first got into the business, but they all finally got here with me.

**What has made you successful over the years?**

Being a landowner and a farmer who knew all of the other farmers here. Being acquainted with land, zoning, taxes, and the owners. I thought I had an upper hand. It turned out very well.

Then I decided I didn't want to list farms, I didn't want to sell for other people. I started doing the opposite; I bought land, invested in land. That's where we're at now. We buy land and represent ourselves.

**How long did it take before you really felt like you were successful?**

It didn't take long because I was comparing it with wheat farming and dairying. It felt successful relatively quickly.

In farming there'd be years I wouldn't make anything. One of the early sales in real estate I made $7,000 and I thought, "Wow, that's wonderful. How could I not like this?"

**What are some of the challenging things you've had to go through? Have you had some years that were a little leaner?**

Yes. I learned a long time ago working with my dad and being a farmer how to borrow money. In those lean years you borrowed against your land and continued to put your kids through college and stuff like that.

Certainly there were periods of time in the economy when nothing was moving. You go through those low periods and, with a little help from borrowed money, you carry yourself through. I think that's what my dad taught me. If you know what you're doing, know how to borrow money, and you think you've got it figured out, you'll do all right.

**B:** *So it was wise borrowing?*

Oh yes. You can't say it wasn't speculative, but it was a growing market and land values kept going up. It was a good time to start.

**How did you know you were going to be successful?**

I had some little successes right from the start. I really liked land and knew land and water rights and taxes and how to annex and how to get land zoned. It was a challenge, but I loved it.

**When you got your license, did you immediately move to real estate completely or were you still farming and dairying?**

I dropped farming. Even if you farmed real hard you never made any money. I went into this knowing this is where I wanted to be.

**Who was your mentor or your model as far as success or in real estate?**

My dad. He bought land to farm and he made some very good land buys. Then he started selling some of his land.

**How did you balance time with your family?**

That was easy. I was my own boss and I didn't have salespeople to manage. If people joined with me I wasn't their boss, they were on their own, so I didn't have to spend any time with them. I could spend whatever time I wanted or felt I could. I don't know if I ever kept office hours, but I was at the office most every day, at least eight hours a day.

**B:** *Were there some days you put in a lot more than eight?*

Not necessarily. In that business I was in control. I owned the land and made appointments during business hours and didn't have to work afterhours or on weekends.

**What other help did you have or what was your support system as you got rolling?**

I started out as a salesman for a fella by the name of Richardson. I didn't like that so I opened my own office and got a secretary. My sons and sons-in-law eventually got their real estate licenses and joined the business.

**What should people who want to be successful know?**

The main thing is to have a vision of where you want to go and stick to it. Certainly you have to have a certain amount of success to really stick to it. If you can't make a living, you're not going to stay with it.

**How do you know when that time is? It seems like so many people who are trying to be successful have to stick it out for a long time before they hit it.**

Yes, they do, and that's part of the stick-to-it-iveness.

I don't know how to put it. You have little successes and little successes. I've brought my sons and sons-in-law in and they've traveled the same road and they were successful. You have to have some successes, some real victories, to keep you going.

**Other than have a vision and stick to it, what should people who want to be successful know?**

Jump into it and learn as much as you can.

If you feel you're deficient in some areas, go to school, get some books, get acquainted with other people who are in the same business. Get some success stories from them and find out how they became successful.

And get into a business that you enjoy. You'll probably enjoy almost any business if you're successful and make enough so you can take care of your responsibilities. Although I can imagine some things I wouldn't be cut out for.

**What dreams or goals did you have when you were a young kid?**

I grew up on a farm. My dad was a successful farmer and I was going to be a farmer.

**What would you say about your personal spiritual belief system?**

My personal belief system is honesty and integrity, which I felt my dad and mother taught me.

**What do you want people to know about you or what legacy would you like to leave?**

Have a dream and roll after it. Work hard and learn all you can about the business you're going to get into.

**What's the next step for you?**

I don't have a next step such as retiring. I can't fathom sitting at home in a soft chair watching TV and not having my mind active in making deals and meeting people. My dad retired and he sat in a soft chair for several years. I think because of that he didn't live as long as he could have and that's no fun.

I don't care much for TV; I just listen to the news. I read all the time.

**What do you read?**

News magazines, the scriptures.

We've got a big library. I'll pick out a book and in a week or so finish it. I love reading.

**What do you wish someone would ask you?**

People who know me, my kids, our family, and our situation here in this area sometimes ask, "What can you attribute your success to?"

[The answer is] being honest, working hard, and learning as much as possible about the business.

Then circulate with those people that have been successful in the type of business you're in.

**How do you define success?**

Taking care of your responsibilities, taking care of your family; feeding them, clothing them, and getting them started in life.

**What is the best use of your wealth?**

I've donated a lot of money to the LDS Church and to BYU-Idaho.

Certainly you want to have all of the bases covered and make sure that your kids are always taken care of.

I've given some large donations to some charities. It's a good position to be in, to feel that you can do that.

**What other things would you like me to include about you?**

The life that my wife and I have together is so intertwined with our seven children and bringing them up right. I can say unequivocally they are all honest, hard-working, successful, good people and they're training up our 31 grandkids the way they should go.

That's a pretty good feeling to have.

****

# Millionaire 2 Jeffrey Luftig

Founded an international consulting company; University professor

Two children

Bachelor's, Master's, Ph.D.

*Ashley Andrus referred me to Jeffrey.*

## You started your career in teaching?

Absolutely.

I started my education thinking I was going to be a junior high school shop teacher.

I graduated high school with a 69 average; I barely made it through. I did hold one record: I graduated from Spring Valley High School owing the most nights of detention.

I went to SUNY Buffalo and studied to be an industrial education teacher. That's what I thought I was going to do, that's what I trained for, and I did my student teaching in that area.

I had a professor at SUNY named Tom Morrisey who asked, "What are you going to do after you graduate?"

I responded, "The school where I student-taught has offered me a position."

He said, "You don't want to do that. What you should do is go for a master's degree."

"I can't afford it."

"I have a place that will give you a graduate assistantship and it's really a good school."

He sent me to Bowling Green State University to work with two professors, Dick Swanson and Jerry Streichler.

That program was specialized for people going on for a Ph.D. I wrote a master's thesis and learned to write and do research. That was a turning point. Now I was pointed toward teacher education.

After I went to Bowling Green–I developed some pretty non-conventional, cutting edge stuff for teaching in public schools–I taught at DeVilbiss High School, an intercity school in Toledo, Ohio, for a year. I started a new curriculum and taught the other teachers how to do it.

After a year I thought that I had enough experience with public schools, I understood how they worked, and Dick Swanson sent me to the University of Minnesota where I got a graduate research fellowship. My objective at the time was to have a Ph.D. while I was still 25 and I made it with two weeks to spare.

I left Minnesota and took a job as an assistant professor teaching ceramics technology at SUNY Oswego, a teacher education institution. At that point I thought I was going to be in education for the rest of the life.

After a year I became the supervisor for industrial education for the New Hampshire State Department of Education. Then I became the director of the research-coordinating unit, two steps below commissioner.

I did that for a couple of years and then went to the University of Northern Iowa, another teacher education institution, to teach manufacturing. I became an assistant department head. The department head moved to Eastern Michigan University where they had started a college of technology. The year after he left he hired me as a department head.

I got a call one day and was asked if we could offer continuing education classes in statistical methods and process control for General Motors. I found out that on my faculty I was the only one who knew anything about it.

This was a really significant turning point in my life because I got a call from the dean of continuing education. He said, "I understand you're going to teach the continuing education courses for GM."

I said, "Yes, on a weekend."

He said, "You're not faculty, you're administration, so you can't be paid if you do that."

I responded, "I was hired to grow the program and do outreach activity and that's what I'm going to do."

So I did it.

They loved it and asked for another one, then another one. Then they asked for an advanced one and pretty soon we were renting out the Hilton ballroom. We opened it up to everyone and some folks from Ford came.

Ford said, "How about coming and doing it for us?"

I started doing that and they were making gift contributions to the school, to my department, because I couldn't be paid.

One day I went to Ford Electronics Division [FED]. This is when Dr. W. Edwards Deming was brought into Ford by Don Petterson to help turn the company around. They had set up a center for quality systems in Dearborn, and that day they said to me, "Deming has said that every division has to have their own consultant. We'd like to offer you the job."

I said, "I'm really committed to higher education."

They said, "We'll double your salary."

"You don't understand. I have tenure, I'm a full professor, I'm an associate dean; I'm committed to this."

"That's perfectly understandable. We'll triple your salary and you only have to work 35 weeks [a year]."

Now they had my attention.

I talked to the dean then went back to Ford and said, "Instead of hiring me away, how about creating an endowed chair? I would work for you 35 weeks a year full-time, but you wouldn't have to bring me on as a full-time employee and pay benefits. You'd simply give the university a big chunk of bucks for the chair."

That was the first chair that FED had ever endowed and it was the first endowed chair in the history of Eastern Michigan University.

In order to take that position I had to be interviewed by Dr. Deming. He was in his 80s at that point. He asked, "Where did you get your statistics background?"

I said, "I went to the University of Minnesota."

"Who was your professor?"

[When I told him the professor's name he responded], "Well, I don't need to worry about whether you know statistics."

He knew [that professor], so I got lucky.

I worked with Dr. Deming for two years and then woke up one day and said to myself, "I've got two really smart kids. They're going to want to go to college. I'm doing OK, but…"

I had started a consulting center at the university. I was consulting for Alcoa, Oregon Sawchain, IBM, and a couple of other companies. I said, "I think what I should do is start my own company, consult by myself with a part-time secretary for a year or two, put some money away, and then go back to higher education."

I gave up full professorship, associate dean status, and tenure and started my own company. All the faculty at Eastern said, "You're out of your mind. You've hit the epitome of where we all strive to get and you're giving it up."

I didn't see it quite that way.

I started my company and it got out of hand. People wanted more and more and I had to start hiring employees. Fourteen years later I had an international consulting firm, which annually employed 30-35 folks.

In the 14 years, we did over $100 million in gross revenue. We had our main office in Southfield, Michigan and I had satellite offices in Chicago; Charlotte, North Carolina; Wales, Great Britain; Geelong, Australia; and then Perth, Australia.

I was at a crossroads. I had enough money set aside for the kids and everything else.

I woke up one morning in the Regent Hotel in Sydney, Australia. It was Sunday morning, the sun was shining and I had one of the rooms overlooking the Opera House in the harbor. I was really lonely, really tired, and I wanted to be home. I wanted to be any place but there.

When you're in a place like that and you've had enough, you've really had enough.

I had achieved the objectives I had set. I said, "I'm ready. I'm going to execute my original plan," which was to go back to higher education. I sold my interest in the company.

The first thing I did when I got home was made up a matrix of all of the places I had ever been and thought I might want to retire to. I put the criteria along the top in columns and then rank ordered all of the places within each column. Then I calculated the median rank weight–I'm a statistician–and Denver, Colorado, came up number one.

I found all of the colleges and universities in the Denver area and sent away for their catalogs. I sent five letters to department heads, chairs, or deans saying, "I've looked through your catalog. Attached is my resume. I'm retiring to Denver. Is there any part-time teaching available? Here are the courses I think I could teach..."

I got three full-time job offers.

This position that I have now is an endowed chair: the Deming professorship. It felt like I was going full circle.

**Did you ever expect your business to grow to the level it did?**

It would depend when you asked me.

The day I started it, I didn't see it as a business. I saw it as a way to do some consulting and teaching and make a significant amount of money in a relatively short period of time. But "significant" changes throughout time.

I didn't think I would have 35 employees, that we'd have satellite offices all over the world, and that I'd be flying around in my own plane; no I never saw that. I wasn't surprised when it happened, but I never saw it.

**B:** *Tell me more about that: you weren't surprised when it happened.*

I worked really hard and we were really good. We had a value proposition that was different than a lot of other people as well.

**Your foundation to be able to experience that success in business was your education and your 12 years in higher education?**

Yes, mostly the education.

**B:** *The Ph.D.?*

All of it.

When I was going through my undergraduate degree in Buffalo, in order to get a degree in industrial education there were eight subject areas: woods, metals, ceramics, textiles, electronics, graphic communications, power and transportation, and plastics.

I had to take a class in every one of those areas. A class was a class plus a lab. I met for each one of those subjects two hours a day, five days a week, and then I had to take advanced in five of them.

I never walked into a factory where I didn't know about the equipment that they were using; that served me extremely well. The research that I was doing, and teaching engineers to do, in applied statistics and advanced research came right out of my Ph.D. work.

Understanding the equipment, the materials, and the technology from my undergraduate degree, combined with the statistics and applied research that I got when I trained as an applied researcher in my Ph.D., plus the education expertise that I picked up in developing teaching materials from my master's degree all came together in a very serendipitous way. I could not have planned it. But that's the way it came out.

However, a lot of people probably have that kind of background so the question is in the application of it. I executed the opportunities that came along that allowed me to leverage those three things. Edison once said that in life everyone is presented with the same number of opportunities; most people don't take advantage of them because opportunity usually shows up in overalls looking like work.

**Tell me about some of those points of execution that you took hold of and made the most of.**

The first one was when the dean of continuing education told me that I couldn't be paid.

Most people would have said, "You're right. I'll call GM and say I can't do it. I'm not going to work for nothing."

A couple of years after that I was teaching the National Seminar Series for the Society of Manufacturing Engineers [SME] in statistical methods and was getting an honorarium of $500 and paid travel. I was doing it because it was exposure to people from lots of different companies, lots of different places, and it was good exposure for the school.

I had a guy sitting in front of me one day [who] by the second day was shaking his head.

At the end of the day I asked him, "What's the matter?"

He said, "I wish I could get you in front of my management team so you could explain to them what quality is and is not."

I said, "Well, bring me to your company."

"I haven't got it in the budget. I can't afford it."

"You pay my travel and I'll do it for free."

I traveled out to Omark industries and gave a presentation. They were our first client when I started my consulting company.

They had classes I was teaching that they opened up to other people. One of the people that came happened to be from IBM. The guy from IBM went back and said, "There's a guy who's teaching up there, he teaches for SME as well. He knows more about this stuff than anybody I've heard talk about it and he understands technology.

He's not an academician. This guy understands equipment and machining and all that other stuff."

They invited me in to do an overview and that was my second client; IBM. In the 14 years I had my consulting firm, I never spent a cent on marketing. One hundred percent of the growth of the company was word of mouth.

**Did you ever feel, as you were going through this process and doors opened up, that you were where you were supposed to be?**

Yes, every day that I went to work.

**Are you a member of a particular religion? Do you believe in a higher power?**

I'm Jewish, but I'm not what you would call devout. I'm not a fan of organized religion, but I consider myself spiritual.

**B:** *Did you believe God was leading you?*

No.

**B:** *Who do you think was leading you?*

I didn't think about it.

**B:** *These doors just opened up, you walked through them, you took advantage of these–*

Well, they didn't just open up. I looked for them, figured out ways to get them open, and when they opened I was willing to do the work required to walk through them.

**What was the work that you did?**

I've written about 40 training manuals and quite a few other publications. I have about 75 publications.

Here's the key: There were a lot of people out there selling services. Our value proposition was, #1) You don't come to us, we come to you. #2) We provide training and consulting when you need it, not when it's convenient for us. We did training on midnight shifts; we trained midnight to eight if you needed it. #3) We're not selling a service. What we want to do is provide you with an opportunity to solve your problems.

There were not a lot of people trying to find out what problems existed. A lot of stuff we developed was cutting edge and the reason it's cutting-edge is that it was developed before anybody asked for it because they didn't know to ask for it.

One of the really interesting things I learned from Dr. Deming about success in business and industry is a success continuum from low to high.

How do people establish businesses? In one group, it's what we might call a "me too," like restaurants. Restaurants have an extremely high failure rate. The value proposition for restaurants is me too, but better, different. This point on the continuum is where people know they have a problem and you are offering a different solution than those that already exist.

Higher on the continuum you find companies like L.L. Bean, which was started because L.L. Bean was tired of coming back from hunting and fishing with wet feet. He couldn't find a waterproof boot, so he developed one. Here's where people know they have a problem, but there's no solution. You can get really big and really successful there, but you have to worry about staying ahead because somebody's always going to come up with a "me too but better."

Higher on the continuum is where true genius comes from.

You're solving problems people don't even know they have. There's no problem until they see the solution.

I was sitting with Dr. Deming one day at Ford Motor Company with the R&D [research and development] folks. We were talking about things that customers were asking for in surveys. Dr. Deming had been quiet for 45 minutes or so, which was never a good sign, and finally somebody worked up the courage and said, "Dr. Deming, what do you think about what we are talking about?"

Deming was in his 80s and he knew the giants of industry. He knew Edison personally. He knew Firestone. He said something very interesting.

"Nobody ever asked for a light bulb."

It was very quiet.

Somebody said, "What does that mean?"

He said, "If you had done surveys in the late 1800s of home lighting consumer preferences and asked, 'What do you want?' they would have said, 'I want a cleaner burning gas jet,' 'I want a gas jet that throws off more light, but uses less gas,' and 'I want gas jets that are easier to clean soot off of.' Nobody would have said, 'I'd like a glass bulb with a tungsten element filled with an inert gas that casts off light without gas and that runs off of wires that come to my house.'"

Nobody ever asked for a light bulb. Nobody knew they had a problem with gas until they saw that they didn't need it.

You really stay ahead and you really create business by giving people solutions to problems they didn't know they had until they see the answer. It's the most profound thing I ever learned from Dr. Deming and I leveraged it myself.

**Is success attainable for everyone and is it that they need to find their own niche to do it, or are there just some times that people have opportunity over and over and the mindset isn't right?**

First, let's define success.

**B:** *Go ahead, I'd love to know.*

No, you asked the question "is success obtainable for everyone?" What do you mean by success?

**B:** *Finding their place in the world, making a contribution, and getting paid to do that.*

Absolutely, I believe that's obtainable for everyone.

I was talking to a woman who was a homemaker. Her husband died suddenly of a heart attack; he had owned a heavy equipment construction firm. She took over and grew it beyond what he had ever had. She became the first woman appointed to the Fed [Federal Reserve System].

She was talking to my university class one day and somebody asked her that question about success: "Can everybody be successful? Why are there failures?"

She said in her experience she believed that everyone in their lifetime has the same number of successes and the same number of failures. Yet there are people who we point to and say, "They're really successful, but here's this other group and they're failures in life."

She said, "The successes and the failures have the same number of success incidents and failure incidents in their lives. What's the difference? People who are successful learn from their failures but build on their successes. People who are failures learn nothing from their successes but build on their failures."

I'll bet you know somebody who has struggled all their life in their work and has not done well. If you talk to them what you'll eventually get to is something like, "Yeah, I had this job and I got cheated out of this." And they talk about it like it happened to them yesterday. They've built on that failure. Everything that comes after that, it's because of that.

I didn't get every contract I ever went after. I made mistakes in contracts I had. I offended a person here, I offended a person there, and lost business. I made mistakes, but I didn't dwell on them. I figured out how to learn from them. It's what you do with them and how you react to them that makes the difference.

**You didn't get every contract, you offended some people; what were some other tough times that you had?**

I didn't have any tough times. Right there's the difference; I can't say I ever had any tough times.

The work was hard, and the travel was grueling, particularly before we had our own plane. Those were the challenges, but as Woody Allen says, 90 percent of life is showing up, five percent is attitude and the other five percent is unexplained variability, there's nothing you can do about it. I think it's showing up is 75 percent, 20 percent is attitude, and five percent is unexplained variability.

**You've told me a little bit about some of the people who helped you in your journey, you mentioned Tom Morrisey.**

Dick Swanson, Jerry Streichler at Bowling Green.

Dave Pucell, my advisor for my doctorate work.

And then I would suppose Dr. Edwards Deming.

**B:** *What did you learn from him other than what you've already shared?*

I learned an awful lot from him about consulting, integrity, the things you do, and the things you don't do. It's hard to explain everything he meant to me, but I spent 14 years of consulting trying to implement the kinds of ideas he was talking about. I'm still doing it. I'm still teaching his ideas in the courses that I teach.

**Did you have any advisors while you were building your business?**

No.

**B:** *You had them it seems throughout your schooling and then with Dr. Deming.*

On the academic side, not the business side.

That (success on the business side) was just natural. You can make somebody a good entrepreneur, but you can't make them a great one; there's something innate about that. I was fortunate to have it. When you asked me earlier was God leading me, no I never felt that, but obviously I got that from someplace.

## What did you learn from some of your failures?

Speed bumps. Every one had a different lesson.

A new quality manager in a company had been appointed. I had been working with that company for some time and I didn't think much of the new quality manager. I was talking to two folks that I had worked with for quite a while. What I knew, but not consciously, was that one of the people that I was talking to had applied for a job with us and I had not hired and was still grinding an ax over it. I just didn't know how big [of an ax].

I made an offhand joke about this new quality manager. He immediately went to this person, told them, and we were eventually eased out of working with that company. One thing I learned from that little activity was to keep my mouth shut unless I knew who I was talking to, and then think twice and keep it shut anyway.

I learned a second thing from that. That company had been doing very poorly until we started working for it and we were credited by many people in the company with saving it, and yet it didn't help us. What I learned is as a consulting firm, no matter what you do, no matter how well you do it, always remember that just because they seem to love you today, doesn't mean you're getting married. As soon as they think they can do without you, you're gone. Never get emotionally involved with a company. You're a consultant. A lot of my people had a hard time with that.

## What is success?

Reaching a point in life where you're doing exactly what you want to do, when you want to do it, in the absence of fear.

Financial independence is not important for the money, it's important so you can do what you want to do, when you want to do it, without being fearful.

I don't go to work. I come to school. The fact of the matter is that I love teaching, I love working with students. I'm doing what I really like to do. When you reach a point when you're doing exactly what you want to do when you want to do it in the absence of fear, you're wealthy, you're finally successful.

My aunt used to say, "No one on their deathbed said, 'I wish I had spent just a couple of more days in the office.'"

I said, "That's probably true, except that I'm not built that way."

On my deathbed, I'm likely to say, "I wish I could have mentored just two or three more students. I wish I could have changed the lives of two to three more students."

Periodically, I'll get emails from students or people in industry that I taught, 15, 20, 25 years ago saying, "You changed my life."

That, for an educator, is the definition of success.

**Does success always follow your passion? Were you passionate about your business when you started it?**

Yes.

**If you were to go back, what would you do differently and why?**

I'd have invested in Microsoft when it was introduced; I'd be a kazillionaire. I didn't have any money, but I would have found some.

**What's the next step for you?**

I have no next steps. I fly fish, I motorcycle tour, and I teach.

**When you stood up to the dean about doing the classes for GM, you were in your early 30s?**

I was young. I had confidence in myself.

For somebody who's entrepreneurial in nature, I don't think you mentioned the most important attribute.

I think the most important attribute, the key to what you've been referring to as success, is a complete and absolute inability to even contemplate the possibility of failure.

I decided that I was going to take what I was doing at the university–I basically started a consulting firm in the university–and start a consulting firm outside the university.

When people ask me, "How did you plan for if things hadn't gone so well?" the answer is I didn't. It never occurred to me to do so. I lined up the clients and I did it. It never occurred to me that I wouldn't be able to go back to higher education. I didn't plan for it. I didn't lay out a strategy.

A lot of riders on sport bikes end up going over guardrails around here. The paramedics will ask them, "What's the last thing you saw?" and they always say the same thing – the guardrail. The thing about riding a bike is the bike will go where you're looking.

If you lay out a strategy for how you're going to deal with failure, you'll fail. You'll go where you're looking. A complete and total inability to even contemplate the possibility of failure significantly diminishes the possibility that you'll have to deal with it because that's not where you're looking.

Then you're building on your successes and you're learning from your failures. That's where you're looking. You never have a chance to build on your failures because they're all life lessons.

**B:** *Did you have any clients when you started the company?*

I had three.

## What advice would you give someone who's looking to be successful, however they define success?

The first thing is to distinguish whether you're attempting to be successful or you're attempting to have people think you're successful.

I have no advice for the second. I do have advice for the first. What is it that you're passionate about? How do you define success? What would make you feel successful?

Once you define that, which I think is the hard part, it's a matter of figuring out how to get there; the strategy you're going to use. Lay out a strategy and plan for doing those things that will get you to that point at that time in your life. Do not spend any time at all making contingency plans for when you fail.

I think about things a little differently than some. One of the things that students are told a lot is that entrepreneurs are risk-takers. Entrepreneurs are not risk-takers. Entrepreneurs are risk-traders.

An entrepreneur who says, "I'm going to leave this big company I'm safe in and start my own firm," is trading the risk. They're trading the risk that they will not be successful working on their own depending on themselves for the risk of being in some big company that gets bought up by somebody else [who then] closes that firm.

So do you want to feel safe and not exposed for many years and then wake up one morning and find out that you work for Enron and everything you ever worked for is now gone, or do you want to depend on yourself? It's not taking a risk, it's trading a risk.

It's more a matter of figuring out what success means to you and how to get there. And always make the distinction between a job, a vocation, and a career. Never focus on a job or vocation to get there.

If you had said to me in my junior or senior year [of college at Buffalo State], "Someday you're going to be flying around the country in your own King Air plane, consulting in advanced statistics and research and the quality sciences," I would have laughed in your face. That develops.

In other words, career development is a matter of seeing an opportunity and saying to yourself, "This is the kind of thing that I'd be really good at, I would enjoy, and I really want to do it," and then leveraging your tools and continuing to study and learn.

It's not the job, it's not the vocation; it's the ability to take multiple paths to get to what you define as success.

**What's your passion?**

Teaching.

Changing lives, getting those kinds of emails about changing someone's life.

It didn't matter if I was in a classroom or graveyard shift in the middle of the Inland Steel factory in East Chicago, Indiana. It never made a difference, I was always teaching.

**What do you want people to know?**

I'm just a teacher, just an educator; nothing more, nothing less.

**What do you want your mark on the world to be?**

I've already made it; all the students I've had, all the students I've mentored, and the lives I've changed. I won't even know about most of them, and yet it's out there. If that's what success is to you, then I'm done. I'm just continuing to do more of it. I'll be on my deathbed saying, "I wish I could have mentored just two or three more students."

It was never important to me to have the biggest quality sciences consulting firm in the country; I always wanted to have the best. It's not important to be the next Anderson Consulting, that's not how I define success. It was never important to me to have a hundred million dollars. Having got a hundred million, it's not what's important and neither is power. What drove me was impact.

****

# Millionaire 3 Matt Given

Founder, Silverline Business Systems; Founder, Matt Given Studios

www.mattgivenstudios.com

Married, four children

Bachelor's, MBA

*Matt was a customer of mine when I worked at CompUSA.*

## Tell me about your background.

I went back-to-back undergrad and grad school so I was in college for seven years straight and left with an undergraduate business degree and an MBA. I don't necessarily recommend the back-to-back because I think I would have gotten more out of the MBA if I would have had some real experience versus just book learning to that point. I was working with a professor and he offered to pay for my grad school if I stayed, so it was a no-brainer.

I went to school in a very small town and lived there year-round because I had my own tree business in the summers.

## Were you an entrepreneur growing up?

No, that was my first swing at it.

That was a pretty good gig. A friend and I bought a truck for about $1,000, bought a bunch of used chain saws and stuff like that and started this tree business. Over the course of five years it grew to where we had a couple trucks. If you needed a tree cut down in your yard, or a limb taken off your garage, you'd call us.

We stored the wood at a farm this friend had. We'd split the wood over Labor Day weekend and sell it as firewood by the truckload all through the fall, so it was a good deal. I was making more money than most kids.

I got into it by total luck. We were working with a guy who had a tree service and he got out of it. When he got phone calls, he would tell us, "Go out and do this job." That's what started it. We became known as the tree guys at Clemson.

It was total college stuff: we had no insurance and were cutting down trees over people's houses and cars, we didn't have workers' compensation insurance, nothing like that.

When I got out of Clemson, I moved to D.C. and took an advertising job. It was culture shock because I had been living in a small town in South Carolina for six years. Having to adjust to life around the D.C. beltway was a different sort of deal and it didn't really take.

Over Christmas break 1993 I came out to Colorado and visited a friend who was living in Telluride. I had my notice in at my job by January 3$^{rd}$ and was living on his couch by January 10$^{th}$. I skied with him the rest of that year, then moved to Steamboat and lived there for five years.

At the beginning of my time in Steamboat it was the ski bum existence. I was $40,000 in debt from school loans making $6.25 an hour loading chairs at Steamboat Ski and Resort Corporation with an MBA.

**B:** *Were you happy?*

Yeah, it was great. If my kid said, "I want to take a couple of years off and go be a ski bum," I would fully endorse it because for me, I just wasn't ready for the real world yet. I needed to grow up some more. Looking back on it, it's how I got into what I'm doing now.

In a ski town you have to figure things out; you have to scrape a bit to make it. I was looking for something to make some more money and answered an ad for a sales rep for a credit card processing company.

I called this guy about five times before I got him. I said, "Hey, I'm Matt, I'm in Steamboat. Saw your ad, I'm interested in a position."

He literally right there said, "You're hired. What's your fax number?"

He faxed over 40 pages of the sales manual. He called me a day later and said, "Let me know if you have any questions." And that was it. That was the extent of my "training."

I didn't have a clue what I was doing, so on my own I went and spent time with this other rep of his in Ft. Collins. She gave me a 48-hour crash course on what to do. From that point, it took me a few more months of figuring out the business on the street before I started making any decent money.

After a few months of doing OK, I figured out that credit card processing is a very lucrative business and people were making a lot of money in it, but I wasn't one of them. During ski season, I took a couple of months and figured out the industry and started my own company to sell credit card processing services.

That business is set up so a one-man shop can do it pretty easily, you just have to know who to contract with to do all the money moving, the network applications, and where to get terminals.

I was the only guy in town who was doing that so I got a lot of the merchants. It was a pretty sweet deal. I was making good money riding around on my bike, visiting merchants. I was known as the "Steamboat credit card guy." I started traveling to some of the other little towns around there and did some work in the Glenwood Springs area.

At trade shows I met a couple of guys from around the country doing the same thing; lone rangers who had figured out the system and set up their own companies. We took three or four of these individual companies from around the country and smashed them together as one. That company became a nationally known credit card processing company.

**B:** *You were about 27-years-old when you started your own credit card processing company?*

That's about right.

**B:** *Did you involve lawyers when you got together with these other guys, or did you just say, "Let's get together?"*

Legally, it was very formal, but it was a good group of guys; we were of a like mindset.

**How much money were you making at that time?**

In Steamboat, towards the end of my own company, I felt like I was the richest guy in the world because I was single making $12,000 or $13,000 a month. When you're used to making a quarter over minimum wage for a couple of years that seems like a lot of money.

That all got swallowed up into the new company. We were just on normal salaries at that point and we had equity in the company. I maybe made $200,000 a year when you threw it all together.

That company grew pretty fast. None of us had really been involved in growing a company that big and fast before. We made a lot of dumb mistakes and there was a lot of blood in the road on the way there.

We started a payroll division within the company and I was pretty heavily involved in that. When I left, part of my deal in keeping some equity in the company was that I had a non-compete on credit card processing, but I was freed up on payroll. I started Silverline Business Systems, which ended up being a locally based payroll processing company. Since we had started a payroll division at the other company I just used that as a blueprint.

My goal was to not grow that as fast or as big as the first company. I wanted to keep it smaller, more regional, and have less travel, at least on an airplane.

I started out with my payroll processor and me. I walked around town and sold merchants myself and then eventually hired a couple of sales reps. I guess we developed a pretty good little company here in this region. We got into Denver and started working with lots of banks and figured out a channel strategy that was pretty effective.

At Silverline, we licensed software for different companies and one of them wanted to buy all their licensees. We started talking the middle of 2006. I was doing some combination of playing hard to get, effective negotiating, and or just playing dumb, so the price kept going up. They wanted to buy me because I was one of their bigger licensees.

My kids were getting a little bit older and I was getting more involved in their sports and activities. I was also getting sick of running the company. We were up to about 20 employees at the time.

My wife looked at me as I was complaining about it one day and said, "Your business ADD is kicking in isn't it?"

"Yeah."

She's said, "You should probably sell that company."

"OK."

It all came together pretty quickly in the summer of 2007. We started seriously talking in June and closed the transaction by August 30th.

Since then I've just been doing a hodge-podge of things, which I like.

**You wrote a business plan when you started Silverline, I'm sure.**

I probably wrote less of a business plan than you might expect. It was more of a sketch, maybe on a white board.

**B:** *You didn't need any outside investment so you didn't need to put together a formal business plan?*

Right.

I thought initially it would only take $100,000 to start it. It ended up taking $400,000 to start it and luckily I had the resources to do that because the previous company had gone public, but if I didn't have that, I would have needed investors.

If I did it over again today it wouldn't take that much because I wasted a lot of it. You can't go back in time and figure that out. You don't know that until you go through it.

**B:** *What did you want to get out of it when you started it?*

I don't know that I ever thought that way. I think I just looked at it and said, "This is what I know how to do, there's a need for it in this area, I feel like I've done this before and can do it well, so I guess I'll just do it."

I don't know that there was that deep of a thought process that said, "What am I going to learn out of this or what am I going to get out of it?" It's just like, "Oh, this makes sense, I'll go do this."

**What kept you going during Silverline is that you were having fun building a business, doing what you were good at, knowing that you were going to sell it in just a few years. What kept you going along the whole path?**

I think that's a similar answer. I don't think there's a part where I said, "What's keeping me going?" It's more just, "This is what I'm doing now."

I certainly had forks in the road where I could have taken a corporate job with somebody. I got offers like that, but I always felt I was doing better on my own. When I left that previous company, I had some offers in the industry that I could have taken, but I just felt like I had some idea of how to build a company and the resources to do it, so I might as well try.

It's easy when you look back to say, "These are the lessons I learned," but there's no way I was thinking like that as it was unfolding. There's no way I said, "This is what I got out of that." The lessons are so subtle, there's no "ah hah" moment that's really meaningful. It takes time to appreciate what you went through.

**Did you ever say, "Making a lot of money is my goal" or "Before I die I want to make X amount of money"?**

No. I never had a number on the wall that said if I get there I've made it or anything like that.

It was just more doing stuff that I found interesting and following the next step in what I felt was my business maturity process. "OK, I started a little goofy company in Steamboat, now maybe the next thing is I need to move to a big city and do it there," or "I've been doing my own thing, maybe I need to work with these other guys now and learn some stuff from them that would be a bigger hit."

Then it was, "OK, I helped grow this national company and helped start a payroll division, let's see if I can do that on my own, on a smaller scale."

I don't think I've ever been one to follow the axiom of put your goal on the wall and look at it every day and you'll achieve it. I never said, "I want to make this much money," or "I want to do this" or "I want to do that."

I think it's more about looking for the next challenge in the maturity road, I guess.

**You had confidence, didn't you?**

I don't know if confidence is exactly the right word. I just always had this idea that no matter what happened I'd at least be OK.

**B:** *Where did that come from?*

Probably the process of thinking through, "What's the worst that can happen?" I got some early wins that gave me some breathing room to think like that. Some of those points I was single, living on my own, so I could have lived off $500 a month. It's not like I was broke living in Steamboat with four kids. I didn't have to endure that kind of stress.

**B:** *Do you think it's a different world if you do?*

It might be, but I don't know. When you look at guys that have been successful, none of the roads were easy. You don't necessarily in the moment think about it this way, but at some point you have to take a risk; you have to put yourself out there.

Not that that's the only road, but when I talk to guys starting businesses who have been somewhat successful, it never was a rallying cry moment where they said, "Alright, I'm going to do this." At least for me it wasn't. It was just, "Alright, I'll give this a shot and what's the worst that can happen? I'm 30 and I'm broke. Big deal."

**B:** *During those two seasons as a ski lift operator, it doesn't sound like you were beating your head against the wall trying to figure out "Where am I supposed to be?" Rather it was a calm, cool, "I know there's something more. This is fine for now, I'm having a blast, but where am I supposed to be?"*

That's a good way to represent it.

I definitely had my radar on to make sure that if there was an opportunity I was taking the steps to figure it out. I was somewhat cognizant that I was going to do something. I stumbled on the credit card processing and it turned into a bigger thing, which turned into a bigger thing, which got me on the road to the other stuff.

I think it's some combination of serendipity and luck and then being somewhat proactive in two senses: One, understanding that I was not going to be a lift operator forever, and two, once I started to figure out that business and got a little bit of success, I said, "Let's do this for a while."

**How did you balance time with your family as you were building all of this?**

That's been at some points hard and at some points easy, depending on what was going on.

When I was traveling a lot it was hard. I've consciously made decisions to travel less at certain points. I've made decisions now to create a lot of flexibility in my schedule so I can do things like coach soccer on a Thursday afternoon or stay home with the kids for breakfast in the morning.

But it's hard. There's no finish line to that one. There's always a balance you have to strike. Luckily, now I can afford to take a day off, if I really want to.

**You're a multimillionaire, why not just hang it all up and go to Hawaii?**

First of all, I need to be productive. I can't at 39-years-old go home and hang out.

The other part of it is I'm finally doing something that I really like; consulting for other businesses.

**How do people, before they get to that point of being financially set, do things that they really enjoy and create financial success doing it?**

I have no idea.

Part of the irony is that you only get perspective when you can look back and can say, "Maybe that's why that worked."

I was fortunate in the late 1990s when a lot of people were going through the dotcom stuff. I had my head down in this little obscure business that wasn't sexy. It wasn't like we were this great technology and we were gearing it up to sell to Microsoft or go public.

We never wanted to be the next eBay or any of the success stories. In retrospect that was good because I think a lot of those guys have a different idea of how to build a business.

**That leads to the farmer story.**

The farmer story is an analogy I use in some of the classes I teach or if I run into someone who's looking for that secret sauce or magic bullet and they think that if they learn this one little thing or if they learn the secret to success then they'll make it, or then they'll be able to employ that.

When you think about how farmers do their work, they follow a very systematic process year in and year out; it doesn't change much. They know what to do in the spring. They know they've got to plow their fields and fertilize them. They know on a certain date or timeframe they've got to plant. They've got to nurture those crops over the summer and make sure they water them. It's a very repeatable process.

As an outsider, if you go visit a farm for a couple of days you would not be able to tell the difference from one day to the next. If I went there today and then tomorrow they would look the same to me, but the farmer knows that if you trust the process those principles are going to yield; in the fall he's going to have a good crop.

The analogy is when many people start businesses they think, "I've got to be fast, I've got to be nimble, I've got to turn on a dime," which in some cases is true, but not at the expense of trusting in the principles and the process that you need to go through to build a business.

If that entrepreneur or that person visited the farm and said, "I was here yesterday and I'm here again today and there's no change, we have to make a shift, we've got to do something different. The crops aren't growing fast enough. We're not ready to harvest yet. No customers are showing up" – clearly that's silly, right?

The other funny story that comes out of that is imagine if you were a farmer and you acted like many entrepreneurs act. You decide in the spring to plant corn and then sometime in June you get bored with corn so you rip out the corn and plant soybeans. Then you heard that there are other "can't miss" plants and so you throw some magic beans in there because you read about it or saw it in some seminar. Then you got tired, so you took two weeks off in July. You didn't water your fields for that time because you deserved a vacation.

Then around September 1ˢᵗ you have this epiphany that your crops are going to suck, so you go to this seminar called "30 Days to Good Crops." How silly is that? Of course it's not going to work.

It's interesting how many people think that way; that there's some sort of accelerant or magic bullet out there that's going to get you there. I think the sexy stories of the early 2000s where a bunch of people made tons of money have skewed a lot of people's thinking that that's the way to get there.

I think if you dissect all the people who have started companies and made a significant amount of money, 99.9 percent of them have done it through just coming in every day and making a few more right decisions that day than wrong ones. The get-rich-quick guys are the exception, not the rule.

When I work with entrepreneurs that's the hardest part for them to understand. Google is not the business model. That could happen, but I would never count on it happening that way.

I would count on following the principles of the farmer. Understanding that if you do the right things day after day consistently, you're going to wake up in 10 years and have a nice little thing in front of you. It's not to say it doesn't suck along the way, but, too bad, life sucks sometimes.

**When was it the worst for you along the way?**

In Steamboat there were some lean financial years, that's for sure.

When I left the previous company, that was a hard decision because there was so much of my work and identity wrapped up in that company. And certainly there were lots of good friends and people there.

**Was there someone or something that inspired you along the way?**

Not really.

**Is there a system that you have for organizing your life and your thoughts?**

It's not really fully employed right now. I'm not an organizational nightmare, but I'm not Type A, so I'll tend to have a couple of different notepads I'm working off of at any one time and go back and forth depending on where I am, depending on what pad I have in front of me.

The funny part is that I teach people how to become more organized, but I'm not necessarily uber-organized myself.

I certainly keep a high level to-do list of important stuff, but I guess if I got caught up in the minutia day after day I don't feel like I would spend time on important stuff.

**B:** *What is important stuff?*

Non-urgent stuff. It might be researching something, or spending time with an individual, or those types of things. Strategic stuff.

Taking care of the really important stuff and then making sure to appreciate the idea of not getting caught up in the thick of thin things all the time.

[Back to the original question about organization], I would say "seat of my pants" is the way I operate a lot of the time.

**What part of what you do is most enjoyable?**

Professionally, right now I like doing a variety of things and getting plugged into different situations where maybe somebody's going through what I've been through before and I'm able to help them a bit and they'll actually pay me for it.

I feel like this is exactly where I should be.

**What's your passion?**

I really don't know.

I've been asked that question before and I honestly have never sat down and thought about what am I passionate about, I just haven't.

I enjoy what I'm doing; I tend to make decisions that way.

**If you were to go back, what would you do differently and why?**

I think that's a red herring question. There's no other road I could have followed to get me exactly where I am today.

There isn't anything I would change except for one thing: my dad was in the Navy. If I could go back, I would have spent two, maybe four, years in between school and graduate school in the Navy.

**Did you have a mentor or a role model?**

Not really. Not until recently.

What we've been talking about is a boiling down of my conversations with him: trusting where you are and where you're going. Trusting the process and having faith that you can handle whatever's in front of you.

**You believe in God?**

Yes.

**B:** *You pray?*

It's more subtle than that. A lot of the principles we talked about you find in the Bible. If you talk about a role model, there are probably a good couple of role models in there.

**How do you define success?**

I don't think I have that perspective yet. I haven't figured out where the finish line is yet.

**B:** *How would you define it along the way?*

I think it's just making progress. Sometimes you have to ask "progress towards what?" but having that little bit of ambiguity is probably a good thing.

**What do you think is next?**

I hope to keep mental engagement in this consulting work that I'm doing and keep growing it a bit. I guess I have faith that if I just do that, whatever's next will reveal itself.

****

# Millionaire 4 Jeffrey Hill

Founder, Hill-3 Investments, LLC; JH Distribution Co, LLC; Meridian Consulting Group; Investor in Papa Murphy's, Gelazzi; Philanthropist

www.teetimewatch.com, www.gelazzi.com

Two children

Bachelor's in Marketing

*Ashley Andrus referred me to Jeffrey.*

**I'd love to hear first about your background and childhood.**

I grew up in Massachusetts. I had an older brother and younger sister.

I had some very serious leg ailments and that was very challenging for myself and my family. We spent a lot of time in the hospital, which I have no doubt had some impact on my personality.

My dad owned a jewelry store. He worked six days a week from 9:00 a.m. to 6:00 p.m. The only time he had an employee was the holidays. He had a tough retail life.

**B:** *What impact do you think that had on your work ethic?*

I think it had an important impact, and my dad was a great salesman. He had a lot of friends. That had a lot of impact on my life, watching how he handled people. People believed in him and trusted him. He could sell anything. He was a very effective salesperson, and that was his strength.

Unfortunately, he chose to run a jewelry store instead of selling jewelry. Running the business might have been a little challenging because it requires many other skills beyond selling. Watching my dad I began to figure out that you should focus on what you are good at and find verticals or businesses where that strength is rewarded and respected.

My mom had a lot of energy and was entrepreneurial in her own way. She started a lot of businesses while bringing three of us up.

I also had many businesses when I was younger. I started mowing lawns at the age of 12 or 13. Probably the most notable [business] was when I got to college. I became a lifeguard on a beach in Holliston State Park and ran the beach. The guys that worked with me were teachers and this was their summer job.

One of the guys was a marathon runner and he had several age group world records. He would run every week and would win stuff every week. One day he invited me over to his basement and there was a whole basement full of stuff; TVs, radios, anything and everything he had accumulated by winning amateur races.

I said, "There's a deal to be had here," so we brought that stuff down to the beach along with a bunch of sunglasses I had accumulated and before we knew it we had a barter business. By the end of the year, we accumulated an enormous amount of stuff. We opened up a flea market stand and sold the merchandise for almost $25,000.

**B:** *Did you have to get a permit?*

We should have. In those days I lived by a philosophy, "Errors of commission are always better than errors of omission." I was 17, I didn't know any better.

Then I got to school at the University of Massachusetts. I got a nice break in that I met a gentleman who was on the GI Bill, had two kids, was much more mature than the rest of us, and was graduating a semester early. He was very focused on getting a job.

I got close to him and began to go with him to the placement department. He helped me get motivated to look for jobs a semester early. I got my resume ready and worked with him to understand the companies that were coming onto campus and one of them was Procter & Gamble [P&G].

The way P&G worked the interview process was that for every three rounds of closed interviews they had one round of open interviews. The open interview was first come, first served. I thought, "P&G is coming, they're the best marketing company in the land, I'm going."

I got there at 4:00 a.m. The next guy showed up at 7:55 a.m. The interviews started at 8:00 a.m.

I went through five rounds of interviews, three trips to Cincinnati, and I got a job as a marketing guy. That was a huge break. That whole thing: my friend being a GI Bill guy and having kids, getting there at four in the morning, those were a series of good breaks.

I got promoted and worked my way through the ranks at P&G.

**B:** *Just by working hard?*

I worked hard and was driven and motivated. I was very competitive as were they. But competition in those days was done in a fun way. We all became friends.

I was running Joy dishwashing division and then a friend, a P&G guy, approached me and said, "There's an opportunity to go back East"–which was a goal of mine because I grew up in the East–"to work for a company called Tampax."

Five P&G managers all decided to go to work for Tampax: the head of R&D, head of research, head of finance, and a few others. That was very appealing to me because I was 29 and it was an opportunity to get a bigger job at a serious company, be able to make a difference, and go back East.

It was a very interesting story as to what happened. P&G had launched a brand called Rely Tampons and just beat [up] Tampax. Tampax had 65 percent market share before P&G launched. P&G launched this massive marketing campaign and it took 30 share points from Tampax in the first six months. Tampax went from about a $600 million business to a $350 million business in six months and P&G probably would have continued to [beat up on] Tampax.

Then an unusual thing happened that changed the marketplace. Toxic shock was identified.

P&G's number one marketing technique in those days was household sampling, an execution they used with Rely. Eighty percent of menstruating females were sampled at home. So when Toxic Shock was identified and post-research was done with regard to what tampon brand the victims had used, virtually everybody answered, "Rely."

P&G had two options. One was to show the testing, which proved that they were not the problem; reinforcing the several years of testing they had done before launch. The other was to say, "The consumer energy is against us, we're a consumer company, let's just bite the bullet and take the high road."

They withdrew the entire Rely brand; a $75 million after tax loss. They had spent a fortune on this thing, they had been working on it for years, but they did it anyway because they're a high ground company and they always do the right thing; very impressive.

I was 29-years-old, didn't have a passport, was running the marking department for Tampax, and our CEO said, "Get on a plane and go find technology anywhere around the world." I flew to Germany, I flew to Belgium, I flew to Paris.

I had no idea what I was doing. I was a smart marking guy, but I wasn't ready for this. It was great. I loved every minute of it.

We found a super absorbent technology in Japan and we created a brand called Maxi Thins. It became an 11 share, $110 million business virtually overnight. Then we did some other fun stuff. We found another thing called a monoclonal antibody. It turned out to be a superior fertility- and pregnancy-detection device and we created a brand called First Response, which is still around.

After being at Tampax for three years, I got a call from another P&G guy who said, "We're about to buy a consulting company called Glendinning Associates from the founder Ralph Glendinning," also an ex-P&G employee.

He had an enormous reputation. He had built a $300 million consulting company with offices all around the world; very exciting business. These guys knew how to have fun and work hard. I caught the disease and took the job.

The other six guys who invited me to join are really players and I was the last guy down the line. Eight years later I was one of the partners.

Most of my partners decided that they wanted to go back into industry and become senior management of various companies. I didn't want to do that; I loved consulting. It was very entrepreneurial, no politics, a lot of money. It was great.

I started my own consulting company called Meridian Consulting. I started it with three clients, all of whom I had developed at

Glendinning: Schering Plough, Chesebrough Ponds, and Nabisco. I had no staff [other than a] secretary.

We did a lot of good work and almost all of the people that [later] worked for me, and almost all of my clients, were in my P&G network. The P&G network had grown and grown. People would leave P&G, become a superstar somewhere else, and they'd hire us. Then they would leave that firm, become a superstar somewhere else, and hire us there.

In consulting, the secret is to win for your client from a business and career standpoint and we were good at it.

I sold the firm in early 2000 for cash to the second largest French Holding Company, Havas, and their U.S. subsidiary Euro RSCG.

There was money everywhere to buy firms like mine because everybody wanted a strategic think-tank consulting company to lead their enterprise. The Big Three accounting firms wanted it, all the advertising holding companies, and several others.

**B:** *You had put virtually no money into the company?*

I had no money in the company, but I had 25 years of my life, which was the equity.

Money is a lot less important than the equity you bring to the table, whatever your equity is. Intellectual horsepower, your skills, your inventions; whatever they are, that's the value of the firm.

What makes a firm successful is the ideas, the intellectual capital; that's what runs a company. Then anybody with high net worth can be approached and if you've got a good idea and you're passionate about the idea, you can sell the idea and get yourself funded. I'm oversimplifying, but the real essence of what makes a successful company is the idea, not the money.

P.S. Without the money, the idea is not likely to percolate, so you do need the money, but the important thing is the equity, or the patent, or whatever it is.

After I sold the firm, I started a foundation helping kids with the same operation I had when I was a kid. We do it for uninsured families.

I did that for a year-and-a-half and it wasn't quite as intellectually stimulating as I thought it would be. I then started making investments. My first investment was in Noodles and Company in Boulder, Colorado.

I also invested in Papa Murphy's and helped run the business for a while as the Chief Strategic Officer. I started getting more entrepreneurial and starting to do other deals. I started a real estate development company.

Then Jan Horsfall whom I knew from consulting at Valvoline called me up and said, "I want to get into the gelato business."

I asked, "What do you know about the gelato business?"

"Nothing."

"So what gives you the license to go into it?"

He said, "I've done a lot of due diligence."

I said, "That makes you a smart guy, but I'm not investing in the gelato business on your word. If you get involved in the gelato business for 12 months and call me back and tell me you've been in it for 12 months and now you know it, then maybe I'll invest." I knew he would not do it.

He did it. That's why I got into the Gelazzi business.

**What would you say is your greatest success?**

My kids, because I think they are going to do very well. They've got a good sense for both sides of life. They understand what it takes to succeed and they're diligent, committed, and motivated. They also have a soft side, which is great.

They increasingly understand philanthropy and what it means to be somewhat more disadvantaged than they are and how to feel responsible to people other than themselves. It's very unusual with kids.

That's probably the best work I've ever done.

Certainly the work with the foundations is a close second.

Maybe someday my kids will take over the foundations, which I hope they do, but they always laugh at me and say, "Dad, stop writing the future of our lives before we've even started thinking of it because we're not doing anything you tell us to." After all, that's how kids are.

**What's the difference between you and others like you who have plenty of money, who have accumulated a lot of worldly wealth, and those that just struggle?**

I can speak to it in the entrepreneurial context. I think there are certain "what counts" factors. Motivation and drive are absolutely fundamental. And knowing what you don't know and seeking out help from people to fill in your voids.

I also think vision is critical. I don't mean vision in a big lofty context. I'm talking about vision as it relates to your ability to see how you can fit into something.

**Would you say that passion equals success?**

No. I think passion is important though.

The most important thing to success is you've got to have a good idea, or you've got to work for a company that has a good idea. Then you have to be able to execute in that environment.

If it's your business, you've got to figure out an executional plan for your business. If it's somebody else's business, you've got to figure out how to execute in that space.

So having a good idea and being able to execute are the first two things.

If you've got passion on top of that and good people skills, then you have a lot of the basics.

**Did you have written down goals?**

Not really.

**B:** *Did you ever set out to be a millionaire?*

No.

My economic goal centered on where my dad came from. I thought $100,000 was all the money [in the world]. Then my goal was to have enough money so that money was not an issue in my life.

I didn't need to have lofty goals. I didn't grow up with a lot of things. My family had a lot of love and we worked hard.

**B:** *Do you have goals now?*

Absolutely.

**B:** *And you have plans to get there?*

Yes.

**B:** *But you didn't along the way?*

I did as I got older.

You asked me if I did when I started. No, I didn't. Did I have the goal of being a millionaire? I had the goal of being successful. I didn't know what that was.

I tripped over the P&G work, that wasn't planned. If it weren't for the guy who was on the GI Bill, I may never have gotten there.

**What would you go back and change, and why?**

My normal answer to anything like that is I wouldn't change anything. I'm not a big "rear view mirror guy."

We can't go back. I've done some things that I would have done differently had I had [different] information, but you never do.

I might have gotten into philanthropy earlier.

**Did you know you were going to be successful?**

No.

I believed I was going to be successful because I'm the eternal optimist. If you don't believe it's not going to happen, so you better believe. The other thing is if you don't believe, then no one else will. In all my start up ideas, I believe and I try to get a contagious belief instilled into others.

**Would you say your journey was relatively easy or hard?**

It was fun, but I wouldn't say it was easy. It's not easy; it was difficult.

**Would you say that you've built what you've built through hard work?**

Yes, without any question.

**Is there a belief system that guides your life?**

I don't know how formal it is, but on balance it's the "do unto others" philosophy. I try not to do anything to others unless I would feel comfortable having it done to me.

I wasn't always like that, but I am now.

**You live a pretty non-ostentatious lifestyle. Tell me about that.**

That's because you're seeing me now. I went through another life stage at one point. I was accumulating things as my career was moving along. But after a while I realized what was really important was friends, family, and giving back.

**What do you consider success to be?**

I have more than one definition depending on what area of my life it is.

**B:** *At the time you were becoming a millionaire, what was your definition?*

Being able to support my family. That was the number one issue. It was never a number, it was addressing needs.

**How do you know an opportunity when you see it?**

The question is do you capitalize on opportunities when presented? Example: P&G was coming to my campus, so "the break" is now presented, but am I going to capitalize and how? I decide to get there at 4:00 a.m. while everyone else arrived at 7:55 a.m.

I was talking to a guy the other day that I was helping in a career context. He said, "I used to work for Starbucks and I got my MBA at DU," and on and on.

I said, "You're a very talented guy, very driven. What you need is a break. When you see it, you'll know what it is."

He said, "Well, I got a chance to work at the U.N., but I didn't take it."

"Really, why not?"

His answer was, "Because they didn't offer me enough money."

I asked, "What did you do instead?"

"I went back to Lebanon where I grew up and visited my family."

I said, "Well, that's an example of not realizing an opportunity that you were presented. You have to be able to identify and capitalize on opportunities when they're presented to you. How many guys have on their resume 'Worked at the U.N.'? Plus, then you would have been in New York City working for the U.N. That's going to expose you to a whole world of opportunity and contact. The next time an opportunity comes along, don't find a reason not to take it, find a reason to take it."

He said, "I didn't have enough money to live in New York."

I said, "I lived in New York. I can't tell you how many people live with five other people in New York City just to be there. All these starving actors and actresses and everybody else, they're waiting on tables. You would have done fine there. You're an industrious guy with an MBA for heaven's sakes. If these guys can survive, certainly you can."

He just chose not to. Not enough motivation and drive there.

A) He didn't have the vision to see the opportunity, and B) He wasn't driven.

**Did you have a mentor or a role model?**

Not really.

I picked up role models along the way, but not any one person. Wherever I was I was looking at people and trying to replicate their approach, style, and skill. I would watch anybody that looked like they were successful and embodied an approach I was comfortable with.

**B:** *Do you get together with people and kick ideas around?*

I do.

A network is one of the greatest assets that you could possibly build. I've maintained my network, many of whom live in the Greater New York area, Connecticut, Boston, and so on.

**It sounds like you're not only not afraid of challenges, you enjoy stretching yourself and growing and learning.**

Right. If you don't push yourself, you never reach your potential.

## What advice would you give a 5th grader?

You have to put yourself into uncomfortable situations, in areas that you know you need to improve in.

Do the things that you are uncomfortable doing until you become comfortable. When you stop growing you stop developing.

Everybody's got friends that when they retired they got old almost immediately. Not that they had to get old immediately, but they stopped everything.

I've got a lot of young friends who are between the ages of 40 and 50 who retired and some of them did it brilliantly. Those were guys that were involved in philanthropy, boards, and this and that. They had plenty to do, which keeps their minds sharp and keeps them focused.

The guys that did what they thought was retiring are all working now, every one of them, because their brain turned to sawdust. They realized they needed to get reengaged.

## How would you describe your passion?

Being very committed to things I love. I don't know what else to say.

## What drove you along the way?

I'm not sure.

I would just say two things. This endless desire to achieve, and to establish goals and achieve those goals. Then once I achieve those goals to raise the bar.

## How did you balance time with your family while you were building your business?

I was good at it. I didn't miss anything.

**B:** *How?*

Mostly because I made sure everybody got what I was doing and knew where my priorities were.

For example, General Mills was a client of mine in Minneapolis. There was a 6:00 a.m. flight for which I would have to leave my house at 4:00 a.m. If I could get to Minneapolis by 9:00 a.m., I could get to the meeting by 11:00 a.m. The meeting had to have a disciplined end point because I had to be on the field by 6:00 p.m. to coach my daughter's softball team.

**B:** *These companies understood? You just laid it out on the table and said, "I coach my daughter's softball team, I'm getting back"?*

I didn't say it quite that way. What I would say is, "We're all parents, right? How important is it for you to spend time with your kids at important events?" – "Very important." – "So it is to me. Let's have a meeting at 11:00 a.m., I've got to be done by 2:00 p.m."

**Were you always looking for the next step, or were you focused in the moment?**

Both.

You need to have a plan. Once you develop the plan, then you've got to focus in the moment. If you don't focus in the moment you'll always be wondering why you don't achieve things.

**Was there anyone who inspired you along the way?**

I'd say many people inspired me, but no one individual in particular.

My parents were inspirational in their own way. They don't even realize they were in some ways. My dad, deep down in his heart, doesn't think that he added value to my life, which is totally untrue. He taught me the family values that I've integrated into my lifestyle.

My daughter wrote a beautiful essay that embodies the essence of what I'm trying to teach her. It proves to me that she got it and got me. I love that essay.

\*\*\*\*

# Millionaire 5 Heidi Ganahl

Founder, Camp Bow Wow

www.campbowwowusa.com

Married, two daughters

Bachelor's, MBA, CFP

*Ashley Andrus referred me to Heidi.*

## Tell me about you.

I grew up in southern California until I was about 13, then our family moved from Irvine to Monument, Colorado, a small town just north of the Air Force Academy near Colorado Springs.

**B:** *What was the impetus for the move?*

My parents wanted my brother Patrick and me to have the experience of growing up in a small community where we would know our neighbors and classmates and live in a more rural environment. I went to middle school and high school with only 70 kids in my class. I had great friends, many of whom I'm still in touch with.

Of course, by the end of high school I was ready for the big city life, so I took advantage of a scholarship at SMU [Southern Methodist University] in Dallas. Later, I realized that my roots were in Colorado, so I transferred to CU Boulder [Colorado University].

I always thought I'd be an advertising account executive and live in San Francisco, or Chicago. I did internships through high school and college in advertising. I was very focused, and really believed that's exactly what I wanted to do, but I was very entrepreneurial, too. I wanted to own my own agency eventually.

## Does that come from your dad who owned a business?

Yeah, my dad's very entrepreneurial. He was always in sales so even when he didn't own his own company, which he eventually did, he was all about creating your own success, being super optimistic, and having a great attitude. He always told us that that we should get a good education. Neither one of my parents finished college, so they were pretty key on that.

My mom, she's kind of his alter ego. She's the accountant/bookkeeper type, realistic. It drove her absolutely nuts at times that I didn't have a stable eight to five job and work for corporate America.

When I graduated from college I moved to San Diego and went to work at an ad agency as a receptionist. I was ready to get going. I did that for a couple of years and moved up to Junior Account Executive and ran out of money out there. I couldn't afford to keep up with the Joneses.

I came back to Colorado. There were no advertising jobs here so I went into pharmaceutical sales–I answered an ad in the paper–with a small pharmaceutical company. I was one of their original 12 sales reps.

I had a blast, but a couple of years later thought I wanted to go work for the big guys, so I moved on to a huge national company and absolutely hated it. That was my first big taste of corporate America. Great training program, I learned a ton from them, but it was brutal.

In the meantime, I met Bion, my first husband, and got married. He was very entrepreneurial too. He put himself through school and worked for my dad. We were the typical yuppie couple.

I got laid off from my second pharmaceutical job and started to realize maybe this was a blessing in disguise. I wanted to start my own medical distribution company, Achoo Allergy Products, so I took a job selling asthma equipment for kids to pediatricians.

About the same time, Bion and I would go over and hang out at this doggy daycare next to my folks' business; we took our dogs there. Kennels just weren't good enough for the dogs, we just didn't want them stuck in a box all the time; they were very spoiled. We had two big dogs and had abused our family and friends with requests to watch them when we were away. We thought, "Wouldn't it be cool if the dogs could go to a camp, play all day and have a great time, and then stay overnight, like a vacation for them, too?" So we built the business plan for Camp Bow Wow.

Bion was finishing college, I had this medical distribution thing going, and we had no money in the bank. But we thought, "Let's try to start Camp Bow Wow." We started looking at sites and the landlords would say, "You want to do what? Put 50 dogs in a room?

Are you crazy? They're going to kill each other." We couldn't find a landlord that was open to that or get any kind of financial backing.

Bion died in a plane crash while we were looking for a site. My world totally changed. I got a large settlement a few months later, a million dollars, and managed to quickly blow through that. I made a lot of loans to friends and family members. Once you learn more about the psychological impact of getting a settlement you discover that you're actually trying to get rid of it because there's so much guilt attached to it.

I was always of the mindset that I was going to be a big success and all the sudden people were saying, "You're going to be a success because you have all this money."

I thought, "No, I'm still going to do my entrepreneurial thing and be a big success some day."

I was experiencing that on top of a quick rebound marriage, which was a disaster, and lasted only a year. The blessing from that was my wonderful daughter, Tori.

I then started Nursery Works, a baby bedding company. I thought that would be a cool idea. I hated it; it was order taking, basically. Then I started doing consulting for people who received sudden wealth, trying to help prevent them from making the same mistakes I did. That's when I created the Maginot Group.

I ended up doing most of it for free because I felt like I was taking advantage of these people just as much as the people that were charging them to give them advice. Half the time they didn't listen to me; they thought they were not ever going to make those mistakes. These are folks that have received $1 million to $20 million dollars. Seventy-five percent of those people blow it within three years.

In December 2000 my brother came to me and said, "You don't like charging people for the Maginot Group and you hate pharmaceutical sales. We're digging up the old business plan for Camp Bow Wow. That's what you were always passionate about, let's make that happen."

My immediate reaction was "I can't, I'm too overwhelmed. I'm a single mom. I don't have any money left."

He said, "You have $85,000 left, let's do it."

We went out and found a spot. He ran the day to day and I continued to do flextime pharmaceuticals to support Tori and me.

**You were doing flextime pharmaceuticals, you were speaking a little bit for Maginot Group, and then you start Camp Bow Wow because your brother said, "Let's dig this up"?**

He had been working for my parents' janitorial supply company and my dad sold the company. I think we had a glass of beer and away we went!

**B:** *What if you had tried to do it in 1994 – would it have caught on? Did the market need more time?*

I think the market needed a little more time and I think I had to have those other experiences with starting and closing down Nursery Works and getting my master's degree; lots of life experiences that helped me be ready to start Camp Bow Wow.

We started Camp Bow Wow and I was in charge of the marketing and getting the business rolling and Patrick was there to hang out with the dogs and keep the business going every day.

It started off with a bang and things went very well until about six months into it. The zoning folks came in and said, "You don't have a use permit for this place."

We're like, "What's a use permit?"

I got my first lesson in zoning and permit approvals.

We had to move the facility a couple blocks away. We found another building, which was totally a fluke. That's our Cherokee street location that's still in existence today, one of the busiest Camps out there.

Things just started evolving. I was a hard-core perfectionist about the brand and how I wanted things done and the customer service. We went through a lot of employees, but the customers loved it.

**You were a perfectionist, but you got slapped with a zoning violation.**

Didn't know what I didn't know.

**B:** *I think so many people are afraid to get out and pursue their dream because they think they need to have all of the pieces in place before they do it.*

That's a good point. I think you're right.

I get asked this a lot, too: "If I knew then what I know now, would I do it all over again?" and I always hesitate. It's exhausting to think about going through all that again, but I didn't know what was up ahead, so you just deal with it when it happens and you take one day at a time, one fire at a time, and try to put it out.

**Why is focus important and what does it mean to focus?**

Everybody and everything tries to derail you from your vision; it's like a video game. Franchisees want to do their own brochures. Your employees think they have a better way of doing things or they want to follow their vision instead of yours.

You've got to keep everybody on the same page. Your website, all the technical parts of the business, your customer service, your front line, the Camp counselors that are talking to the customers; everything has to permeate that brand for it to be successful. If you think about the best brands in this country–Coca-Cola, Google, Starbucks–it's consistency. Somebody can have an experience with that brand and it's consistent day after day.

But my goodness it's almost like a cult; you have to get people to buy into that. We call it drinking the Camp Bow Wow Kool-Aid, whether it's working here, being a client, or a franchisee. The beauty of franchising only lies in the cohesiveness of everybody in the vision. If everybody's off doing their own thing, it doesn't work.

That's been one of the biggest struggles; I could have taken short cuts, it would have been cheaper to do things a different way. From the very beginning I felt it was very important to have a [great] website. It cost a lot of money when I didn't have any money, it's continued to cost money when I didn't have any money, but I'm very stubborn about it.

The thing that I will not compromise on is taking care of the dogs. I will shut down an operator in a heartbeat if their heart isn't in the right place or they are not completely focused on the dogs' safety because that's our brand.

I'm trying to create Disney for dogs; a place where the dogs can have an incredible time, and the franchisees have an incredible time running their business. I want to make it as easy as possible for them to run the business so they can focus on the dogs.

But at the end of the day, it's got to stay true to what my vision of the brand is. It's worked this far. When people try to derail me, I'm going to follow my gut because my gut's gotten me pretty far with what the customers really want.

You have to listen to that and respect it even if it costs money, or if it means making a tough decision about firing somebody, or bringing on a program that's controversial.

**Did you ever set out to be a millionaire?**

I always wanted to be very successful. I wanted to be a great leader or a female entrepreneur. I always had that drive, but when I set out to become a millionaire was after I lost the million dollars from the settlement. I knew I had to earn it back, so my whole goal has been to create a company that is worth at least a million dollars.

**You had a business plan, but did you have written down, specific goals? "In year one I want to make this much, in year two this much, the company this much, me this much." Did you have it crystallized?**

For my Camp I did, for the franchise part of it, no.

**B:** *You just fell into that?*

By the seat of my pants.

We had a client who was a regional sales director for Mrs. Fields Cookies. He said, "Have you ever thought about franchising this?"

This was after I had opened my second Camp.

"No."

He said, "Why don't we go to the IFA [International Franchise Association] meeting. I want to introduce you to some people and let's see if franchising Camp Bow Wow is a viable concept."

Nobody had franchised a dog care facility yet. It was bizarre; I can't imagine why they hadn't.

**B:** *Earlier you had tried to talk that lady who opened up her dog care facility next to your dad's business into doing it, right?*

Yep, and she said, "No, I just want my one little place." She's still there. She's still doing it.

I just thought I would have four or five Camps in Denver and that would be the end of it or I'd do the sportswear part of it [selling doggy-themed clothing].

We went to the meeting. He wasn't super knowledgeable about how much it actually cost to start franchising a business and all of the implications of doing it, so I paid my attorney to put together the paperwork. I took out a loan on a credit card of $25,000, put up a couple of signs on the counters at the two Camp Bow Wows, and went for it.

It was a couple of weeks, I think, after I put that sign up that a lady named Nancy walked into our central Denver location–she had been to Camp once with her dog, Daisy–and [saw the sign]. She called me up and said, "Heidi, I think I want to do this, can we meet?"

We had breakfast and a week later her parents financed the whole thing. She opened the first franchise in Castle Rock. She's such a trooper and we got to be very good friends. I couldn't have asked for a better first franchisee; she was so tolerant of everything.

My dad, my brother and I worked at her place for two months straight going back and forth to Home Depot helping her build it out. Her parents came, her brother, everybody pitched in; it was fabulous.

**Did you do all kinds of demographic studies and surveys or did you just say, "You want a franchise, let's go"?**

I did everything you shouldn't do when you franchise a business, but I was just so tenacious and so starry eyed about, "I'm sticking to it, this is what's going to happen."

A lot of it was luck.

**Did you practice a formalized version of visualization of where you wanted things to be, or did you just have this general concept?**

I am the poster child for *The Secret*, but I didn't know about *The Secret*. I didn't have any formalized education on visualization but my dad and my grandfather taught me that. My grandfather was a chemical engineer; he was involved in the Manhattan project, brilliant man.

He taught me that you have to have passion for what you do and vision, but you have to step it out; you have to have a plan and work your plan. He was all about having an idea of how you're going to get there, but knowing what the steps are to get there. In my head I had it, I just never put it down on paper necessarily.

I always knew I wanted to make Camp Bow Wow a household name and I wanted to change the way people took care of dogs in this country. I realized that the Camps were the business, once I got away from the retail idea of selling sportswear.

**B:** *And that was two years into it, do you think?*

I think it was when I opened Camp Bow Wow Broomfield and I saw the response was tremendous; way better than the first Camp even. I thought, "Oh my, this is huge. People love this concept and they love what we're doing."

I think it was about the time I decided to franchise. I knew if I'm going to do this, I'm going to do this right and everybody's going to know what Camp Bow Wow is and we're going to have fun with this. We're going to make it a fun concept that blows the mom and pop kennels out of the water so that dogs don't have to sit in a little box 24-hours a day and get a bowl of water.

**B:** *And that's when you caught your vision?*

Yeah.

**B:** *You fell into the franchising part, which is where you're really hitting it big?*

Yes.

Life has certainly not taken the path I thought it would. I always say if I'm going to write a book about my life it's going to be called *The All American Girl Gone Wrong*, because I was the epitome of the All American Girl. I was a cheerleader and I wanted to be an ad exec. I was like Reese Witherspoon in *Legally Blond*, I was just too naïve to know any different.

I had a great family, a great upbringing. I got married to a great guy and was ready to have my 2.5 kids and do pharmaceutical sales when all [heck] broke loose. But I'm such a grounded person. I have a stronger faith, [but I'm] not religious.

**What belief system guides your life?**

I was raised quasi-religious, the typical "we go to church on the [religious] holidays."

My mom was Catholic, my dad was Baptist and they didn't want to go that far, but did want to give their kids a taste of it.

When Bion died I felt very lost. "Is there something out there? What is it?" I read all kinds of books in the first six months about spirituality, different religions and beyond death and that kind of stuff; it gets kind of morbid. I finally came to a really comfortable place where I knew that there is a higher power and I do believe in God.

I don't know if I believe in the stories the Bible tells, but I believe there's a reason why we're here. We're supposed to learn certain lessons, we're supposed to become responsible for ourselves and the rest of human beings and take care of each other. I think that's the lesson that we're supposed to learn, but man it's hard.

I think that's why I'm so attracted to dogs and kids. They're so innocent and have that all loving, no judgment, unconditional peace about them. So I think that's the spirituality piece for me.

**Who were your mentors?**

[Two friends.] Deanna is a very good friend of mine. After going to high school together, we both ended up at CU. We became very close. [Another friend], Dawn Marie, and I have known each other since I was born.

Those two girls have kept me grounded through everything that has happened. Those are two people in my life who will never go away.

**How would you say you got where you are, if you had to distill it?**

I'd say my lack of fear, my vision and my sheer, stubborn tenacity. I'm not going to fail. Failure is not an option for me.

Yeah, I piddled around with these other companies doing these other things, but this is what I'm supposed to do and I'm going to be a big success. You just have to believe that in your head.

**How did you stick to the business, stay tenacious, grab the results that you've gotten and still focus on the family time?**

I think involving my family in the business was a big part of it. It wasn't either or, it was always blended. And I think my energy level.

I have tons of energy. I've never been one to sit around on the couch and watch TV. I'm always making the most of every moment, whether it's with Tori, with my friends, or my family. It's certainly swayed toward the bad side where my mom and dad had to sit me down and say, "Hey, pay attention to your family and your daughter." That has happened several times.

**Would you say the journey–this is a loaded question–was it relatively easy, or was it hard?**

Oh my, it was harder than...

It was so hard. That's why when people ask me would I do it all over again, in that sheer moment I go, "NOOO!" Yet again, I can't imagine my life without doing this, but it was really hard.

**Why are you so well respected?**

I don't know, maybe because I'm so real. I'm very open. I am what I am and if people don't like me or don't get along with me, that's OK. We can't all get along, but I just have fun. I try to be good to people because I'm a firm believer in Karma. What you put out there comes back to you.

**What's your greatest joy in life?**

My daughters, my husband, my dogs and my family. Spending time with people that I love and making a difference in dogs' lives.

**What should people who want to be successful know?**

That it's a [heck] of a lot of hard work and that cash is king. Cash will rule your life: not having enough of it, having too much of it, knowing what to do with it, how to invest it, how to build the company with the cash that you have.

**B:** *Cash will rule your life?*

Cash flow management, I guess I should say.

**B:** *OK – cash flow management. You said earlier that money doesn't make you happy.*

Yes.

**B:** *When you can't pay your bills, you're not happy.*

You're right.

**B:** *So money does make you happy to a degree?*

It's a tool.

**B:** *But once you have enough, is that when money ceases to make you happy?*

It's Maslow's Hierarchy of Needs pyramid: once you have your basic needs met, you realize money's not important, money doesn't create happiness.

**B:** *When you're managing your cash, no matter how much you have, if you're managing it well and living below your means, you're still falling in that happiness zone. Is that right?*

Yeah, and you're not stressed out because you're maxed out on all your credit cards and living in a house you can't afford with a car you can't afford. It's the American way, and believe me, I'm the biggest offender.

**What advice would you give to somebody looking for a break? They're beating their head against a wall and they're wondering, "Where is it? Where's success?"**

For me, sometimes the best thing to do is just to ask God, or the universe, for what I want, and then put it away for a little while and stop thinking about it.

I think that sometimes we get bogged down in the minutia and you've got to just give your brain a rest and it will figure it out. If you have a question before you go to sleep and you ask yourself the question, usually in the morning you wake up with some clarity, so keep it simple.

If you watch *The Secret*, the people that have used it successfully talk about visualizing what they want, really thinking about what the end result looks like, then putting it out there and putting it out of your mind and seeing what happens. I know that sounds a little bit crazy, but I've done it in some cases and it works.

When you're analyzing something too much or you're buried in something, let God figure out what's supposed to happen. Quit trying to figure it out. You can do the same thing with God and prayer. When you pray, you pray for what you want the end result to be and you leave it in God's hands. It's the [idea from the poem] *Footsteps*; He'll carry you if you let Him, if you quit worrying about it and trying to let your mind run your life instead of that current or that energy.

**What do you wish someone would ask you?**

I wish my franchisees and the people in my company would ask me what they do at their job that makes me happy. They get so focused on what they think they should be doing.

**What is success?**

Success is loving what you do, enjoying getting up every day, jumping out of bed, being excited about life. The day I get bored or don't enjoy what I'm doing is the day that I'm not successful.

**What else do you want people to know?**

I think after talking to you, and hearing where you are in your series of becoming an entrepreneur and becoming successful, it's that you just take one day at a time, one step at a time, and don't overwhelm yourself with the whole thing about opening a business or being a huge success at work.

[Just ask yourself,] "What can I do at work today to get there? What small step can I take? When I finish this day, what do I want it to look like when I look back and know that I'm working towards that goal?"

Just not making it too complicated. It's that keep it simple thing again.

**Bonus Question**: Have you ever stopped to think about: you lost Bion and that taught you huge lessons, you lost a million dollars and that taught you huge lessons?

Yes. I think part of the reason Camp Bow Wow has been successful is that I don't have any fear. I can lose everything and I'll be OK. I've lost the person that is most dear to me in my life and I'm OK.

I'm not happy about it, but you survive. My therapist used to say, "You wake up every day and you decide if you're going to die or if you're going to live. You're going to act as if you're dead or act as if you're alive."

I feel like life isn't always what you expect it's going to be, but it's an adventure. It's a wild ride. You never know what's coming.

I hope I can instill that in my daughters. Don't have such rigid expectations. Just go with the flow and have some fun. It's going to twist and turn, but you've got to be flexible and just enjoy the ride – which is so not who I was before everything happened.

I've learned faith in myself and my abilities to overcome bad things. At the end of the day, it's OK. That's what life's about, just learning and growing and having confidence in yourself that you can overcome obstacles.

\*\*\*\*

# Millionaire 6 Steve Rosdal

Retired: Co-Founder, Hyde Park Jewelers

www.hydeparkjewelers.com

One son

Bachelor's in Economics

*Theresa Byrne[1] referred me to Steve after hearing about the book from Ashley Andrus.*

**First, I'd love to get to know you and your background.**

I was born and raised in Queens New York. I went to school in upstate New York and then got a job on Wall Street, but the market back then was awful. There was no volume, it was a different market; there was no money to be made.

**Was it your dream to work on Wall Street?**

No. I got into Cornell and was pre-vet, but then I worked on a farm one summer and realized I didn't love blood or suffering and it wasn't for me, so I never went on.

I graduated with a BS in Economics. My first job on Wall Street paid me $11,000 a year, and it really wasn't enough in New York to get an apartment, to go out and have a life.

One day I figured the only way out of New York was to escape. I wasn't able to have a good life there and decided I would start over. It didn't matter where I went, I really didn't care.

**B:** *Did you know what you wanted to do once you got there?*

No, I had no idea.

I was in a rut. You don't have a lot of friends in New York because people at work might live in another borough. It's a tough city in a lot of ways.

I already decided to move to either Denver or Atlanta. Then I saw the Robert Redford movie, *Jeremiah Johnson*, that was filmed in the Colorado Rockies and thought, "I like the four seasons and I'm a skier" so I came to Denver.

I came at summer time and I wanted to take a month or two off. I moved to Capital Hill, within blocks of Cheeseman Park. A bunch of people played volleyball there every day and I met some of them.

One of them, who went by the name of King, a doctor at Denver General, was collecting Indian jewelry. I didn't know anything about Indian jewelry. I didn't even know there were Indians that made jewelry, but he was collecting it. He was going to the mountains to Frisco to check out this old pawn store that had a lot of old Indian jewelry, which, when that was around, was good stuff. I had never been to the mountains so I went up there with him. I got interested and thought it was really neat.

I was told basically you get on I-25 and there are Indians in Albuquerque. I had nothing better to do. My life's savings, which at the time seemed like a lot more than it would today, was $1600. I took $800 and went to Albuquerque to buy some Indian jewelry.

There were tons of places to buy Indian jewelry; I don't think I bought anything from the right spot. I just went into stores and I spent $800. I came back, got together with three or four doctors from Denver General and sold half of what I brought back and got all my money back, so I kept going.

I used to commute from Denver to Albuquerque on a regular basis. This was during the old road system. It was a longer trip than it is today, but I'd commute like that was nothing. I actually looked forward to the commute.

It seemed to be a good business, but it wasn't a great business. It was a lot to do, but it was a growing business. Everything I got I put back into the business. It's not like I ever had a lot of money, but I had a growing stash of jewelry.

I started trading with the Indians. I got to the source; I got on the reservation. I was able to buy much better and about a year after I started I was selling to the same stores that I originally bought from.

From King and his doctors, the business grew from various people along the way. Caribou Ranch was a major recording studio in Nederland at the time. All the big groups came through Colorado and recorded there. I met somebody and became known as the "Indian Trader."

I had a store in Aspen. It got to be very tedious because I had to travel to Albuquerque, come back to Denver, and then drive to Aspen.

**B:** *You were savvy enough after a year that you were selling to the same people you had bought from previously?*

What really happened was about a year into it, I believe it was *Time Magazine* had Jill St. John on the cover and she was bedecked in Indian jewelry: earrings, necklace, Concho belt. It was a fashion statement. There was an explosion of Indian jewelry. People wanted it after they saw her in it. The designers started using it, Ralph Lauren started to use it, and it just became this thing.

It's still the only fashion I know of that started in the middle of this country, worked its way to both coasts and then oversees. It started basically in Aspen, with the Jill St. John thing.

I would go down to the reservation and did most of my trading off the Santa Domingo Reservation. I moved to Albuquerque and lived there for about a year-and-a-half because you had to be on the reservation at 9:00 a.m. or else you weren't going to buy anything. Once the department stores got in, it was crazy.

The people that were buying right off the reservation sold to stores and to other traders. I could have walked off the reservation and sold everything I had.

We had a system. I would take this shoulder bag and about $10,000 or $20,000 in cash everyday, go to the reservation, and spend it. I would then go to the Albuquerque airport, pack it all up, and put in on a Continental Airlines jet. They would open the package in Denver and there would be people that were there to buy.

It was every single day, seven days a week. We started with my $800 and about a year-and-a-half out we were at a $1.5 million in sales.

**B:** *How did you do that?*

Just the way I told you. The biggest thing was probably right time, right place.

I was this pseudo-hippy guy making a living, but not much more, from doing something that all of the sudden everybody wanted.

In saying that, I had friends down there that went out of business in the same time period. They just didn't get the right things, didn't have the right contacts, didn't know what to do with their money.

Some people made it, some people didn't make it, but it was the easiest thing I ever did. If you worked hard and you were honest and fair, you built a business. It was hard not to, even with no money, which is where I started. You can't really look at $800 as having enough money to start a business.

### Did you build the business step by step or did you have a master plan in mind?

I had no master plan. I was playing volleyball.

**B:** *Did you just take the next logical step at each turn?*

Yes.

I think you make mistakes.

When the department stores hit, it was the best time and the worst time. We were selling truckloads of Indian jewelry. However, we were ending the fad.

The way I feel about things like this is when it gets big enough, the department stores take it and that's the last step. They will take it and do it and do it and do it. They don't have the same kind of integrity because they just want it cheaper and cheaper.

The department stores wound up buying stuff that wasn't Indian, stuff that was made in Hong Kong and Mexico, and selling it for Indian. They were buying turquoise that wasn't treated. It was the beginning of the end.

We chose not to do that. We wanted to be our pure selves – right answer and wrong answer. We end lined the business for ourselves; we couldn't compete. American Indians don't work as cheap as people in Hong Kong, who at the time were working for pennies an hour.

It was not a situation that we chose to play in. But we found scrimshaw in the Northwest on whales' teeth and walrus ivory the Eskimos made. We bought a mastodon tusk and got with a company called The Alaska Silver and Ivory Company. We went back to all of our department store customers and said, "This is the next thing."

They bought into it.

**How did you know this was going to be the next big thing?**

We didn't – it wasn't.

We had come up with our own brands of jewelry and everything we did was successful, so we thought that this was something that hadn't happened yet. We came out of jewelry, put all our money into scrimshaw, and sold it into the stores.

All those department stores do the same thing: if it doesn't sell, they send back the items. It started backing up on us. We were out of money; we were very close to bankruptcy. We were too big of an organization to just go back to selling to little stores. Our business went from the top of the line and one of the biggest in the country to very little money.

We didn't know we were making a huge mistake. We made a bet because we felt that we knew better. We'd run these ads in Indian Jewelry magazines: "Change or die, Scrimshaw."

In our minds we were the pioneers, we were the big guys. We had a national reputation. We just never thought that we wouldn't be successful.

We had a lot of scrimshaw and no place to go with it so [on someone's suggestion] we opened up a gift and jewelry store in Tamarac Square.

Many stores in Tamarac Square were jewelers and we were the smallest. We had no fine jewelry; we had ceramic, lots of scrimshaw, and stuff that was out of the realm of the 1970s. We had small ticket items so it was a longer haul. We worked very hard for a number of years. Michael, my business partner, and I were the salespeople along with one other person.

In business today, I think you can't make a lot of mistakes. We made tons of them through the years.

**Why did you have that luxury and it's different today?**

Competitors back then weren't as strong as they are today. If you had a lot going for you in the way of your personality, relationships, integrity, and working hard, you had a shot.

Today, if you want to open a clothing store, you're going to have to compete with Polo Ralph Lauren. Starting small in a retail situation unless you have a new product nobody else has, how do you compete against that kind of competitor? It's hard and you stay small.

Today if you pick the wrong location, you're probably not going to be there. We picked the wrong location, but we survived it.

When we were picking a location we could have pretty much been anywhere we wanted. The Bagel Notch, a bagel deli from New York, picked backside of the mall. We said, "Bagel Notch, they know what they're doing. If they want to be back there, we want to be back there."

The Bagel Notch survived a few years and went out of business. They didn't know what they were doing and we didn't know what we were doing either because we followed them.

We survived [though]. There was an opening in the city for a jeweler like us. We had an eye to what was going on and we picked the right lines, worked really hard, and about a year-and-a-half in we started selling watches. Every jeweler in this town was traditional, meaning they had no eye to fashion, they didn't do designer jewelry; they did just the classics. We were doing designer bands and things that today are commonplace, but back then people weren't doing it.

The 1980s were a very opulent, fashion forward time, and we were the guys. We picked the brands out as they developed. We were able to have relationships back then and we picked whom we wanted to represent, which carried and carried so that today if you're a designer and want a store in Denver, you're going to come to Hyde Park first.

**Is that because of your reputation in the previous business?**

No.

**B:** *You built all new relationships with these designers?*

Absolutely.

**B:** *You built a name there.*

We were young, in our 20s. Every other jeweler in this town was second generation, 50-years-old, and did it the way their fathers did it. We were able to just do it differently. Nobody taught us it. We were first generation and just did it.

We made a lot of mistakes, but we also did unique things. I had a friend who was selling Famous Amos cookies when Famous Amos just stared. Nobody in town had them; not a grocery, nobody. In our store we built an island for Famous Amos cookies and sold them. It was the only place in Denver you could get them.

I don't think we made a penny on Famous Amos cookies ever, but the amount of traffic and conversation that we garnered from having this island of Famous Amos cookies was huge.

**B:** *Was that the intent, to drive traffic?*

No.

**B:** *The intent was to sell the cookies?*

I don't know what the intent was...Here was the intent: I'm friendly with you, and you tell me, "I've got this unbelievable cookie and I'm trying to find stores to sell it to in Denver," but you haven't sold it to anybody. I try the cookie, I love the cookie. I say, "Wow! Let's sell it at Hyde Park."

We made a lot of mistakes, but we built a place people wanted to come and they wanted to see and we always had something different and new. Thirty some-odd years later it has a national reputation.

I left last year, but Michael got "Jeweler of the Year" this year in the multi-store category in the country by one of the big magazines who has that contest every year. It's not like I'm bummed out that I wasn't there, that I didn't get it. It was something that I could feel good about because that was part of me; it didn't happen in one year.

**Did you have a spiritual background growing up or do you now?**

I was brought up in the Jewish religion, although I don't think I'm very religious. I don't go to the synagogue every week. I go during the high holidays. I do believe in God, but I believe in people.

[For] some people I've met along the way in different industries, and in Bazi too, everything is God: "God wants me to do it, God gave me the talent." You see athletes that way. The way I look at that is although I believe in God, I believe that that comes from the person; either they create it or they don't. I think anybody could be successful, but the only ones that will be successful are the ones that believe. Not only believe they can be successful, but create it. Have a game plan. Know what is takes.

I didn't and I was lucky. Today, I couldn't have done that. Well, maybe I shouldn't say that. Maybe in the Internet you can put in $800 and with your brain come up with something that somebody buys for $100 million in two days. In any other traditional industry or business, I could not take $800 and parlay that into what I did. I don't think I could today. I don't know how you do that today.

You get some breaks and then you make some mistakes. It's how you take advantage of the breaks and how you deal with the mistakes that will probably get you to success or not. It probably is not as easy as it was to do things. But on the other side of that, I believe that anybody can do anything they want. It's a principle that you first of all have to take responsibility.

If you want to be successful, find out how other successful people that do what you do, do what they do. You want to try to make it easier on yourself. Find out what it is and then create it happening.

That's the mistake we made with scrimshaw – it was new, and nobody was doing it.

But then again Indian jewelry was new and nobody was doing that. I guess because we did it with Indian jewelry we thought whatever we were going to do was going to work. Looking back at it the smarter thing would have been to do a little scrimshaw and test it with one department store; put $250,000 into it instead of buying $1.5 million of inventory.

**Did you ever set out to make a million?**

No.

At the same time, if you were to have said to me when I started my business, "Are you going out to make a million?" I would have said, "Why not 10?"

Who wouldn't, if they're young, think they're going to make a million, which, by the way, isn't that much any more.

**It doesn't sound like you had a concrete plan where you said, "We want to open up the Hyde Park store and we're going to be at $2 million by the end of three years."**

We never had a concrete plan, but those days I believe you didn't have to have a plan. Now, I think you have to have more of a plan. It's very competitive and your competitors have a lot of capital. There's not a lot of open space, meaning places that are working where people aren't in them.

**You had a lot of hutzpah, a lot of belief in yourself. Where did that come from?**

I think I developed it. I don't think I had it in college or even in those Wall Street days. I think it probably happened with the 33 years in the business, of building the business of having a lot of employees, of finding out what was important to myself and people I dealt with.

**What are you passionate about and what were you passionate about as you were building your business?**

In the beginning I was reactionary, it was just minute-to-minute: "This seems like a good idea, let's do this."

Now it's interpersonal dealings; relationships; creating things, whether it be a relationship, or having a new conversation. I've always been interested in politics, although these days I'm kind of turned off with it. I can have political conversations with people or debate certain things.

**How did you balance time with your family as you were building your business?**

It was tough. We were very socially engaged, very charitably engaged, and there were always meetings or events or this or that. During bigger times of the year and holidays I'd work until 9:00 p.m.

If I went back, I might have changed some things that way. There were a million meals I missed with Aaron and my wife at the time, Lynn. There were a lot of things that didn't happen.

It's really hard to say, "I want to put this much time into family, this much time into work." When people have your number and they call you and say, "I'm coming in after work, I want to buy a diamond ring, be there," you're there. You have a payroll of 70 people; you've got to keep it all going somehow.

**Would you say your journey was relatively easy or hard?**

It was easy for me because when I look at it I think I'm fortunate. I'd have to say my life for the most part worked out.

**B:** *Did it work out like you ever thought it would?*

I never thought of the future much. It was the 70s.

**A lot of the literature out there says you need to have a firm goal in mind, you need to plan your steps, and you need to know step by step what you're doing.**

**The people that I've talked to so far are more geared toward flying by the seat of their pants. They know what they want, but a good number have just taken the next logical step and said, "Whatever's right here in front of us, let's just deal with that; whatever comes is in the future so why worry about it?"**

But wouldn't you say that most of the people you've talked to, if they were giving advice, would say, "plan."

**B:** *Yes. Why is that? Because you do now?*

It could be a number of reasons. One reason could be most of the people you're talking to are probably a little bit older and like me they might not think the outcome would be the same for them today. I guess I've been saying I think it was easier back then, in the 1970s. There were openings; there were spaces you could fit into.

The other reason is if you're finding entrepreneurs, the entrepreneurial story is different than other people that are successful. The entrepreneurial story happens where people are floating around in life and something presents itself and they just go for it. I don't think you can plan that. I don't know how you plan that, because you don't know what it's going to be.

In somebody's life there have got to be maybe two or three, maybe five or six, major opportunities that they stare at right in front of them. It depends on if they take the step, which is the belief, that starts them creating their experience with that opportunity.

I think that's an entrepreneurial-type person and I think that if you're speaking to entrepreneurial-type people, and I put myself in that realm, we probably all have a similar story about right time, right place; but the answer is not that that right time, right place would have worked for everybody. It worked for the people who grabbed it, seized the moment, and went with it believing they would be successful, full speed ahead.

In some of these situations people crash and burn. Probably every one of those entrepreneurs will tell you when they were close to bankruptcy. It's just part of seizing it, believing it, doing it, and then maybe you made the wrong choice, and then you get through it and the next one it hits.

**Your moment wouldn't have worked for other people, but there are five or six moments in everybody's life that if they grab them can turn into something?**

Maybe somebody has 10 moments in their life and somebody has one, and that might be the luck part of it. It's not just being presented the opportunity, it's making it work, it's creating it working.

There are opportunities and it's a matter of that moment in time that probably is defined when you make the decision to either go forward or not to do it.

**Who is it that takes advantage of it: Is it a personality type? Is it a work ethic type?**

I think you need a work ethic.

There's a lot of ways to skin a cat. You just have to know the important ones to make it right. It's a matter of the belief and creating it, knowing you can. Just knowing you can.

That's what an entrepreneur does. He sees an idea, and says, "With that you can do this and that." Then that guy, instead of doing a major study on it, takes it and runs with it and does what it takes without the plan.

The plan comes around after you've done it and you're successful and if you do another product, you say, "OK, now we're going to have a plan."

**The first go round is just gut and energy, hard work and enthusiasm?**

Do what it takes.

**B:** *Then the second go-round involves the due diligence?*

If somebody asks me about opening a store in a mall I'd have 40 questions for them. But when we did it I didn't have 40 answers nor anybody to ask any questions.

**How do you know when you're making the right decisions?**

Evidently I can't tell you that – scrimshaw.

I don't think you can run things that way. If you have to make sure you make the right decision, you probably won't make the right decision. You won't feel comfortable because you don't know if it's the right decision.

You have to be willing to take that chance. You have to have the leap of faith. You have to have something out there that makes you an entrepreneur. Otherwise, put your money in treasuries and collect the three to four percent the rest of your life. And that could be the right decision if you start out with enough money.

**You didn't have a mentor along the way?**

Not really.

**What is success?**

Being happy.

If you're poor and you're happy you're in better shape than if you're rich and unhappy. I see both. I see a lot of people with money that are absolutely unhappy, and if you're unhappy, so what? What's money going to do for you? But if you don't have money and you're happy, surrounded by happy, loving people in your life, I'd take that.

**Is there anything that you would like people to know?**

I don't think so. It's not as much about me doing this interview for other people; that wasn't part of my thought process. When you called I thought, "Sure, I've got an hour-and-half for you. Why not?" I have an hour-and-a-half for almost everybody.

\*\*\*\*

# Millionaire 7 Vance Andrus

Lawyer; Co-Founder Sonoma Corporation

www.AHW-Law.com

Married, four children

Bachelor's, J.D.

*Vance's daughter, Ashley Andrus, referred me to him.*

**Your father was a lawyer?**

My father was a lawyer and his father was a judge. My eldest brother is a lawyer.

**B:** *This runs deep in the family?*

Yes. My daughter Lori is a lawyer. We've been lawyers for a long time. My brother Alec says, "I get up every morning and get on my knees and thank God for inventing the law because I have no merchantable skills." I feel much the same way.

**B:** *When did you know that you were going to pursue law?*

I didn't so much know, as it was foreordained.

I grew up in a family of six. I was number two and we had a very matriarchal household. In south Louisiana, which is very Catholic, the women run the households and it was simply foreordained that I was going to be a lawyer and my brother was to be a lawyer. My younger brother was allowed to be a doctor.

I really gave it no thought, it was just one of those things that was going to happen.

I even recall my mother taking me to the college that she picked, dropping me off at the dorm, and saying, "I'll see you in four months." I never had this big vision of being a lawyer. I just went forward.

I graduated from college in 1969 and that was the year of the first Selective Service draft numbers. My draft number was seven. My mother said, "You always have to be in the Top 10, don't you?"

It was a foregone conclusion that I would be drafted, so instead I volunteered for the Army and wound up in an officer training program that allowed me to become a 2nd Lieutenant but also go to law school, after which I was going to be [in the] regular military; it wasn't a JAG program. I had an opportunity to go to law school in the middle of Vietnam. I was assigned to the ROTC unit at LSU Law School.

After law school I had the opportunity to clerk for a Louisiana Supreme Court justice before the Army finally got their hands on me. By then they had ended the war and didn't need us, so they let me go relatively quickly. As I recall, they trained me and the day I graduated from training they let me go.

**B:** *Did you at least get some marketable skills from the Army?*

I did. In fact, I could have stayed in the Army. I received the Legion of Valor Bronze Cross medal–I was the outstanding 2$^{nd}$ Lieutenant graduate in the 3$^{rd}$ United States Army that year–on the 50-yard-line of the LSU-Ole Miss football game. I had a future in the Army. I was a good soldier, but it wasn't what I wanted to do.

I clerked for one year for Justice Al Tate, the smartest, brightest, most humane person God ever put on this earth. After that I came home to Opelousas, Louisiana, to work for my dad. It was my father, my big brother, and me.

All the brothers got nicknames in college: Stick, Twig, Branch, Stump and Root. I realized if I stayed there I would always be Twig, so I left and went to a Lafayette and began practicing defense law there with a defense firm.

I was defending insurance companies. There was a lot of heavyweight litigation in south Louisiana at the time because the off shore oil business was very dangerous.

A lot of the work was maritime law, so there was a higher quality bar. Federal courts are generally of a higher standard; they push harder, they demand more of you than state courts so I got to practice a high level of trial work in Louisiana for 30 years.

**Was it during that time that you accumulated a good amount of wealth?**

Wealth is an interesting thing. I accumulated and lost wealth a number of times during that time.

One of the clichés about capitalism is the flow of capital; cash flow. There are allusions of capitalism to flow and the reason is this:

capitalism creates a giant pool of capital. What is capital? We think money—and it is—but what it really is is individual effort and energy, which is reflected as money.

You don't get paid unless you work. What is money but evidence of work? That's all money is – frozen effort. So capitalism creates this vast pool of capital, and that capital flows constantly.

Imagine the largest river you've ever seen. A capitalist is one who tries to dam off or block off a small portion of that giant stream. Then this little whirlpool of money comes in and will continue to circulate into it, potentially forever, unless the rocks are washed away by changes or circumstances, or unless there's some reason why you lose it.

The laborers are those who are swimming in the river. They're just out there floating along with the capital and trying to grab a little bit for themselves. But the capitalists are standing on the bank. The ultimate example of that, of course, is Bill Gates who threw some big rocks in the river and that got a pretty good little whirlpool going.

So to answer your question, "When did you acquire wealth?"; if you talk about net worth, while I was practicing law in Louisiana in the late 1970s, early 1980s, I had become wealthy by those standards.

Then we had the oil crunch. In 1974 oil fell and there were gas lines. Then again in the 1980s there was another giant oil collapse. South Louisiana was fueled by the oil economy. I owned a lot in oil and gas interests and real estate and lost all of that. My net worth went negative on at least one occasion, maybe two.

As with most people of an entrepreneurial bent, you go up, the bottom falls out, and you've got to fight your way back in. That just happens.

**Did you ever set out to make a lot of money in your life?**

No, I really didn't.

Justice Tate–he loved me and I loved him–said, "My boy, you're going to be incredibly successful because you've got all the skills and talents, but you're never going to be really rich."

I said, "Why, Judge?"

He said, "Because you don't have that burning desire to be really rich. I know people," he was 62, he had met people, "who are really rich, big rich, and all they care about, all their waking moments and all they like in life, is focused on accumulating wealth. You don't do that. You love to spend money, love to make money, and love to be successful, but you don't have the drive to be really wealthy."

Although I've done all right, I'm not really wealthy. I'm not wealthy like the guys who fly around in the G5 jets. The trade off to that is I have a life, I get to do things that interest me.

**B:** *Tell me more about that.*

Starting when I was 18, my mother sent me out every summer to do something different. I continued that with my children. For example, I sent all of them to Washington to work for a congressman.

She sent me out to fight forest fires in Wyoming and Canada. When I moved to the mountains of Colorado 10 years ago, I was 50-years-old and I took up skiing. At 51, I became a ski instructor. In the second year I was here, I became a volunteer firefighter.

I was the oldest volunteer firefighter in the history of the force. I went from practicing law in south Louisiana with no hobbies to being here and having a whole new life. That's because I had the wisdom to obey my wife and move here, and the courage to believe her and do what she said, which was walk away from a very successful practice and move to another state with no practice whatsoever and no future.

**B:** *Why did she recommend that?*

She came here to be with my son who was in school at the time. She loved the mountains and wanted me here, but she also knew and intuitively understood that I had really become stuck in south

Louisiana. The proof of it was, if you asked me, "Why don't you move?" I would have said, "I can't move, there's no way."

There's a way for everything, so that proved that I was stuck.

Everyone thinks of themselves as Tarzan swinging through the jungle on a vine. Everybody wants to be on the other vine and they think they're going to swing the vine a little harder until they can grab it, but they can never quite get there. If you watch a Tarzan movie, he *lets go* of the vine and sails through the air and then he grabs the other vine. There is nothing in life that will invigorate you like walking away from your job with no prospects. That's sailing through the air.

I didn't relish that, I didn't want that; my wife ordered me to and she's smarter than I am so I did what she said. It was scary, but it also turned out to be the best thing I ever did. It reinvigorated me, got me unstuck. I was in a new city, a new environment.

I had two things I had to walk away from: my law firm and my oil services business, the latter being the more difficult one, but I walked away from both.

It was my law firm, I was the senior guy. When I got to Denver they said, "You can have an office there, but you can't quit." That made that transition a lot easier, but that hadn't been promised before I left.

My business partner and I sold our oil field service company right after my move to Baker-Hughes for a lot of money, but that wasn't in the cards when I moved.

So it turned out to be OK.

What's interesting, you'll hear this similar story from a lot of people, that's by my count the seventh business that I was in. The first six failed. They failed for every conceivable reason. One of them was too successful.

I was practicing law full-time and wanted to get in business. I had no concept whatsoever of what "in business" meant; I was a simple laborer. A lawyer is not a capitalist, a lawyer is a laborer. I decided I needed to get into business, so I did; a whole series of them before it worked.

**Why did you decide you needed to get in business?**

In part because I wanted an interest other than practicing law. Second, I saw that the people who were really wealthy, who could retire very comfortably very early, were in business. I looked around and said, "I see 80-year-old lawyers. I don't see any 80-year-old oil field service company owners."

I did it mostly for family security, but also because I wanted to learn, to try something different.

**B:** *That seems to be a theme throughout your life.*

One of the most difficult things in life is the fear of fear, or the fear of panic. We tend to live very closed lives, so as not to expose ourselves to fear. Fighting the fear of fear has been the theme of my whole life. I don't know why, it's just something I'm driven to do. I don't like to do it; it's my lot in life.

I had a good friend who was a psychologist tell me that I would never be satisfied. He said, "Oh, you'll be happy and you'll have joy, but you'll never have satisfaction because you have a restless soul."

That's a question that you ought to add to every one of these interviews: "Do you have a restless soul?"

A restless soul is one that just has to keep pushing.

**Was your journey to millionaire easy or hard?**

It was no harder than anyone else's journey who gets up and goes to work.

**B:** *You believed all along you'd be successful in whatever you did, right?*

Yes, but I always had to seek approval of others. I've been told that one of the reasons that I work so hard is simply because people praise me. You praise me, I'll keep going, I won't quit. They say some people work for the money; I work for the praise.

## Who or what inspired you throughout your life?

The "what" would be fear of being afraid and the restlessness of my soul inspired me to keep going forward. The "who" would be all the people in my life who demonstrated to me that hard work and kindness can be rewarding. It isn't always. It rains on the good and bad alike.

## How did you balance time with the family?

You have to make conscious choices to do so.

"The law is a jealous mistress," is a phrase in our business. She will seduce you, especially if you get a lot of feedback from the law that affirms [you]. "You're so good, you're so smart, look at all the money you're making." You're getting that from your profession. That call is there. You have to consciously fight it so as not to become a workaholic.

## If you were to capsulize it, how would you say you got where you are today?

Persistence. Learning new skills and talents and then applying them constantly. And generosity.

My mother, an old battleax Catholic, came to me one semester on a Saturday morning and dragged me, hung over, out of bed at my dorm. She said, "I'm worried about you. My intuition says you've been partying with those fraternity boys too much and I am really worried about you."

I said, "Oh mom, don't worry. I'll be OK."

That semester I had a 4.0. I brought that home and showed it to her and said, "Mom, I told you not to worry, I made a 4.0."

She said: "Imagine how much you would have learned had you really studied."

That story epitomizes the kind of drive that all of the kids were under in our household, so I'm sure that has a lot to do with it.

**Was there a system of success that you had in mind that you followed, or did you follow your gut and your heart as you went along?**

My only system was to be aware of my surroundings at times. Be aware of where you are, what's going on, what the opportunities are. Beyond that it was all following my heart and my gut.

**What do you mean being aware of the opportunities around you?**

I don't think opportunity knocks once. I think opportunity is banging on the front door, the back door, the roof, and the walls and multiple opportunities are right there. We have to lift the veil of tears to see them, so you need to be aware what's going on. Ask questions of yourself and others.

I'm constantly curious. I'll be talking to a CPA and he'll say, "I'm selling so and so's business." And I'll ask, "What kind of business is that? What does he do?" – "They buy [widgets], paint them orange, and then sell them." – "That's all they do?" – "No, they also repair them." – "OK, fine."

Simply ask questions of other people constantly; "What does that do?" It leads to more knowledge and the better your knowledge base the more you'll be able to observe opportunity knocking and the better choices you get to make.

**What are your greatest successes in life?**

First, being smart enough to marry my wife. Second, raising four wonderful, loving children. Third, being able to practice law and help people. And then fourth, amusing myself.

**B:** *By amusing you're not talking about entertaining yourself through life, you're talking about those different interests, careers, and things that you've always taken yourself to the next level with?*

Right, that's exactly it.

**Did you have written down goals along this journey?**

I never did. I always just stayed awake and alive.

Here's an example:

I was walking across campus and I ran into my acquaintance Edwin Price.

Vance: "Hey, Edwin, what's going on?"

Edwin: "Nothing much, Vance. Are you getting ready to graduate?"

Vance: "Yep, I am. Did you get a draft number?"

Now what is that? Being aware, asking questions.

Edwin: "Yeah, I'm number 22."

Vance: "Oh, man, what are you going to do?"

Edwin: "Well, Coach knows the coach at LSU and they talked to the Colonel over there and they have this deal. They can get me in the Army and I can then go to law school."

Vance: "Really? Do you think there's a spot left open?"

Edwin: "I don't know. Do you want me to call?"

Vance: "Please."

Edwin did. The next day I was talking to the Colonel.

Vance: "I'm Edwin's best friend."

Colonel: "Coach Blanco wants us to do it, we're going to do it, son."

There was no plan. I didn't sit there and say, "I've got to plan how to get to law school and try not to get killed." I stayed awake, I stayed aware, I asked questions, and an opportunity presented itself.

Instead of making goals and trying to fill them, I just went through life finding opportunities and taking them.

**What did you learn from your failures?**

There is a speech I give to young lawyers I call "Andrus' Aphorisms." It summarizes a lot of my philosophies.

The question is, "What did you learn from your failures?" Here it is [reading from Andrus' Aphorisms]:

"You're momma doesn't live here, clean up your own mess. You have to be honest with yourself with respect to failures and honestly appraise to what extent were outside influences responsible versus some failure on your part. If it was outside influences, to what extent did you fail to anticipate and react or act proactively to reduce or stop those outside influences from affecting your performance?"

Beyond that, you just pick up and move on.

Don't pass judgment on yourself such as, "I'm a bad person." Instead say, "I made a mistake. I didn't see that coming. I need to get a little better because I need to go back in."

You know you're not going to quit, so why not just learn something?

Clean it up, that's number one. Number two, try to learn something from it.

That's it. It's not great philosophy there.

**What is your passion?**

Life.

Go to number eight [of Andrus' Aphorisms]: "Grab life by the throat.

"From the day you were old enough to walk you were faced with a choice: either you grab life by the throat and give it a shake, or life will grab you by the throat and give you a shake."

That's my passion. To me it means trying to be honest with yourself and commit to trying to be successful in life, whatever that entails.

**B:** *Did you ever have a passion for law?*

There was a Charlie Brown cartoon in which Linus is saying, "One of the greatest burdens in life is great expectations." I didn't so much have a passion for law before I became a lawyer as I had resigned myself that it was my fate. It's only in the last 10 years that I've really gotten passionate about it.

**B:** *But all along you've had a passion for being successful and making the most of life?*

Right.

**B:** *So whatever you did you were going to be successful?*

I was.

**B:** *Part of that is your upbringing, part of that is you were resigned to it?*

Yes, and it also has to do with playing with the cards I was dealt; it has to do with recognizing what my skills and talents are.

In high school, all I wanted to do was be a jock [but] I was a second-class athlete. I was skinny; I weighed 138 pounds.

My senior year we only had 21 kids on the football team. The coach came in and with a gleam in his eye said, "As you know, Marvin went down yesterday. I have a golden opportunity for someone to play cornerback."

I had never played cornerback, but he was staring at me and he said, "a golden opportunity." I raised my hand and said, "I'm it." He called me in his office and said, "You're the only one on this team smart enough to learn almost every position. Someone is going to get hurt every week and I'm going to need you to be able to play every offensive and every defensive position. Here's the book. Learn the plays this week and you're going to be our starting cornerback on Friday."

I played every week for 11 weeks. I played six or eight different positions, none of them particularly well. I played guard – I weighed 138 pounds. I played defensive end, I played cornerback, I played linebacker and I lettered.

That's what I mean about opportunity; being aware and using the skills that you have. I wasn't much of an athlete, but I was really bright.

**What should people who want to be successful know?**

They need to know their own personality.

Mine is a personality that works best on a team. In fact, it works best leading a team, but I'm a team guy.

You can be successful without being a team guy; I think it's a lot harder. The vast majority of people who have been successful are on a team. Who's not on a team? A brain surgeon maybe, but he's got a team. I'm talking about a team of people who help do all of the lifting.

You have to know your personality, that's the key, and you have to be committed.

I never ever intended to replace anyone, or to even be the next so and so. I wasn't going to be the next anybody.

**What advice would you give to someone looking for a break in their chosen field or in life?**

They asked Bear Bryant one time about luck. They said, "Coach, what's the role of luck on the football field?" He said, "It's funny you'd ask that. Seems to me the better athletes I recruit, the more luck I tend to have."

If by "break" we mean a lucky break, there is no such thing. You make your luck; luck is made by people. Luck is a result of hard work and awareness.

If you work hard and you're aware, you will spot opportunities, which will seem to be lucky to you, but there is no such thing as luck.

## Why did you do what you did and why do you continue to do what you do?

Because it's better than the alternative. To live an unexamined life is a waste of protoplasm and I don't intend to do that.

## What is success to you?

Being loved and receiving life affirmation from others.

## What do you wish someone would ask you?

I think you have; all these questions, because one of the problems with life is that everyone thinks that they're on an island, that they're the only person facing these choices and these difficulties. That no one else understands and that no one else has ever been through any of that. In truth, all of us have.

When I look at an old photograph I try to make myself appreciate that those people had the exact same fears, hopes, and aspirations that I have; exactly the same, not any different.

I think the worst thing that can happen to anyone reading this book is that they feel alone.

**B:** *Why is that the worst thing?*

Because they're not. And all they have to do is lift the veil of tears and they'll see that we're out there, folks. We're there, we're one of you.

## Is there a belief system that guides your life?

I'm a non-practicing true believer in the Catholic version of God. It only guides my life in the sense that the very humanistic values that we learn from any religion, that are instilled in us in any religion, the stuff I learned in kindergarten, all those things were touchstones for me my entire life and are used by me in my business endeavors.

An example is I don't lie. I deal with very, very powerful people and a lot of them at one time. I have to be politically judicious and kiss this one and spank that one…but the one thing I don't do is lie to anyone. Never, never, never, never.

Do I do that because I was raised as a Catholic and they told you not to do that? Probably. Do I do that because it's really efficient to tell the truth because as Mark Twain said you don't have to remember what you said? Yes, probably. Do I do it because it's very detrimental to lie because the truth will be known no matter what? Yes, that's part of it too.

So my belief systems would be characterized as generic Christian, I think.

**When I called you to set up the interview you said, "I don't know that I've done anything special. I've just worked hard, which is no different than my maintenance man." Tell me a little bit about that.**

One of the finest people I ever met in my entire life was Howard Riddick.

Howard was a real jack-of-all-trades; he could do a little of anything. He would come out here and stay for weeks or even months at a time and we would do projects.

Howard worked harder and with more calm than I'll ever do in two lifetimes. His life was physically and economically much harder than mine and yet he simply accepted life.

I don't think I've done anything special that Howard didn't do. My training and my education gave me an opportunity to do good for more people at one time than Howard would do, but I'm not any different. I'm certainly not any better than Howard was.

**B:** *What's the difference between those people who seem to be successful financially and those that aren't? Howard was a success by the means of being happy, wasn't he?*

Oh yes. Howard was a success by every means possible.

I had more education than Howard, so I had an opportunity to be more efficient in the capitalistic system of capturing a small flow of the capital stream that Howard simply wasn't equipped to do by his training and education. That's the only difference.

**Bonus Information**:

*Two additional things worth knowing about Vance:*

*One, he has a philosophy that the only things you own are those you can give away: your time, support, advice, and assistance.*

*The second is that he leads by consensus and does not allow voting. The decision must be unanimous and he allows the veto of group decisions by any member who demonstrates good faith without any outside agendas.*

****

# Millionaire 8 Barry Hamilton

Founder, Red Canyon Engineering & Software; Real Estate Investor

www.redcanyonsoftware.com

Married (since the interview), one daughter at the time of the interview, three children now

Bachelor's, Aerospace Engineering


*Theresa Byrne referred me to Barry after hearing about the book from Ashley Andrus.*

## You've grown up here in Colorado?

Yes. I was born in Sterling, Colorado, and then grew up in Colorado Springs.

My mom had me when she was very young. We lived in a trailer park on the east side of Colorado Springs for the first five years of my life. My mom was going to school at UCCS [University of Colorado Colorado Springs] and my dad was a student teacher.

They were young teenagers with a kid trying to get by. I watched them pursue the American dream and go through the ranks. My dad was a high school teacher and a football and baseball coach. Eventually he became a college coach. I watched my mom rise up the ranks at Hewlett Packard from the bottom of the rung electrical engineer to running the marketing division for all of Southeast Asia.

I was recruited to play football at the Air Force Academy and attended for two years before I tore my ACL [anterior cruciate ligament]. I wasn't flight qualified and I couldn't play football anymore. I didn't want to disappoint my grandfather who was a retired colonel in the army, but I couldn't hack it anymore. I left the Academy, went to the University of Colorado [CU], and graduated in 1991 with an Aerospace Engineering degree.

## What made you choose that path?

I wanted to be an astronaut since I was five-years-old. When I couldn't choose that path because of my knee, I decided to help us get there by being an aerospace engineer.

I started working on the vehicles that help explore the solar system and I went out to Silicon Valley, where my parents were.

I had a blast out there. I was working at Lockheed Martin in Sunnyvale and the first year I lived with my parents in Palo Alto. The second year I lived in San Francisco. It was just a blast, but I couldn't afford a house out there.

After about four-and-a-half years, I found an opportunity to come back to Colorado and jumped on it. I got a 15 percent increase in my salary and became a consultant for a contractor of Lockheed Martin's called Advanced Systems Engineering [ASE]. I worked for them for three weeks before Lockheed Martin lost the contract at the site.

I had given up my stellar career at Lockheed Martin in California to join ASE and then that happened. It really taught me how to think on my feet and bounce back. I got a job on another program on which I worked for six months, and then I transferred to Omaha, Nebraska.

I was supposed to be out there for three months, but it kept dragging on. It was a good experience and I was around great people, but Omaha is not my cup of tea, especially after going from San Francisco to Colorado Springs to Omaha. I felt like I was going in the wrong direction.

My boss got me a job at Hughes, which is now Raytheon, in Aurora, Colorado. I worked there for a couple years and then went to Lockheed under ASE.

I had been working mostly on defense programs, which is fine and helped me feel like I paid back my dues from the Air Force and that I served my country, but my passion is to explore outer space.

ASE helped me get a contract job at Lockheed Martin working on the Mars '98 program. We crashed both of those satellites. The orbiter got too close to Mars and burned up in the atmosphere and the lander did not land correctly. I actually wrote the entry descent and landing logic for that.

That was the biggest disappointment of my business life.

As we were building the craft I was in our lab all the time; sleeping on the floor, running simulations, and working with the Ph.Ds. at Jet Propulsion Laboratory. Once the satellites went into the atmosphere, my job was done. I came home and slept for 24 hours.

When I woke up I called in and they hadn't heard anything. I went in and worked for the next three days straight.

We never established a contact and then we had the NASA review boards come in to determine what could have gone wrong. We found some problems with our testing and engineering. Anytime something like that happens, it's not one person's fault. It is the whole systems engineering process of building a spacecraft. So I learned a lot of great lessons from that experience.

A company called Cyber based in Englewood, CO, bought out ASE and there was a stipulation in the contract that wouldn't allow me to contract through ASE anymore. I either had to become an employee of Lockheed Martin to continue working on the project or find another contract vehicle.

I had already been an employee of Lockheed Martin in California and being an employee just wasn't my bag. I knew that my skill sets were not on the corporate, political side. There were a lot of people in Lockheed Martin that tried to guard their data or their domains because of job security and I always wanted to find the best solution, the most efficient solution, that made sense for everybody.

Also, I wasn't the smartest engineer. I was decent, but my skill set was more geared toward being able to get all those engineers together and look at the big picture, shine a light in the corner and make sure we weren't missing anything.

I've always been lucky, so I jumped at the chance to start my own company as an alternate contract vehicle to keep working on the project. That was where opportunity and hard work met.

A year later, my boss said, "We've got two other contractors who are in the same boat. Do you want to join forces?"

We got together in February 2000 and called it Red Canyon Software. That's when I started doing sales. I sold our services to Ball Aerospace and built up six employees there. At the time we were building that project, I had been bringing over some buddies from Hughes and Raytheon to help out and we built up [to] seven employees [working on contract] at Lockheed Martin.

In 2000, I was working 50-60 hours a week writing altitude determination control software while I was trying to run the company. My business partner and I had to do statements of work, proposals, respond to request for proposals, deal with payroll, healthcare, benefits, and still write software.

At one point I worked at Lockheed Martin for six or seven hours, then went to Ball Aerospace and worked for another six or seven hours. I was commuting two-and-a-half hours a day and working 14, then trying to do everything else on the weekends. It was a rough period.

In 2003 when I was doing all of this, I split up with the woman to whom I was engaged and I split up with my partner from Red Canyon Software. Those are some of the negative effects of being an entrepreneur. I was probably not focused on some important things in life. Maybe they would have worked out, maybe they wouldn't have, but there is a lot of sacrificing to build a business.

To make a business successful you've got to commit a lot of hours, a lot of energy, and a lot of passion. I think sometimes you lose sight of other things in that pursuit like family and friends.

The summer of 2003 was the last time I wrote a piece of software. Now I just work on building the business and our revenues are about three times what they were then. I'm not working as hard and I'm able to concentrate on some of the more important things. One thing that helped me with that is Entrepreneurs Organization [EO]. I joined in 2004.

I joined to improve the bottom line, but it's given me much more than that. It's like group therapy for entrepreneurs. The group is oriented much more toward work-life balance and I gain so much from these other entrepreneurs. I can't say enough about the organization.

We have a group called Forum, which is like a board of advisors on life and entrepreneurism. It's helped me put things in perspective such as enjoying the journey while you're here and spending quality time with family.

**You said earlier that your passion is exploring what's out there in space?**

Yes, absolutely. I do it here, too; I love to travel and meet new people and to learn from them. It's all really a part of my essence and being.

**When did you get into real estate?**

I tried to buy a place when I lived in San Francisco, but I couldn't even afford a one-bedroom condo anywhere in the whole Bay Area. I had even looked into multi-unit buildings because the mortgage company would count the income that the building was generating to help me qualify for a bigger loan.

When I moved back to Denver, I caught up with one of my friends from CU, a real estate broker, who taught me the ropes. I bought a four-unit building and lived in one of the units while renting out the others, mostly to buddies. I fixed them all myself because I couldn't afford to pay someone else to do it.

It was great because I had my mortgage paid plus some [extra money]. I refinanced the mortgage in 1997, got some cash out, and bought a three-unit complex around the corner from the building in which I was living. I fixed that up on the weekends and then rented it out.

I kept borrowing money because during the 1990s interest rates went down and real estate values went up. I could buy something and it would be worth more six months to a year later. Then I could refinance it, lower my payment because of the lower interest rate, and get money out to buy something else. I kept leveraging and got really lucky.

I bought duplexes, legally split them into townhomes, and then sold them. I remember my first $20,000 check from a sale in 1998. I thought, "This is amazing!"

I joined up with a few partners and we combined resources to buy units, fix them up, and sell them. That's how I started building up some capital in real estate.

It's been a good thing because I'm not totally dependent on just one business. And because each of my businesses is so different, they complement each other well. I don't have to worry about having a single income source.

**You could sell your current real estate assets and make $10 million and you could sell Red Canyon Software for a significant amount and then do whatever you wanted to. Why don't you?**

What would I do then? Go sit on a beach? What am I going to do with that? Be bored? No way.

**Do you have a restless soul?**

Yes, absolutely.

**How would you say you got where you are today?**

I'm open to opportunity; I'm able to receive it. And my networking skills help a tremendous amount.

Also, good people are important. Once you find the opportunity, the actual building of it is a result of getting great people, smarter people than yourself, to help you.

**Is there a belief system that guides your life?**

I was raised Catholic.

I didn't align well with Catholicism. What I saw there was a lot of hypocrisy. I took an honors world history class as a sophomore in high school taught by Dr. Birshnull who had a huge influence on my life.

I learned about the Buddhists, Hindus, Muslims, and thought, "Wait a second. We're the minority in this world and we're saying everybody else is going to hell because they don't believe what we believe." That doesn't align with who I am.

Through college, I wandered around. I read a lot of books on religion: Siddhartha, King Arthur on Paganism, all sorts of stuff.

I now attend Mile High Church, which aligns perfectly with who I am. They don't discriminate on your sexuality, your background, or what mistakes you've made in your life. They're talking about the present and the future and how to make it better, that it's OK to create wealth, it's OK to be happy and you don't have to feel guilty about that.

Although that's a relatively new part of my life, it's the first church I've ever wanted to attend.

## Did you have written down goals, concrete goals, that you wanted to achieve along the path?

When you meet with a certified financial planner, they ask, "What kind of car do you want when you're 30 or 40?"

I never went through that exercise of planning what kind of car I wanted to drive. I know a lot of people do and they're successful with it. They've got their "dream board" on which they put pictures of cars, boats, homes, etc. and use that as motivation. I've never been like that.

I think I'm probably a little bit different. My goal was to be worth $1 million when I was 30 and $10 million when I was 40. Those were the only goals I ever had.

**B:** *Aside from being an astronaut as well?*

Yes, but I gave up on that.

I still have a goal to get in space. I will get to space; it's probably going to be on Richard Branson's high altitude, hypersonic airplane.

**B:** *Do you have that written down somewhere?*

No.

**B:** *So that's a dream, a vision that you have. Another vision that you had was to be worth $1 million by 30. Did you hit that?*

I did.

**What are some of the challenges you've encountered?**

1) The partner breakup was the biggest challenge businesswise that I've had to deal with. I didn't want to break up. There were some differences of opinions, but I thought we could work it out, so that was hard.

She owned 51 percent of the company; we were a small, women-owned hub zone company. I jumped in with both feet. I found some document on the Internet and modified it to make it an S-Corp document and we signed it. We didn't even use any lawyers to start because we were eager to just get going.

Obviously, I learned from that. Now I probably wouldn't do that because it burned me. She had shareholder rights and board of director rights because she had shareholder majority. I had to get a lawyer and look at minority shareholder rights and different things after the fact.

That's always been my method and motivation: jump in with two feet and go versus worrying about this and that because if you worry about all that you never get going. I'm a risk-tolerant engineer.

2) Work-life balance is hard because as an entrepreneur, especially now with an iPhone, I can work anywhere and I usually am. After I put Loren to bed at night, I get back to work.

I have to make sure that from the time I pick Loren up after school until I put her to bed is all her time. She's six now. Soon she'll be a teenager and won't want to hang out with me. At that point I can go back to working all the time, but right now is her time.

Work-life balance has been a challenge for me and EO has helped with that.

3) Funding right now is a challenge. Luckily, I've got some very good relationships with local banks that have helped ease that problem and I've got such a track record with them that it makes funding easier.

**Who or what inspired you aside from Dr. Birshnull?**

My grandfather, Sabatine Marconi, inspired me.

My mom was instrumental in instilling the desire in me to be an astronaut. I talked to her about that in recent years. It was a dream of hers as well. I think we used to talk about it when I was young.

My dad also inspired me.

I used to tell my grandpa that I had to be as tough as my dad, who was the college football coach, and as smart as my mom, who rose through the ranks of the technology companies in Silicon Valley.

It's funny because they are both risk averse. I remember when I wanted to buy my first fourplex and my dad said, "You don't want to deal with renters."

They were very successful in their life and lived the American dream, but I've done it a lot differently.

**When you hear those voices of caution and when you hear some feedback from the outside world that causes you to think that perhaps you're looking at something differently than others do, do you take it into consideration but ultimately decide yours is the right way? How do you know it's the way?**

If I can see it, then it's going to happen.

**B:** *How?*

Leap of faith.

**What did you learn from some of your failures?**

I keep re-learning from my failures that I need to keep my communication skills and my communication actions at a high level, both in personal relationships and business relationships so that there aren't any misunderstandings of who is supposed to do what.

It's about doing what you say and saying what you do and making sure that you're aligned with the people in your life, whether it's personal or business. You need to communicate it on a repeated basis so there's not a misunderstanding of what's supposed to be delivered when. Failures usually are a result of miscommunication.

**What would you say are your greatest successes?**

My daughter is my greatest success; in particular, trying to give her balance because she's grown up in a much different environment than I grew up in. We couldn't go out and buy me a pair of sneakers anytime I wanted. I want to try to instill the values that I grew up with into her in a more difficult situation.

My other successes include my friends and family and the relationships that we have with each other. A lot of my business associates are my best friends and a lot of my best friends are my business associates. Those waters are sometimes hard to navigate and some people probably would think it would be impossible, but it's natural for me because of who I am.

**If you were to go back, what would you do differently and why?**

Nothing.

**Where did your belief in yourself come from?**

I think it came from my parents. They had me play musical instruments, the sax and the piano, while I was growing up. They also had me in advanced academic courses and sports. The successes I derived out of those experiences helped give me a belief in myself that if I want to be a concert pianist, then I'll go do that. If I wanted to be a football player, I'd go do that.

I wanted to be an astronaut and football player. When those didn't pan out it hurt, but I was able to bounce back.

My parents would strongly encourage me to do things. I finally gave up baseball after seven years. My dad was a baseball coach so he was disappointed, but he understood. I was a failure at baseball.

I had failures and successes early on in life. I think it taught me to continue to pursue things that I liked and if I didn't quite get there and failed, it didn't mean I was a failure. It just meant that it wasn't meant to be and I needed to go to the next one.

I've had real estate deals where I didn't make any money; it doesn't mean we're a failure. Sometimes you have to get out of stuff and learn your lessons and go on.

I think it's a belief in yourself that you can bounce back from adversity. Your last failure was just the last one before you could be successful. It's how we learn as humans. I definitely think that my parents have a lot to do with instilling confidence in me and in my abilities to do what I wanted to do.

**Did you have a mentor or role model throughout this process?**

No.

**What advice would you give to someone who's looking for a break in their chosen field – Their break as in, "I really want to make it, what do I need to do?"**

I would say speak to people about what you want.

Whatever that break is, whatever you're looking for, communicate it. Communicate it to your co-workers. Communicate it to your boss. Communicate it to your friends, because you're not going to get the break unless you tell people what that break is.

**What is success to you?**

I was at an EO event in Omaha with Warren Buffet a few months ago and he said, "Happiness equals excitement."

I agree with that. I think that success is being happy and excited and passionate in life.

**Would you say that you found your passion and therefore you have found success?**

If you combine your passion with a solid skill set, you will make money at it. If your skill sets don't align with your passions, then you have to build that skill set or find the people that have it.

If you have those two ingredients, you'll make money whatever it is, it doesn't matter. If it's picking up poop or growing flowers, if you're passionate and you've got a core skill set in that arena, you can do it.

**Do you think everyone has opportunities in life for success?**

We're all dealt different hands at birth, but this country, of any country in the world, gives you more of an opportunity than anywhere else. It tries to level the playing field more than any other place to allow you those opportunities because of the system; our government and our republic.

I could have stayed in the trailer park my whole life if my parents hadn't tried to do something with their lives. If my parents hadn't instilled that belief in myself, I probably wouldn't be here. I think a lot of it has to do with your parents and your family and passing on those skill sets.

But even if you're born in the ghetto there's still opportunity, there's still ability for you to get out of that situation.

It's not the same situation I had or the situation Bill Gates' children will have, as their challenges will be at a whole different level. Maybe there's opportunity for failure for them. Life is not fair, for sure.

**Bonus Question**: Did it turn out thus far like you thought it would?

I don't think so, but I'm still happy.

I love where I am, I love where I've been.

You talk about the goals and what car do you want and what kind of house and how many square feet – I've never thought about that stuff. I don't really set concrete ideas of where I needed to be.

I'm much more of a person who goes with the flow of karma and energy where it takes me, kind of like a feather in wind. I try not to fight where my next opportunity is coming from or where my next vacation is going to be.

I know I'm different from the guys in EO in that regard because they set that ultimate goal. I'm more into living life at the moment, right now. This 10 seconds of reality, enjoying it, and that's what I try to embrace.

**B:** *We don't have to have all the answers, and an entrepreneur doesn't?*

Absolutely not.

**B:** *An entrepreneur makes a lot of mistakes?*

Yes.

****

# Millionaire 9 Theresa M. Szczurek

Co-Founder, Radish Systems (aka Radish 2.0); Co-Founder, Radish Communication Systems; Author, *Pursuit of Passionate Purpose*; Founder, Technology and Management Solutions (TMS)

www.RadishSystems.com, www.TMSWorld.com, www.PursuitofPassionatePurpose.com

Married, one daughter

Bachelor's, Master's, MBA, Ph.D.

*Ashley Andrus referred me to Theresa.*

**What was your goal in high school? Where did you want to end up?**

I liked math so I thought I was going to be an actuary working for insurance companies.

I grew up in the suburbs of Chicago in a large Polish Catholic family: five kids, two parents, and every pet imaginable. They were really humble beginnings, but I had a strong ethical foundation. I learned to work hard and that "if it's to be, it's up to me."

**B:** *How old were you when you started thinking, "I've got to make my own way"?*

For sure by high school. I realized that there were things that I wanted to do, places to see, people to meet.

**Do you think you have a restless soul?**

Whatever that means, yes, I think so.

There's a level of dissatisfaction I have realizing that things can be better. I feel like I am here to use my skills, background, talents, and gifts in a way to make a meaningful difference. I'm always looking to do that in a bigger, better way.

**You had been at AT&T Bell Labs almost seven years, you had been working on a new product release for three years, and your boss got to go roll it out and take all the credit, is that right?**

Right.

There were different signals over the years that perhaps I was not able to really live true to my values in that work environment and that I didn't really know who I was at that point.

First, I remember it finally came – the next promotion. I heard some colleagues of mine who I thought were my friends talking behind my back.

"Did you hear Theresa got promoted? *She* didn't deserve it."

It was as if an arrow had been shot through my heart and these feelings poured out. Up until that point, my head–the rational, logical thinker–had dominated my life and in that moment my heart– the creative feeler–broke through. I realized that I valued contributing through work *and* I valued having deep, caring, meaningful relationships. I was letting my work (the head) hinder making connections (my heart).

It was painful and that pain initiated some changes. I joined a church, decorated my house, started entertaining, and made friends. That helped for a while.

The next encounter came when my boss, working late one night said, "Theresa you need to kill Larry [a coworker], or Larry is going to kill you" [figuratively speaking].

I said, "I play win-win. I don't play it like that."

My boss dropped me in terms of support.

I determined that I really valued a place where I could work with people of integrity. I think highly of AT&T, it was like a family to me, but in any environment you encounter people who may be less aligned with your values.

The final straw came when after three years of working on my product to bring it to the world market the company sent that boss, not me, to introduce it. I realized I valued contributing, but also being rewarded and getting the recognition for my contributions.

That was the impetus for me to finally say I needed to take a break and move on.

If I knew then what I know now about building passionate workforces and helping organizations grow, I wouldn't have had to leave the organization. One of the things I do now is help people and organizations work through these inevitable challenges, but it was the impetus for me to grow and move on.

## You left AT&T and then you got this crazy idea, "I'll start a company"?

After I left AT&T, I went on a trip around the world. I went to the South Pacific for two months and saw kids and families and became aware that if I had the choice, I did want to have a family.

When I came back to Colorado, I had lined up a job working for another technology company, but that fell through. This was a life opportunity for me to do something else so I started my consulting firm, Technology and Management Solutions, and I started the Ph.D. program at the University of Colorado.

I also started working on the "Man Plan"–attracting the right man into my life–which would ultimately lead to the "Baby Plan" and the "Family Plan." I call these different phases of my life "plans."

It was impossible to do all of those at the same time so really I started working on the Ph.D. Getting my Ph.D. was something my math teacher at Western Illinois University, Paul Humke, had inspired me to do.

In 1989, I turned in my Ph.D. dissertation and then Dick, my business partner and friend, and I jumped into his Porsche. We drove it cross-country to sell it to his friend to use the money as seed money to start the company. We knew at that point we wanted to do something entrepreneurial.

**B:** *But you didn't know what at that point, right? You just knew you wanted to do something.*

That's right.

So we searched for the idea. We were open, set a big intention of finding it, and then we started thinking about it using our head, feeling passionately about how it would be when this technology was there, and took action.

We stopped at Pizza Huts and other little restaurants as we went across the country and scribbled down notes. We didn't find the idea on that trip, but we did when we had come back.

148

Dick got a call from a travel agent and they were talking over the phone. Dick realized what was going on was stupid. He was asking for information and the person was bringing it up on the computer screen and then reading it to him; this was previous to the Internet really proliferating.

He got this idea–he was the technical visionary–about transmitting data as easily as voice. He invented the VoiceView protocol, which was the foundation for our company, Radish Communication Systems. That then started us on our way to founding, funding, and growing the company.

We used initially what I call the "Attraction Strategy": Set a broad intention and then work with your head, heart, and hands to attract to you that which you want while being open to the possibilities. The idea came.

Then we worked to build the right team of people. We used what I call the "Connections Strategy," another part of the six strategies that help you pursue your dreams and be able to successfully attain them. Build relationships with self, proper people, other beings, and spiritual sources. Minimize the impact of improper people. The right people make a huge difference.

In the first year, we brought everybody together and put together "our values to live by" statement because values are so important to understand what's meaningful to you.

When you connect those values with your gifts, your core competencies, you will find your passion. Then align that passion with a clear purpose and pursue it with a plan, until it is time to assess progress. Here is when you appreciate and celebrate, continue, or make course corrections. Those are the four stages of the "Pursuit of Passionate Purpose" process and the six success strategies help you move along the way.

**Did you have the four stages and success strategies consciously in mind as you were pursuing it?**

No.

I was using it; however, I hadn't articulated it as such. After we had sold Radish, I had this calling to distill the approach that had helped me so it could help others. Then I looked back at what it took and discerned the success formula.

**B:** *You started the business by just following your heart. You started relying a little less on the head, which was heavy for the first seven years of your career. You were open to the path and without a conscious plan you went through what you felt were the right steps in building the company. Is that right?*

We had prepared, it's not like we just started with a calling. We had prepared for years and years at AT&T; one of the best telecommunications companies in the world gave us a foundation of successfully bringing new technology to the market. It also gave us a depth of knowledge. We had connections with really great people, many of whom joined us or helped fund us. I had a Ph.D. in business, so I knew a bit about business planning and running businesses. My co-founder had a Ph.D. in engineering and was a brilliant technical strategist, and both co-founders had management experience.

So all this experience, what I consider some of the gifts, came together and allowed us to start the company and do well. We also had connections with some very successful entrepreneurial friends who served as advisors to us, who gave us suggestions, and opened doors along the way.

We started with the intention, we got the idea and knew it was a good idea, and then we found the courage to begin. Many good ideas are never pursued because the courage is lacking. We started out by putting together a plan. I encourage people to have a plan, both in their personal life and in their professional life. If it can be written, you have a higher probability of success than if it's not.

We started looking at things: What would the product be? We needed to have a way to show it, so we built a prototype. Then I took the prototype on the road and conducted market research to get people's feedback. We asked them, "How would this work for you?

What was your reaction to it?" People liked it and felt there was value. We were getting the substance to justify the business.

I recommend to my consulting and coaching clients to follow your heart along with your head and take the right steps to ensure that you're going to succeed. Having a good plan and then executing on that plan are two of the ingredients.

**You and Dick worked the company for six years?**

Dick and I were the founders and we initially put in founders' capital.

We knew we had a big idea and needed more capital. We brought in friends and family as investors through a private placement offering and we still needed more money. We raised money through some very good venture capitalists.

In that process, we were getting feedback to broaden the management team so we brought in a consultant who became the CEO. We brought in a vice president of sales and a vice president of manufacturing. Dick's and my roles changed in terms of the day-to-day operations, although we remained founders.

We built that core team and got them on the right seats on the bus and then brought in some other people to help. We gave everybody a stake in the company to help keep people motivated. We continued to work on the business model because you have to make midcourse corrections and changes along the way; that's what we found. It's part of the "Polarity Strategy."

I call it the "Flow Approach," go with the f-l-o-w. You first find a polarity. Then you learn how to manage it by allowing a dynamic flow, or a dynamic movement, between these two interdependent poles. Next you oscillate; you allow that flow to happen so you don't get stuck only in one side of the polarity. Then you watch for warnings that you might be stuck on one side and use those to make needed changes to stimulate movement.

**You had a plan for the business, you had a plan for the book, you had a husband plan. How concrete were all of these plans?**

They were concrete and yet things keep evolving, too. I tell people you may not know when you're getting out of college exactly how the plan will evolve and what it's going to be like when you're 50, so you have to be open to the opportunities and be flexible. Have clarity on where you want to go, but allow the way you get there to evolve.

Sometimes you don't get exactly what you thought you would, but [what you get] is what was intended; [in other words] what you get is perfect. You may not know why [it's perfect] but if you have the attitude that it is perfect and if you have an acceptance that at some point you may understand why it was perfect, you can take what you receive and make lemonade out of lemons.

Then take hold of it and try to make what you want to have happen, but realize along the way other things will evolve and come and that's what synchronicity and serendipity is all about.

**Why are there so many people that struggle in our world to be successful?**

Part of it revolves around what I call the "Pack Strategy." In life, people make more progress on their journey if they pack the energizers into their bag that they're taking along the journey and unpack the hindrances or those things that are weighing them down.

In my research, I found one of the biggest hindrances that people carry is self-doubt – the internal, negative, nagging voice that is so difficult to quiet. Even some of the most successful people I interviewed feel that they have self-doubt.

Passionate Pursuers [those who pursue their passion] have nine traits that align with the word SUNFLOWER; first and foremost is self-esteem, self-confidence – believe in yourself and hold confidence that no matter what, the right thing will happen. This is why there is a large sunflower on the book cover of *Pursuit of Passionate Purpose*.

I tell people to use the Pack Strategy and unpack self-doubt. How do you do that? You build your confidence. How do you do that? Build a positive feedback loop. Take some task that needs to be done, break it into smaller and smaller and smaller pieces, and then work on one piece of it until you make progress and succeed. Then savor that moment and say, "Yes!"

If you were climbing Everest, you would look at your goal and then break it into steps. You get to the first base camp, rest a little while, look up at your goal, and then continue working toward the next base camp and so on.

The number one hindrance holding people back is self-doubt. The second thing that people need to unpack from their bag, and it's interrelated, is fear. If you're in a very dangerous situation, yes, use that adrenaline and fear to get you out of it. However, many times people are hit with fear and it's irrational.

I use the approach that Phyllis Postlewait used to train newly blinded adults who were fearful. She would give them their cane so they had some support. She would stand with them so they were not alone. Then she would help them take the first step. You have to just do it. Take the first step. Learn that you will survive and then take the next little step. Break through the fear.

Life is short and each of us has the choice to turn a good life into a great life. How do you do that? Ignite your fire, keep it burning, unpack those hindrances, pack the energizers, and keep moving. Lord knows we need, in this world, the energies, the spirits, of every person.

**Do you believe every person has a passion to contribute to the greater whole?**

I do. They may not know what it is. Many people are striving to find it. Many people do know what their passions are, but are somehow blocked in pursuing them. Other people, thank goodness, know what their passions are and are pursuing them.

## What's the first step in finding your passion?

The first step is getting to know and nurture yourself, the person. The sages since antiquity have said, "Know Thyself." Think of Joe Jackson's song, "You Can't Get What You Want (Till You Know What You Want)." Well, you can't get what you want till you know what you want and you don't know what you want until you know who you are.

When I was at AT&T I wasn't getting what I wanted because I didn't know what I wanted; I didn't know who I was. It was through that process, painful at times, that I discovered my values. I wanted to be around people of integrity, to be rewarded and recognized for my contributions, and to have balance of head and heart. It was only through discovering who I was and what I wanted that I was able to find my passion and pursue it.

Discern your values and gifts, also known as your core competencies. Explore how you can align these two in a way to unleash and ignite your passion. The intersection of your values and your gifts describes what you are passionate about.

**B:** *For some people is that to be an individual contributor within a company and for other people it is to be a worldwide success story?*

Everyone has his or her own path. There's no right or wrong.

You don't have to be the top of the company in order to contribute. You can contribute and make a difference in smaller ways. Let's say you smiled at someone or gave them feedback that helped them do what they needed to do. The mother who's caring for the child, the individual contributor who has some brilliant idea on how to improve the performance of a product, and the person who is caring for others: we all have a way to use our gifts and our values. We may not know the impact we are having [and] we may sometimes not appreciate that it's our way.

You have to find your own path. Realize you have been given your own gifts, you have your own values, and so therefore there is your own passion to pursue. Don't compare yourself to others. Know and nurture yourself. Find out what's important to you and who you are.

**How do you know if it's time for you to change or time for the environment to change?**

You wouldn't know it necessarily, but you should ask your heart.

Our schools and work environments too often close down peoples' hearts. It happened to me being in a technical arena.

I ask people, "What helps you listen to your heart and hear it?" and for many people it comes from quieting down, perhaps meditating. For others it's being out in nature, giving yourself a chance to exercise, being around people who might stimulate you; whatever it is for you, find it. Give yourself permission to do some of those things and when that little voice, that you don't know where it's coming from, speaks up ask, "What is this? Give me more clarity." Then follow that message.

I was in Africa, coming back through Greece and Paris before I came home. This was prior to cell phones. Nobody knew my itinerary and no one would have been able to get in touch with me. I was standing in line to get on my flight to Paris and got this feeling that came through my gut, into my heart, then into my head. It said, "Go home. Go home." I didn't know why, but I went [directly] home.

When I came home I found out that my dear uncle who was like a second father to me had died at just that moment and I was needed back home. By following my heart and listening to it, I was there for my family.

The same thing happened in a work situation. I was getting ready for a business trip and I got this message, "Back up your laptop." I hadn't backed it up in a long time. I thought, "I don't have time, I'm going to miss my flight."

About an hour later, I got this same message, but louder, and still didn't follow it. I wasn't really open to my heart. If I had been, I would have at least backed up some of my [critical] files. On the plane, I opened a magazine. The first article I saw was, "PC Security While Traveling."

When I arrived in the rental car lot, I got off the bus and put down my suitcase and briefcase with my PC in it. This car zoomed by, drove over my PC, and smashed it.

I really regretted not listening to my heart. We all can do exercises to strengthen that heart muscle and allow it to speak and be heard.

**B:** *You have similar promptings of what to do in business?*

Yes, absolutely and you have to trust it. Ask for clear messages, give it permission to speak up, and then listen.

**B:** *Whom do you ask for those messages?*

My inner, wiser, older self, which to me is God speaking through me. Life is a spiritual journey. I consider my work my ministry, so God is speaking through me, through my hands, my heart, and my head.

**What is your belief system?**

I grew up Catholic so I have a very structured, formal educational foundation. Since that foundation, I've branched out and grown and combined other beliefs, including Buddhism. I'm a long-time meditator.

I consider myself a Unitarian Universalist. We are open, questioning people from diverse religious backgrounds who create our own theology and believe in the worth and dignity of all people, the democratic process, the interconnected web of life, and that it is fine to have your own search for truth and meaning.

**Let's talk about your book. You interviewed 80 people. You went in from the research perspective trying to find what is the difference between those who pursue a passionate purpose in life and those who do not? You didn't have any preconceived notions as to what they were?**

I had hypotheses from my secondary research and life experience that I tested and they were the basis from which I generated certain questions to ask.

After defining what it meant [to have a passionate purpose] I asked the questions, "Have you ever have a passionate purpose?" "If so, how did you find it? How did you know it was right? What was your means for pursuing it?" and then I would dive in to learn more. I was trying to understand if there was a universal process. I knew that there was a method for me and I wondered if other people had the same or a different approach.

**B:** *And it seems that it's the same?*

There were a lot of similarities, yes, and it was distilled down to the formula in my book.

**Did the people you interviewed consciously know they were following that formula?**

No, not necessarily. Some people had their own version of the formula; they had different words to describe it. Most of the successful people had an approach that they could articulate when I talked to them. They may not have taken it upon themselves as their life mission to explain it to others.

**How do you define success?**

A combination of making a difference, contributing, and having deep, caring relationships in a way that I can support myself and my family while living with integrity. I have five overall goals in my life which define success.

One is being a strong, healthy, authentic self at the emotional, physical, psychological, and spiritual level. Another is loving connections with myself, fellow beings, God and spiritual forces, and nature. Third is contribution, my professional endeavor and meaningful work. Fourth is financial serenity and divine prosperity. I like making money and I want to make more to be even more financially secure. The fifth has to do with being in the flow – enjoying life in a joyful, passionate, optimistic state while being open to the opportunities. Those are the main five goals I have in my life and I feel if I can attain those, I will be successful.

## Would you say your journey was relatively easy or hard?

I read Scott Peck's book, *The Road Less Traveled*, and the opening words in his book are, "Life is difficult." I read that 20 years ago and said, "I totally disagree with this. Life isn't difficult. Life is easy." However, I learned that life brings adversity.

[Yet] adversity is a gift. Karen Bernardi, one of the most successful realtors in the country, when I interviewed her said, "If I would not have been so hungry, I would have not been so motivated to pick myself up by the bootstraps and make changes. Adversity has been a positive force in my life. People and purpose rise out of adversity."

Yes, at times life is difficult. I like to have a positive attitude that even the worst of times can be turned into the best of times and that maybe there is some purpose behind hardship or it will help in some way in which I may not even be aware. The most successful Passionate Pursuers have the trait of optimism, the "o" in SUNFLOWER.

Belief is essential in terms of continuing on the path and getting what you want in life. Believe in yourself. Believe in the process.

To strengthen my ability to believe, I say positive affirmations and visualize optimal outcomes. Some of my favorites include: "my self-talk and my public talk are always very positive," "I easily visualize in living color and attract those things that I want in life."

I had set a goal after the first baby plan delivered to have a second biological child. I called it "Baby Plan Two." Baby Plan Two did not deliver, so I don't want people to get this impression that every single thing that I've set out for has been easy for me to attain. Baby Plan Two did not deliver because I stopped believing it was possible.

## Did you have any formal mentors?

John Hess, my Ph.D. dissertation chair, is a mentor to me. He is also a very successful entrepreneur. There have been others.

I went to my boss at AT&T Bell Labs one day and said, "Nelson, when are we going to sit down and do my career development plan?"

He said, "Theresa, nobody does your career development plan but you." He taught me some important things.

I have a mastermind group, which is a group of peers from different areas. Napoleon Hill in his book, *Think and Grow Rich,* introduces the concept of a mastermind group. I suggest you should have intimates, supporters, and mentors. Set up your own group if you don't have it.

Use the "Connections Strategy" and realize that the most effective Passionate Pursuers build relationships with and bring along on life's journey the proper people and support network and lessen the impact of improper ones.

**B:** *Did you know about* Think and Grow Rich *while you were building your company or is that something you've come to later?*

I discovered it afterwards through the National Speakers Association.

**B:** *Didn't Napoleon Hill have a mastermind group with non-existent people toward the end of his life?*

Oh yes, he did and you can also. That is so powerful, too. You can have this powwow and bring together the optimal set of advisors – consider if you could have any advisors in the world, who would you recruit? Ask them for advice and they will speak to you. I also have another mastermind group of sorts of my chakra animals. For each of my chakras I have an animal and I will occasionally bring them together and ask them for insights.

**Do we all have opportunities presented to us?**

I think opportunities are everywhere and we need to open our eyes to see them and embrace them. That's why one of my affirmations is "I easily find and embrace my right work with the right people in the right location with the right compensation." I don't know all of the specifics of what that will be, but if I can be open to it…

Then there's this challenge of saying "yes" and saying "no."

I'm saying to be open to the opportunities, yet you have to say "no" to many things in order to say "yes" to your passionate purpose. Margot Zaher's passion at one point was to live in France. She had to say "no" in high school to cheerleading and a lot of other things in order to study French. She ultimately became a marketing manager for Proctor and Gamble in France and lived her dream.

I think you can have everything in life, but maybe not all at the same time. It takes discipline. It takes focus.

**Did you have written down goals throughout the building of Radish?**

Yes.

Sometimes they were clearer than others, but we definitely had a clear, written business plan, which we revised annually and turned it into an operations plan of how to guide the firm.

I have had personal goals since my early 20s. I took a course then called, "Achieving Your Potential." This was one of the gifts that AT&T Bell Labs gave me. It was a means by which I learned some important success habits. Get a vision of where you want to go and then set goals both personally and professionally to help you move towards it. Break those goals into smaller chunks. If you have annual goals, break them into what you're going to do this month, this week, this day. Then take action. An important mantra of mine is: Believe, Visualize, and Act.

I do that. Even yesterday I had my list [of things to do] and they were prioritized from one to six. I didn't get to bed until midnight because I had to finish the last one, but I finished it. I don't always get all of them done, by the way. I'm way too ambitious, but that one I had to get done.

**You had to believe in yourself that you were going to be successful. Where did that come from?**

Ultimately it came from my sense of self, my confidence that was generated in the early years of my life and all along the way when I would strive to do something and get it accomplished. I built up this confidence.

With Radish specifically I think there was an inner knowing that this was a good idea and a knowledge that the work was important. Then there was the belief that Dick and I would somehow work it out and achieve a good outcome.

**Were there disappointments or challenges along the way in building Radish?**

Yes, absolutely.

Radish got to a point where we were making sales, but in comparison to where we really needed to be to meet our financial goals we realized that it was not going to get us there fast enough. Some changes had to be made. We looked at it with a force-field analysis – we determined the positive things encouraging us and our technology to be successful and what negative forces were holding us back.

We identified on the negative side that we were the new kid on the block and people wondered if our protocol would become the *de facto* standard. There was a limited set of people who could use our product because we hadn't sold that many units.

We built a strategy that turned those negative forces into positive forces. We did that by deciding to open our protocol to the world and convince off-the-shelf modem and chip and PC manufacturers to embed our technology in theirs.

It was a process of assessing progress, seeing what was working, seeing what was not working, and then making some strategic decisions on what to change and then pursuing those modifications.

We were fortunate. We were at the right place at the right time and Microsoft walked into our trade show booth. That started a courtship. They licensed [our technology] and embedded it in the Windows operating system and that led to other things. They helped us open our protocol and attract hardware original equipment manufacturers (OEMs) to standardize on it.

There are so many challenges you face on an ongoing basis. Another big one for me was when I felt that I could not live true to my values in the organization that I had started. The values on which we had started the company included integrity, customer delight, and financial rewards for all stakeholders.

In my opinion, the way certain people were operating in the company lacked integrity. I tried to change the situation, but I was no longer in a situation where I could. Those people didn't report to me. I tried to live with it, but could not. I ultimately did what you have to do if you want to still survive and keep your spirit alive; I had to leave.

That was another "allowing" experience. I realized I couldn't control that situation, so I had to let go and drop the resistance. I quit and decided to move on. That was probably the biggest challenge for me. I learned to use the "Allowing Strategy."

In retrospect, it was by leaving my first baby, the company, that I was able to heal and get pregnant with my real baby, Annie. Had I not left, I may never have gotten the gift of the most wonderful, precious thing in life. I moved from pursuing the "Business Plan" to pursuing the "Baby Plan." This is an example where you never know when something is happening, even when it feels painful, whether it's good or bad.

*An update from Theresa*:

Dick and I have started a new company with a familiar name, Radish Systems, also known as Radish 2.0. We are pursuing "Business Plan 2." The mobile market has exploded and people on the go want better business information faster. Radish offers ChoiceView™ to allow mobile callers to instantly SEE and HEAR info delivered during a call with a ChoiceView-equipped business, thereby transforming hated interactive voice response (IVR) systems into visual IVRs, reducing online transaction abandonment rates, and improving the technical/customer/sales support experience. Check it out at www.RadishSystems.com.

****

# Millionaire 10 John "Jack" Odom

Retired, Orthopedic Spine Surgeon

Married, five children

Bachelor's, M.D.

*Chris Ware, a good friend, was renting a house from Jack and referred me to him.*

**Did you always want to be a doctor?**

Since I was 13.

**Where did that come from?**

My father.

**B:** *Was your father a doctor?*

My father was a farmer.

**B:** *He planted within you the plan to become a doctor, though?*

When we had hog killing day, he taught me anatomy. The more he taught me anatomy, the more I wanted to learn about it. When I was 13, we had a cow that had a calf hung up and he had three of us hold her down while he did a C-Section on her. After I saw that I thought, "Boy, that's the real thing."

My dad said to me not long after that, "You like anatomy, you like hog killing day, and after the C-Section you were so excited that I think you ought to consider being a doctor."

I said, "No, I don't want to be a doctor."

"Why?" he asked.

We had one doctor in our county, he was a family doctor, and some of the people he operated on died and everybody knew about it. I said, "I don't want to be like Doc Lawson and operate on people that die." I couldn't live with that very easily.

He said, "Well, you should think about being a surgeon."

I asked, "Aren't all doctors surgeons?"

"No. If you have extra training you do surgery every day."

"Really?"

Mother always said that I then said to dad–I'm sure I didn't but this is the story that went on forever–"You mean everyday will be just like hog killing day?"

**Did you really enjoy what you did?**

Yes.

**What did you enjoy best about it?**

Becoming a spine surgeon. There are about 10 sub-specialties in orthopedics; that wasn't true when I finished [school], there were none. I got interested in spine because it is so complicated and I thought, "I can do that complicated stuff and I can do it with ease."

When I finished [school], I heard a report about a doctor from Australia operating on the spine from the front and thought, "I can do that."

They said, "You have to be a general surgeon."

I had two years of general surgery training at the University of Pennsylvania, Philadelphia before I went into orthopedics [so I qualified].

I learned from John Hall in Toronto; he and Doctor Dwyer developed the technique. I visited him and came back and started doing them. I operated on a little girl who had about a 90-degree curve in her spine. I put screws through her on the convexity, put a cable through the screw head, cut out the disc, tightened down the cable, and made her totally straight. It was the first one done in Colorado, and the second one done in the United States.

In the 1970s it was unethical to advertise about anything in medicine; you could lose your license. But Children's Hospital heard about this operation and somebody in the hierarchy of the hospital thought that would be good for the hospital and asked if they could take pictures and put those pictures in the Denver Post.

We had before and after pictures; it was pretty dramatic. Probably the best case I ever did. The next day people started calling in asking, "Who did that?"

Orthopedic surgeons called in and started sending patients to me like crazy. All the sudden I had more than I could handle and it just went like wildfire. I did about six-and-a-half thousand spines in my career.

In the 1970s and 1980s I was in a group with six other surgeons. I brought in more revenue than anybody else, more than double the bottom guy of the seven, but we split it evenly; I didn't like that. I said, "We've got to have some sort of deal where you get money for production and not just because you're a member."

They wouldn't agree to that, so I moved across town. In the first year I tripled my income, the second year I quadrupled my income.

The first year, 1991, we kept a map of where the patients came from. I got patients from 46 states. Now they have changed the insurance system, though, in that patients can't travel. Insurance will pay perhaps 60 percent out-of-network, maybe less, or none.

**I'll bet the insurance was something that frustrated you.**

It was, but I did it for fun.

I traveled all over and gave talks: Rome, England, Hawaii, Canada, New York, San Francisco, and Boston. It was a thrill. I operated in New Mexico, Virginia, Wisconsin, and multiple other places. Other doctors said, "Show us how to do this."

I said, "Let me come on a Thursday night so I can do it on a Friday and go home on Saturday."

Sometimes I'd go stay two days and do two cases.

I went to China a few years ago for a year. I did a little over a hundred cases for free for people who couldn't afford it and would come from a distance.

**Was it an easy journey or a hard journey to be successful?**

It was a great, fun journey. It was not just easy, it was wonderful. Easy is not the word. It was hard work, but it was joyful work.

I started a spine fellowship. Now you can't do spine until you've been trained in a fellowship. I wasn't spine trained except self-trained [as] I visited everyplace that was doing something new, whether it was San Francisco, New York, Chicago, Houston, or whatever. Those first years I'd go [learn from other doctors] about 12 times a year.

They would say, "Yeah, I'll work with you," because they wanted to teach me.

Nowadays, the guys that know how to do it are much more arrogant about it. When I was young, everyone was just doing the best they could and if they had somebody else that wanted to learn, they were honored that somebody would come and spend three days with them. Now it's not that way.

Plus you can't get insurance. Now if I have someone come in, they have to have a Colorado license and at least a million dollars of malpractice insurance.

**Did you ever have written down goals for becoming a doctor?**

Nope.

**B:** *For the amount of money that you wanted to make?*

No.

**B:** *You never had written down goals?*

No.

**Did you ever have a vision of where you wanted to be in life?**

Yes.

I wanted to be known as somebody who knew how to do something better than anybody else in my community. That's what I wanted to do. I wanted to be known by the physicians more than anything else. The patients that's fine too, but I wanted to be recognized by my peers.

When I grew up, we had a little farm in Tennessee, but my dad ran a 2500-acre experiment station and I badly wanted to have some land around my house [when I got older]. I didn't want to live in a place where you could hear the neighbors. I never quite achieved that, but I have 17 acres and a couple of barns. I have horses, and I've had cattle and sheep. I have a big garden, fruit trees, beehives, and all that stuff that I grew up with. I just wanted to have some land and some space for myself and for my children. I wanted them to have the country experience.

**How did you balance time with the family while you were busy?**

I didn't do it that well at first, I guess, but my wife had psychological problems and she spent a lot of time going to the psychiatrist and then she had to go to the mental hospital. She decided that maybe if she got rid of me that that would cure her problems. It didn't.

I didn't balance it as well the first time because I was on-call every third night and when I was on call, I was gone; I worked. In those days, they didn't have an emergency call list. I'd go sit in an emergency room and say, "I'm in the hospital. If you want me, I'll be there in five minutes." I developed a huge practice by doing that.

**What was your income at the height?**

The most I ever made was $1.3 million in a year. That started in the 1990s. I was making about $300,000 to $1 million a year and then the last 20 years I made an average of $1 million a year. But that wasn't my purpose. My purpose was just to have a booming practice and be somebody. And I've always been generous to people, I like to give people things.

My mother always used to grow a huge garden. It was right at the side of our house.

People would ask, "Why do you have such a big garden?"

She responded, "So I can raise things and give them to people like you. Come out here and let's see what you want."

I did that too, because mother did it and they had such a joy in doing that. I just wanted to do the things that were joyful.

## What is your passion?

Probably my family. My passion has been spine surgery for lots of years, but now I'm writing all sorts of history of my family, so that's my present passion. And responsibility is the way I look at it; not just purely a passion.

I'm passionate also about having a nice place and sharing it with people. We started having square dances on the top of one of the barns. Finally we got so many people I built another barn with a whole level that's a dance floor. We used to have three or four dances a year, but now it's one a year, that's all I can handle.

We have a big potluck; I supply all the meat and drinks, they bring the vegetables. It's a lot tastier than hiring it all out and [those who come] feel better about it and enjoy being part of the system. Then we get out the two surreys and two horses and ride around the pasture. Everyone has a buggy ride. We've been doing that for years.

## You like having space and resources to share with people?

Right.

## What did your parents teach you?

Everything I know except surgery, but they started out with that; my dad taught me anatomy.

They taught me values. We were Congregationalists, which were the Puritans. All three of us sons became somewhat non-religious and the two daughters became religious. When I was 23-years-old, my father admitted that he didn't believe in heaven and hell. That's when I told him I didn't either. We believe in the Judeo-Christian philosophy, we just don't believe in the heaven or hell part.

**You still believe the Judeo-Christian philosophy and that's what guided your life?**

Right.

**Did you have a mentor or a role model?**

Sure, I had lots of them. Of course, probably my best two were my mother and my father. Then probably my next best mentor was my younger brother.

**You said earlier the three brothers were very successful and it's because the principles mom and dad taught?**

Absolutely.

**Did they teach it in combination with living it, or did they just live it?**

They lived it and we watched it.

They both agreed early on that education was the way to move up in the world. Money passed down meant nothing; your education would make you successful in life, so they thought it was wrong to give us things.

They taught us to work for everything we got, and that included going to college. They expected us to go to college and because they worked their way through they expected us to work our way through.

My sister Nellie worked and paid her way through three years of college until she met her husband and got married. My brother Bill went to West Point. It cost $300 in those days, now it doesn't cost anything. He had to borrow $300 from Uncle Newt and paid him back when he got out.

I was number three and I was nervous I would have to do like dad did: work for a while and then attend school for a while. In those days, if you were a high school graduate you could teach grade school and high school. He'd teach for a quarter, go to school for a quarter, teach for two quarters, go to school for two quarters. He went like that until he finished college; it took him five-and-a-half years.

Mother was able to graduate in 1929 four months before the Wall Street crash. She graduated in June and then dad kept going to school.

They started us saving money from an early age. We had bank night on Saturday night, the purpose of which was saving money for college. I was two-years-old and I got two pennies. By the time I was five or six I had to do tasks to make money. At age 12, I started working on the agriculture experiment station that my dad was superintendent of for $0.20 an hour. When I was a senior in high school, I was getting $0.70 an hour. From age two to age 18, I had saved $1,000.

I started the University of Tennessee with $1,000 and at the end of that year I had almost nothing. I figured if I stayed and worked the whole summer–mom and dad said I could and they'd pay for all the food and for my clothes–I'd have about $400, so that whole year I was talking to people about summer jobs.

I found a guy that sold Fuller Brushes one summer and he made enough in one summer to buy a car and pay for two years of college.

I sold Fuller Brushes door-to-door and I made enough for almost three years of college in one summer. I saved it and made it through four years of college. I was able to pay everything and finished college owing nothing.

I got admitted to medical school, but I couldn't afford it so I put it off for a year [to work].

I was all set up to go to Detroit to get a job in a Chevrolet factory. A school superintendent, whom my mother knew well, called and offered me a job. My mother didn't tell me until later that she had talked with him about hiring me. If she had, I probably wouldn't have taken the job because I wanted to be independent. I taught algebra and English and helped coach football.

I started medical school the next year. Probably 65-70 percent of all medical school students had jobs in those days, 1958, so I got a job at the blood bank two days before I started medical school. Anytime I had free time, I'd go to the blood bank and work. I worked a little bit at the mental hospital; I didn't like that very much.

Between my freshman and sophomore year I had a bet. I lived in a fraternity house–it wasn't like a college fraternity–which was a lot cheaper than living in any dorm. Some guys had cars and they would charge about $5 week to ride with them to school.

In that day, students didn't ride bicycles and I thought, "What the heck, I'll ride a bicycle." I saw this new type with three gears and a seat so you could tie books on the back for $39.95 at Sears. I figured I could pay for it in a few months. If I were paying $20 a month for rides with others, in two months I would be ahead and would still have transportation. Then I would have the freedom to work at the blood bank more.

I was so excited [about the bike] and these guys called me "Joe College" and always laughed at me. I said, "Look, I can ride all the way from here to Knoxville," which is 430 miles, "in three days."

They said, "We bet you can't."

Sixty-seven of them put down $3 a piece, which was $201 dollars, and I put $67 in the treasury. My bicycle fell apart before I started.

I told my brother Bill about this trip, so he bought me a bicycle. I rode that bicycle 430 miles in 67 hours and got $201. I got palsy at 90 miles, I had numb hands, I was bleeding by the time I got there, I was sunburned; but I made it there and I got $201.

The main thing was I proved to those guys that I could do it. My father and mother say you never gamble, no matter what, that it's terrible. My mother was mad at me for about 10 years.

When I was a junior, I got a job at North Peak Hospital. That was the best job I ever had. I lived there so I got room, board, and laundry and $25 a month. I borrowed a thousand dollars from the Carmel

Clinic, which is in our hometown. Dr. Evans and Dr. Metcalf loaned me the money and I was able to get through medical school.

But there was no doubt I was going to do it.

**Where did that confidence come from?**

Mother and dad, and Bill.

Grandmother's father fought in the Civil War, in the Tennessee infantry. He was a captain. He got badly wounded. The other grandfather got wounded, too. They had been confident and their great-great grandfather before that was a colonel in the Revolution. He was at Yorktown with Washington when Cornwallis surrendered in 1781.

You just knew you were going to do well and parents expected it, so you just did it. There wasn't ever any thought about not doing it.

**What advice would you give for someone who's looking to make it in their chosen field; they're looking for their break?**

Not only work hard, but work smart. Think and plan and listen. In my day, anybody that just worked hard could probably do all right; not do real well, but you could do all right. In today's world, you have to be smart and look at all the issues and plan and think.

**What is success?**

Being happy with that you're doing. And feeling like you've done something worthwhile for humanity. You haven't done something worthwhile for humanity if you've just made money. You've done nothing.

**How do people find their passion, or find something they're happy doing, and then make money at it?**

Look hard, look smart. Don't just take the first thing, keep looking. I didn't just practice medicine. I've bought apartments and rented them. I bought into a bunch of apartments that we've sold for lots of money. That was my side job and that was in the days that I thought I was only going to make $300,000 the rest of my life.

Then when I started doing well while working in the group practice I decided I'm not going to give it away to those guys. The best way to make money is to work for yourself, not somebody else.

****

# Millionaire 11 Mark Sanborn

Professional Speaker, Author

www.marksanborn.com

Married, two sons

Bachelor's in Agricultural Economics

*I knew of Mark for several years since we worked in the same industry. I called his office for an interview.*

**You had an experience with a postman, Fred, and that seems to have really launched your career.**

No, it was an important milestone, but the encounter with Fred came about two or three years after I went full-time as a speaker. *The Fred Factor*, which is of the books I've written my best-selling book, didn't come out until I had been in the business full-time for 18 years.

Certainly *The Fred Factor* has been a wonderful brand and revenue stream for us, but I made my initial wealth long before *The Fred Factor*.

**When you were in high school, what did you want to do?**

I started speaking in 4-H when I was 10. Through listening to professional speakers like Og Mandino and Zig Ziglar I realized that you could make a living speaking and I wanted to do that someday, but I didn't know when or how that would take shape.

I was later the state and national president of Future Farmers of America [FFA]. A lot of people heard me speak in that capacity and as a result when I went back to college, I kept getting invited to speak. I worked my way through college doing $150 or $200 after-dinner speeches.

**You made your millions doing public seminars? I'm just kidding, I [know what the pay is].**

I did public seminars for about three years. Late 1989/early 1990, I went cold turkey and just started working with my own clients. From 1990 on, I've been averaging about 60-70 engagements a year. Probably for the first 15-20 years, I was doing 70 or 80. Some years I would do as high as 90-100 – when I was single and didn't have a family.

**I sent you an email previously and asked how you balanced time with the family. You said luckily you did a lot of your traveling before you had the family.**

Yes, but it's still not easy.

My wife is a stay-at-home mom by choice and because she can be, so that helps with the kids having a sense of stability. I use the concept of "time sovereignty" that says we don't really control how many minutes we have in a day, but we control how we arrange the minutes.

If I want to go to a matinee with the kids some afternoon, I can do that because I'm my own boss. I don't have to ask for permission.

One of the lines I use a lot in my work is, "Nobody has time. You make time for what is important." And for me, family has primary importance.

**What prompted your transition from public speaking with a company to your own business?**

I just didn't want to be doing low-fee public seminars anymore. I wanted to do keynotes and shorter programs. I had a good learning curve and a good win-win relationship with my friends at Pryor and CareerTrack, but it was a growth move, pure and simple.

You only have so many days in a year. You're always going to be limited by the value and revenue you can produce each day. If you know that each day's only going to be worth $500, you always know the absolute most you can make depending on how many days you want to work.

CareerTrack was billing me out to clients for a great deal more than what they paid me, so I already knew my value in the marketplace was dramatically more than I was earning as a contract trainer.

The argument that a public seminar company would use is, "We're doing all the marketing. We're generating leads." They would make the argument that people were buying a seminar and I was an interchangeable piece of the puzzle.

As time went on, people wanted me, and that dynamic shifted. Plus, I knew the business. I had been a member of the National Speakers Association from the time I was a sophomore in college, so I knew the business side of speaking. It wasn't like I was guessing or making it up as I went along. I learned the business long before I went into the business full time, which is an important and useful lesson for anybody.

If you have an aspiration to do something, whether it's starting your own business, becoming a speaker, or winning a marathon, start training and studying now. Don't wait until the year you want to do it. If you want to run a marathon you start training well in advance of the race. If you want to be competitive and do well don't wait until two weeks before the starter's gun fires. You want to start a business in five years? Read the books. Go to the seminars. Develop the plans now.

Preparation is what allows you to make a smooth transition.

The reason it looks like an overnight success is people aren't on your radar until they're successful – they might have been laboring and preparing in obscurity for 10, 20, 30 years.

My friend Michael LeBoeuf inscribed a book to me that he wrote. He said, "The bad news is it takes 15 years for any overnight success. The good news is the 15 years go very quickly." Interestingly, from the time he wrote that inscription until I got inducted in the Speaker Hall of Fame was 15 years.

### Did you have a visualization of where you wanted to be or written down goals?

I'm not the best guy to talk about written goals. I believe in the power of goals, but I have been far more successful personally with having a very clear sense of direction and seizing opportunities as they evolve.

I knew I wanted to be a speaker. I knew I wanted to be a successful speaker. But I didn't have the goal of "I'll be making X number of dollars by this date next year."

I'm not discounting that for people who do, but there are a lot of things in the pursuit of success that are preferences or stylistic. The substance may be shared, but for instance, a lot of millionaires don't have budgets. They just always make sure they spend less than they make and save the balance.

I have never, other than in my business, worked from a budget, but I also have a pretty good head for numbers. I've never operated in deficit in my entire adult life. I had parents who taught me that basic premise of living beneath your means.

I've got nothing against budgets. I just don't operate that way. I use profit and loss and statements and balance sheets in my business and we have some guidelines.

I know the ratios and the amounts that are reasonable and unreasonable for what we do, but I've been profitable for every one of the 24 years that I've been self-employed, including some pretty lean years. There's always extenuating circumstances, but it goes back to a philosophy of prudence.

**Would you say your journey to success was relatively easy or hard?**

It was relatively simple, but not easy.

Simple in that figuring out how to be successful is not complicated, but doing it is hard work. In all due respect to people who read *The Secret*, all the positive thinking in the world doesn't accomplish anything until you couple it to action and effort of some kind.

Certainly the right thinking can expedite or leverage your action, but it never ever replaces it, so I worked very hard and still do. Maybe there are people smarter than me that figured out a get rich quick scheme that didn't require much effort, but I did it the old-fashioned way. And I've noticed that when someone gets rich quick, they tend to get poor quicker.

I was willing to work harder than my competition to become really good at what I do. And that's whether you're making French fries, giving speeches, or practicing law: become so good at what you do that people will choose you over your competition. That's a simple but powerful concept.

## What did you do to get good?

I've always been a great student in my craft. I was always willing to study my clients more deeply, prepare more thoroughly, and spend more time creating. I was just willing to go beyond the easy and obvious.

I didn't have any particular breaks. I got a degree in Agricultural Economics. I grew up middle class with good parents, but nobody gave me a nest egg that allowed me to launch out on my own.

I boot strapped. I never had even a significant lump sum of money to start my business, which is why I'm a big fan of professional services firms. They are less capital-intensive to start.

## How did you gain your first clients?

That was the helpful part of public seminar companies; they provided a steady stream of audiences. The trade off was I didn't get paid much. The benefit to me was I got a lot of experience and chances to speak, which is the hardest part of becoming a professional speaker. The way you become a good speaker is speaking a lot.

Until you're a good speaker, no one will hire you. Keep in mind, I spent from the time I was 10 until I was 18 speaking in front of audiences for free. That's the other thing people forget: before you get paid to do anything, you do it a lot for free.

## Is that one of the key things that holds people back from experiencing the success that they want?

I'm not sure. There are people who have done the research on what holds people back, but I personally think lack of motion is what holds people back. I always tell people I'd rather be splashing around in the ocean than sitting on the shore doing a strategic plan.

The only way you get experience is by doing lots of different stuff. Whether it's bad experience or good experience, experience helps if you learn from it.

Being willing to try things and make mistakes is absolutely essential.

**What were some of your failures that you experienced along the way?**

I worked for most of my 24 years primarily on referrals and bureau bookings. The last few years we've done a little bit of marketing, but for the first 15 years, I just responded to inquiries. I tried to be so good that somebody in the audience would hear me and say, "I want to hire him, too." Speak a hundred times and you'll get a hundred more opportunities if you hit it out of the park.

If I had spent as much time on a really logical, organized approach to sales and marketing, I could have leveraged that. Instead of being reactive, I could've been more proactive. I'm sure it would've been both more strategic and probably more profitable, but you only have so many hours in the day; I put them into improving my performance.

You have to choose the way you're going to do it and there's no singular path.

**Does everybody have opportunity? Is the environment right for everybody to achieve success?**

First of all, nobody "has" opportunities. They don't land in your lap. You seize or create opportunities. You create opportunities by doing well at little things so that over time you'll get an opportunity to do bigger things.

Although we all make our own opportunities, I acknowledge that there are circumstances and environments–poverty, homelessness, lack of education–that make it harder for some to create or seize opportunities. I've seen many people start out either incredibly destitute or overcome incredible odds who became successful, but still, I'd be a little naïve to say that it's an equal playing field.

Even though I didn't have any big early break outside of good parenting, neither did I have any liabilities like drug addiction, abuse, or terrible poverty. While it's true that anyone can be successful, I don't ever want to sound harsh or unrealistic in saying that we all have equal chance to create our own opportunities because we don't.

One of the things successful people do is look for opportunities to help others find those opportunities. One of my passions is programs that teach people skills to succeed.

**You've made millions of dollars. You could retire. Why do you keep at it?**

Despite whatever money I've made, I'm the kind of person who will never completely retire. I enjoy my work too much, and being productive and contributing helps you live longer and better. One of the great rewards of some success in life is you go from doing it because you *have* to, to doing it more because you *want* to. You get to choose more.

I balance what I think I need to do with what I want to do. My goal is to make best use of my time to make a positive difference. I know that sounds a little corny to some people, but it is absolutely true.

**How did you become an expert in leadership? Where does that come from?**

I was the national president of a youth organization with 500,000 members at the age of 21. I was involved in leadership from the time I was 10 in 4-H, FFA, church, and community.

When I say "leadership," I don't mean I was running a Fortune 500 company, but I was accepting leadership roles and I became a student of leadership about the same time I became a student of speaking, culminating in today, being the executive director of a foundation, serving on boards, having been the president of the National Speakers Association, and speaking to and advising 60 or 70 clients a year.

Did I win a war? Did I win a gold medal in the Olympics? Did I lead a Fortune 100 company? No, unequivocally not.

What I've done is lead organizations (like my own, associations, and others) and I've coupled that with the ability to communicate what I've learned to help clients.

I do believe that being a leadership speaker it's essential to be a practitioner. I think the people with most credibility aren't just the ones who talk about it, but the ones who do it and talk about what they learned from doing it. That's why I continue to stay involved in leadership roles; it feeds my business and becomes a laboratory for what I teach. Being a practitioner is key.

**Did you have any mentors or role models?**

Yes, I had several of them and I've acknowledged them over the years in my books.

I was lucky in FFA. I had an early mentor, Dr. Earl Kantner. He was the executive director of the Ohio FFA when I was state president. Another was Ed Johnson, a broadcaster and speaker.

Back then I didn't think in terms of mentor/mentee. That term wasn't on most people's radar. My "mentors" were just people who were investing in me and my success with no ulterior motive other than to be role models and to serve.

Charlie "Tremendous" Jones, in later life, has been a spiritual mentor and dear friend. I learned a great deal from Charlie. And I have many close friends in my collegial group Speakers Roundtable (www.speakersroundtable.com) who are a wealth of wisdom and counsel.

I certainly encourage formal mentor/mentee relationships, but I think when most people stop to think about it, they've had a lot of mentors they've learned from even from a distance. Sometimes a good book is a mentor.

**What is your belief system that guides your life?**

I'm a New Testament Christian.

I hesitate to use terms like "evangelical" because it tends to come with baggage, but I'm a Christian who believes in and follows Christ. After much seeking, study and thought, that is my worldview.

**What's your passion?**

My passion is *helping* people grow. I can't literally "grow" someone, but I can assist them in the process. I can provide ideas and encouragement.

I'm in the idea business. There are many ways to share ideas. I started primarily expressing ideas in speeches. Now I do it through speeches, books, training resources, and the Internet (blogs and social media), but the principles don't change.

The motto of my business is, "Developing leaders in business and life." If I can help someone become a better leader that influences and impacts others, that's a worthwhile legacy. That will last beyond me and beyond my books.

**B:** *Was that your passion when you started at age 27?*

Early on I was driven to prove myself, to succeed.

Hopefully sooner than later you reach a point in your life where you don't have to prove yourself. You're not doing it for the acknowledgement or the recognition. You've got the acceptance of the marketplace.

I grew up as a kid who was overweight and picked on. I didn't have the kind of storybook childhood where I look back with fond memories.

I was successful within my speaking and with FFA, but a lot of my early life was probably designed to prove my self-worth first to me and then to others. Then I got to the point where I realized it shouldn't have bothered me so much.

I didn't have this grandiose passion at the age of 27 to be a difference maker. My maturity and my worldview weren't evolved enough yet. I was probably more fueled by pure ambition more than anything else. Which isn't such a bad thing, because at the age of 50, that isn't my primary driver anymore. If it were, I would still be dealing with some big maturity issues.

**How do you define success?**

At this point in my life, success is living life in the way God intended for me to live it.

He wants us to be more like Him, which means to be more Christ-like. I'm a woeful example of that, but that's the goal. The goal isn't to have more or even just to be more, but to be more like Him.

Whether someone believes or agrees with your worldview, if you can be more like Christ, you're going to positively impact them because His life and example were life-giving and enriching.

For me the question is, "Would God be pleased with how I spend my time?"

**If you had to capsulize it, how would you say you got where you are?**

At the end of my book *You Don't Need a Title to be a Leader*, I included the story of what B.C. Forbes, the publisher of Forbes magazine, wanted on his tombstone: "While alive, he lived."

I thought that was a good start.

I hope I have many years before anyone has to worry about it, but I said if I had an epitaph that was meaningful to me, it would be, "While he lived, he loved. Because he loved, he served, and when he served he led." That to me encapsulates what it's about: living fully but not just for self.

"Servant leadership" to me is redundant. All leadership is a form of service. If you say you're leading and you only benefit yourself, that's ambition, not leadership. Leadership means you've created a better department, a better community, a better family, or better experiences for your customers.

I can only second Rick Warren's sentiment in the beginning of *The Purpose Driven Life*: the navel is not the center of the universe and the beginning of maturity is when we realize that.

When we realize that, we realize that as blessed as we are by the stuff we've got, that's not what gives life value or worth. That's just icing on the cake. For me it is about faith, family, and friends first. The real challenge is as you get more things in life to not let the stuff overshadow the real gifts.

**What advice would you give someone who's looking for a break?**

I'd either look for a problem I could solve or way I could be of greater service. In those two directions are acres of diamonds and fields of gold.

Right now with everything that's gone on in the economy, everybody's focused on playing not to lose. You've got to keep playing to win.

For instance, I did a conference call with a client and we were talking about the bailout plan and the market. This person produces infomercials; a $100 million company. He said, "It's tough, but we've got a show running right now on how to deal with mortgage foreclosures."

He didn't create the problem, but he created a solution: "You got foreclosures? Here's how to deal with it. Here's how to turn lemons into lemonade."

Most people are going, "Wow, what possibly good could come of this?" Here's a guy that said, "Where's the problem and how can we help solve it?" He developed and marketed a resource to help and found an opportunity [even] in this [awful circumstance]. Life's always like that.

Preserve your capital, do what you have to do to protect your assets and your family. Don't stop looking for the opportunities.

The reason I don't want to buy a new house, among many, is I hate to move. If a realtor came to me and said, "I've got a system to make moving painless. We work with a moving company and other professionals to make it easy so you don't have to go through the stress of packing and labeling boxes. We don't just sell your house, we get you in your new house with a minimum of brain damage," that would be a way to give greater service that I'd pay for. Just as a realtor could gain a competitive advantage by increasing his or her value and competitive edge, we could all benefit from thinking bigger and doing the same.

**Is there anything else you would like people to know about success or about you?**

First of all, I haven't cornered the market on success. I'm a student and as long as you maintain a student/learner posture, you'll always keep growing. When you think you've figured it out, that's the beginning of the end.

Maintain a student posture, a learner attitude, and no matter what happens, regardless of the success you do or do not achieve, you'll have a more enjoyable journey.

Finally, I believe that despite the challenges and the pain, life is meant to be enjoyed.

That doesn't mean pain doesn't exist, it just means we can both deal with the pain and embrace the joy at the same time. That's one of the great paradoxes.

If you wait for all your problems to be gone, you'll be dead and in the grave and realize you never enjoyed the journey.

\*\*\*\*

## Millionaire 12 John Simcox

Retired: Founder, JC Keepsake; currently involved in private finance ventures

Married, six children

Associate's Degree

*I knew of John through Ed Reynolds, a friend and former boss, and then met him at a self-employment seminar he taught.*

21 Questions for 21 Millionaires

## Tell me about graduating high school and then what was your plan in life?

My plan in life really started as a boy. I was the oldest of eight kids. My dad worked hard and struggled. Financially it was really a tough battle all the time.

My dad was from the hills of Tennessee. He was an honored pilot in WWII. He flew 104 missions without being shot down and was a very decorated officer.

He came home and started looking for what he was going to do. He had saved his money and had a pretty good amount of money saved up and decided to raise chickens. He was a hard worker. Everything was going great and then a disease, Newcastle's, hit the poultry industry. A vaccine was quickly created, but he lost everything before that could be done. He had 25,000 chickens and they were all dead in a month.

I remember as a little boy, standing there with my mom and dad in tears as they buried the chickens. They borrowed the neighbor's backhoe and pushed these loads of dead chickens into holes. That's all they could do.

My dad [had to then] lease the land and farm it. My whole life as a boy I was working. I was always selling something so I'd have some money; otherwise I wouldn't have anything. I'd raise chickens, fatten them up, and sell them in the neighborhood.

My dad would let me throw in a couple rows of sweet corn in the silage field. I had a place in town under the shade trees where I would sell corn by the dozen. In the morning I would get up early, pick the corn, and do the same drill again until the corn was gone. So that was the start of my entrepreneurial spirit.

I would collect the eggs out of the chicken coops, carried them in buckets or baskets down into the cellar and then my dad would pay me 25 cents a case to case them. I'd do a case a day, some days more, some days less. I was saving to buy a horse. I had $25 saved up and we found a horse for $25 when I was about eight.

**You learned at eight-years-old the value of working for yourself, entrepreneurism, the value of being able to communicate and sell, and working toward something?**

Yes.

Casing the eggs was first. I was probably 11 or 12 when I was doing the corn and the chickens and all that stuff. My dad taught me how to milk a cow at a young age so twice a day I'd milk the cow.

I always felt a little aggravated because I couldn't go do the things my friends would because I always had these responsibilities in the morning and at night. I'd always be missing out on things.

In spite of all the challenges, and it was always a financial struggle, it was still a good life. My grandparents, who I lived with for a few years as a boy, lived just a short walk away. They were wonderful. I had high regard for my grandfather and he taught me a lot.

I had severe hay fever as a boy so I would be sitting there with a handkerchief, mopping my eyes and nose while I was trying to sell somebody corn. That was pretty miserable.

I remember watching the guys at the co-op where all the farmers take their stuff to sell it. I liked seeing these guys sitting at a desk, figuring everything out. I thought, "It sure is a lot easier and cleaner and there aren't [any] problems with hay fever in this office."

After years of farming, my dad went to work as a car salesman. He did very well, everybody liked him and he was the top salesman right away.

That changed everything. We left the small farming town and moved to an area that was very different than what we'd been used to. I couldn't do the same things I had done before.

I went from a small town, farm boy in [a close-knit church community] where everybody knew everybody else and everything was wonderful–I had all the merit badges to get my Eagle Scout award, I had been actively involved in leadership as a boy–and moved over to this new area that was much bigger. I didn't feel like I fit with them.

I backed away from it and never got my Eagle. That was a disappointment I had. For some reason I kept having rubs with some of the church kids in this new ward so I kept pulling away from the church, and the church was different. I didn't go on a mission. I hid from the bishop for months during that time. I didn't want to go to college either.

I had jobs all the way through junior high and high school. I worked for a grocery store as a bagger, then a guy opened a furniture store and hired me to deliver the furniture. As his store got bigger, he had me hire friends and we'd deliver furniture all over Salt Lake.

I went through all those years of working for people and finding ways to do things and then when I met my sweetheart I thought, "This has to change, my life is going to be different." When I met her I was driving a gasoline tanker for American Oil. For a young guy my age I was making great money, but the guys I worked with who were in their 30s and 40s were making as much as I was. [It was good money for a single guy, but not enough to really raise a family on.]

I thought, "This isn't going to work now that I'm falling in love with this great gal. I have to get educated. I know what I want to do. I want to market, I want to sell. I want to be doing some services where I'm the organizer between producers and the users." That was the plan.

As soon as we were married, I enrolled in LDS Business College. The first year I took classes at night trying to transition myself [because] in high school I was much more interested in all my various pursuits of earning money than I was in listening and working in classes; my mind was always somewhere else. If they were to measure my graduating class, there's no question I was in the bottom 20 percent.

College was hard for me. I was more of a conceptual thinker, not a detail thinker. I wasn't used to reading and I had to re-discipline and re-teach myself to become a student. It was hard, but I was motivated. The next year I went full-time and finished up. It was a two-year associate degree program and I finished up in about a year-and-a-half. I did fine and liked it.

First I thought I'd go on to the University of Utah or BYU [Brigham Young University] and get my bachelor's degree, but I was too impatient. When I met my wife she had been married previously and had a little boy. He was six-years-old; his dad was out of his life and never gave my wife any support so I felt highly motivated to get in the work place. She worked as a secretary while I went through school. She'd always been a hard worker; she's very smart.

That was a very exciting time for us. One, falling in love and two, I just knew that we were going to do well in life. I was excited to get out, get after it, and get going. I knew it was going to happen.

**How did you know that?**

I had watched other people.

I knew I had been blessed with a lot of things my dad had. I knew how to work hard and influence people, and I'd been taught leadership in the church as a boy priesthood leader. I had some great leaders that were highly influential in my life that taught me about leadership and organizing; how to have a meeting, to have an agenda, and all those things that they teach us as boys in the church.

That put me, I felt, way ahead of the whole world, even though I felt like I didn't have much advantage in Utah because everybody else was doing the same thing. As a result, I wanted to move out of Utah because I wanted to go out where there were bigger populations and more opportunities.

I went on a lot of interviews before I got a job. I got hired by a pharmaceutical company and they moved me to Kansas.

I liked the job and was highly motivated by it. I'd be up early in the morning. I had a car, expense account, salary, and bonuses; I thought I was on top of the world. I told everybody as long as I would be financially elevated based on my performance, that I didn't care what they started me at.

It was exciting because I was in a professional environment. I was wearing a suit and tie. I'd never tire. I was so energized by the opportunity I'd run everywhere. I immediately started having measurable success. They were highly pleased and I was excited.

Then I met a friend who worked for a company called Farah. Their deal was they gave you nothing but a territory, products, and a percentage of everything you sold. The more you sold, the more you made, and I liked that. My friend was a highly motivated guy and he was doing very well, making twice what I was.

I was still a very conservative, careful, young guy that wouldn't even consider going into my own business at that point. I had a paycheck, I had cash coming in, I had a wife and a son to support and it wasn't long after that that our daughter was on the way so I wasn't ready to start my own business. I was too nervous, too conservative. I knew how much I'd have every month. We knew how to budget. We never out-spent our income, whatever it was, as low as it was.

When I did eventually make the move to Farah, it was a big jump and a big risk. I had to go on a six-month training program. We moved to Montana, and later they moved me to California.

It went great. I was the number one salesman in California after being there six months. Within a year I was number one in the company nationally. They moved me to Colorado to take over.

I knew how to work with people, how to work hard, how to gain others' respect, and I wasn't afraid to ask for the order. I wasn't afraid to be a little aggressive and at the same time I had a good, country, down-home approach. The combination just worked.

[After we moved to] Denver I wanted to have my own business, [but] I had no idea what [it would be]. There were two guys at church who had a diamond ring store [and that was interesting to me because] in the apparel business if you didn't sell an item within the first four months it was obsolete. You had to mark it down to practically nothing and I didn't like that.

I got into the jewelry business, opening a store [while] I was still an independent contractor with Farah.

**B:** *How long had you been with Farah when you started JC Keepsake?*

I think it was nine years. Then we got into the fitness business [Nautilus] and had fitness centers. They were all growing so fast I was trying to keep all three balls in the air.

A friend of mine became the national sales manager for Farah. He knew what I was doing [with JC Keepsake and Nautilus]; it wasn't like this was being done behind their back. They didn't care as long as the orders came through and I always gave them a high order rate.

I told him, "My heart's not with Farah anymore it's with my own stuff. I know this real sharp guy here in Denver and it would be a big boost for him to get the job and he'd do a great job."

I left and they hired the friend. I went full bore into being an independent, self-employed person for the rest of my work life.

**The process of getting JC Keepsake started: Was it as simple as finding where to buy the diamonds and then finding a storefront?**

Yes and no.

The model then was a new phenomenon in the United States–regional shopping malls–and one of the first big successful ones was in Englewood, CO. That's where you wanted to be.

Most of the jewelers were national and internationally owned companies. The malls wanted those well-financed, big companies as their tenants. They didn't want the little guy so we had a hard time trying to find a location where we could get in.

The Aurora Mall was just being built at that time so that's where we decided to try to get in. They turned me down many times, but I just kept after this guy. I became friends with him and worked through the whole process. Eventually he said, "OK, I'm going to give you a space."

I had some partners in the business, two brothers from church who were contractors; good guys.

**What is your passion?**

My passion is multi-personalitied.

I have that inner need for security and financial stability. I think about finances and how to manage money a lot. It has just [been] part of my DNA since I was a little boy. I'm always looking for ways to increase our financial position. Some might say I spend too much time thinking about it.

I was never one to work long, incredible hours, but I'd get so focused. That was all part of that drive, of always having a little bit of the fear from my youth of seeing mom and dad crying because they couldn't pay their bills and couldn't buy their kids the things they wanted to and me never wanting to be like that.

The other thing is I was always motivated by working with people and doing two things: trying to have people around me that were smarter than me and trying to find people that had the same work ethic that I had. That was motivating to me, finding those kinds of people. It was always a wonderful thing when they came to work and they were happy and I was happy. Those people were what built our business.

When I was running the business actively, I had as much fun everyday running the business as I did on any vacations we took.

I said I was never going to be held hostage to our business. Early on there were times when I was, but my wife straightened me out and I wanted to be straightened out. She would see that I'd be with the family, but my mind would be somewhere else. That would irritate her and rightfully so. When that happens, the gospel keeps us in line.

**What's your business now?**

I look for ways to loan money.

Real estate was really good for us for a number of years, now it's a problem.

I make short-term loans to people at high rates where their banker wouldn't loan them money. Some people call it hard money lending.

**We know that, "The love of money is the root of all evil."[1] How have you reconciled yourself to the fact that it is OK to be financially prosperous and think about finances a large portion of the time?**

My approach has always been this: when I was a boy and being taught by my [local] leaders and the leaders of the LDS Church they were constantly encouraging us to get educated. We were all poor farmers; we lived on nothing. We were encouraged to get educated and become solvent, financially secure, and self-sufficient.

I've been doing that ever since. Yeah, it's worked better for me than maybe it has for some and so maybe I have more than some do, but my approach is the same. I pay my tithing faithfully. I've never turned down a calling in the church, by saying, "Oh, I'm just too busy out there chasing the dollar. I'm opening three stores this year and I won't have time. I'm sorry. I can't serve now. After this year's over I'll be able to." Never have we done that.

I've always rationalized that I know the other side and I know that [it] wasn't good for anybody when we couldn't pay our bills, and I know the [LDS] Church teaches us to be self-sufficient. I'm just being self-sufficient. Maybe it's [at] a little different [level] than other people are.

My wife and I have always given of ourselves and we try to be very generous with people and helping others out that aren't in the same position we are.

We've always lived our life as though we were the same young, aspiring newlyweds that are trying to live like students. We've always been those same people.

We've never had debt. The only things we borrowed money on are our house and business. Early on we did have a car payment, but that was only for a while. We made that decision years ago that we'd never borrow money. Now in our station in life we don't borrow money on anything. If we can't pay cash for it, we don't do it. I think that's all part of being responsible and conducting our stewardship in accordance with what the Lord would have us do. I think we're on track with what the gospel teaches us and our circumstances are just what they are.

**Would you say it's your drive that's brought you to the point where you are?**

Yes.

**B:** *Your intense drive to be number one, to be successful, the fear of what you saw when you were a young boy.*

Right.

**B:** *And then your constant focus on, "How do we improve this situation? How do we manage it well?"*

Manage our position and not put us in risky environments. That doesn't mean we don't enter into risky situations, because anytime you invest there's risk. But you do everything you can to minimize it. It takes a lot of thought and planning and research to figure out if it's risky or not. And then I try hard to do due diligence to ensure that I don't put our resources in places that are going to hurt us.

**Did you do due diligence before you were in this position or would you say you learned to do due diligence once you started to really experience success?**

I've always done it. Sometimes it was the little things and sometimes it became big. Before we opened that first jewelry store I planned and plotted and thought and talked for I don't know how many hundreds or thousands of hours before we actually went forward.

**Did you ever expect, think of becoming, or desire to be a millionaire?**

Never thought of it in that way, no.

**B:** *You just always thought of it as, "I want to be number one"?*

I want to be successful. I want to be profitable. I want to have adequate for our family needs. The money was an issue because of my past, but my passion was more about being good at what we were doing, whatever it was. Having our stores be well run, having good customer relations, creating a niche that worked and that had long-term success available to us.

I have no clue when we became worth a million dollars. That was never on my mind. I guess I think a lot smaller than that. I think of the detail of the stuff that will make that happen.

**Did you have written down goals?**

Yes, all the time.

**Did you have a vision of where you wanted to be?**

Yes.

With Farah it was always goals by customer: "Last year I did $50,000 with this customer and I know we should've done $70,000. What do I have to do different for us to realize our potential with this guy and do $70,000 instead of $50,000?" It was always that kind of monetary goal, but never, "If I do $50,000, they pay me $10,000. If I do $70,000, they pay me $15,000." Once it was my own business, it was the same process.

We were constantly thinking of ways to raise the ladder and climb up a little higher, always pushing to climb higher and be better. Always looking for the areas in which we needed improvement, and there were always lots of them. It was never hard to find things we needed to do to be better.

**What were some of the mistakes you made along the way?**

In our jewelry business there were some location mistakes where we should not have gone to that location. We should have said "no" when we said "yes."

**B:** *Even after due diligence?*

Yes. Something else overpowered good judgment and said, "We can make it work," when in fact we can control so much, but that's all we can control. There were some uncontrollables there that we could not overcome.

We made people mistakes through the years. They were painful. Some of the most painful things in that business were people related. Most of the pain I had was through employees.

## What would you tell someone who wants to be successful?

Be passionate and be willing to work hard and like what they're doing.

## Did you have a mentor or a role model?

I had lots of them. I never had a specific one, but I felt like I learned from everybody.

I learned from an alcoholic boss what not to do, how not to waste your life away. I learned from real smart people that did things a lot better than I did. I watched them and I tried to do things as efficient as they did. I probably didn't measured up in a lot of cases. I think I learned from everybody, the good and the bad, and I try to not make the mistakes that I saw others make.

## Do you have a restless soul?

Partially.

## Was your journey to financial independence relatively easy or hard?

Hard work and there were terrible problems through it.

We went through a big recession in Colorado in the late 1970s and early 1980s. People were going broke all the time. Everyday you'd hear about all the companies that had gone out of business and the people that were laid off. That hurt us. We were right out there in the middle of it with a bunch of jewelry stores trying to sell watches and gold and diamond rings when they're telling us they're losing their jobs.

**Why did you stick with it? Why did you not walk away in such a tough time?**

We learned how to stay profitable. I'd meet with my people and say, "It's going to be tough, but we can do it. We won't have the high profits. We're not going to be able to give raises and we're going to all have to work together on this, but if we do and we work hard now, we stay profitable and stay in business and not go out like others are. Then when it gets better, we'll be there ready to make a lot of money and everybody will be happy."

I convinced them of that and I had some good people who worked for very low pay for some tough years when the economy was on the skids.

Nautilus went from being a cash cow to being a bust for two reasons. One, the economy. Two, the bigger reason, was we had some former employees open their own. Ours was called Nautilus Fitness Centers and they called theirs 24-Hour Nautilus.

They sold to some guys who left town with hundreds of millions of dollars of unpaid bills. One day the clubs were boarded up. It was on the news, radio, television, and in the newspaper. Everybody was confused – "Was it Nautilus Fitness Centers?"

We had eight big facilities around Denver. The day that hit the press, our sales dropped in half and we never could get them back up again. We ended up selling. We had people wanting to buy us before that that would've paid us a lot of money. We said, "Why would we want to sell it to you? We're making so much. Plus we like the business anyway."

**How would you define success?**

First, the family. Right now my success is we have five great kids that are good people. They're all hard workers. They have high ethics. All of our kids now have been to the temple, and I'm not putting that as a badge of honor on me, but I'm happy for them, what they are.

## What do you wish someone would ask you?

I think a key question is, "Why do you think you were able to do what you were able to do when there were lots of other people that are probably smarter than you and good people and [they] were not able to do it?"

**B:** *What's the answer?*

Focus, discipline, and consistency.

**B:** *Focus on the end goal?*

Focus daily. Discipline to not get distracted. There's a lot of detail with that: time management, resource management.

## Is there anything else you would want people to know?

The bottom line is you're only as good as your people. You're not going to have much success on your own. You're pretty limited [on your own] so to really have any kind of success there's going to have to be good people involved with you in some fashion. Every circumstance has a little different set of rules, but you just can't do much by yourself.

And I don't think you can do much without the gospel. Obviously there's a lot of people out in the world that do well that don't have the gospel, but I don't think I could. My dad used to say, "This family wouldn't be much without the Church."

**\*\*\*\***

# Millionaire 13 Bill Begal

Founder, Begal Enterprises, Inc.

www.begal.net

Married

*Bill and I got connected after Millionaire 8 Barry Hamilton sent an email through Young Entrepreneurs Organization [YEO] asking if anyone were interested in being interviewed for the book.*

## Tell me about your religious background.

I grew up in a Conservative (not necessarily very religious, but practicing) Jewish home. I was very close to my grandparents, my mother's parents, and quite often celebrated Sabbath meals with them since they lived very close to us.

My parents did not keep a Kosher home. When I moved out of the house and moved to L.A., I started keeping a Kosher home and still keep a Kosher home to this day. I do eat meat [when I'm] out, so I'm not completely Kosher. Some may say keeping Kosher is like being pregnant, either you do it or you don't, but I think Judaism allows you the ability to be hypocritical and do with it what you want to whatever extent. The Orthodox would not agree with that, but many others do.

I question God tremendously. I've been very active in Jewish communal and Jewish youth work. I used to take 65, 16-year-olds to Israel every summer on a six-week tour. On one of those trips we went to Poland for a week first and I questioned God a lot that week.

My parents had a dry cleaning business and my grandfather had a dry cleaning business. My father also worked full-time in the automotive business as a salesman, in addition to the dry cleaning store.

I didn't know what an entrepreneur was, I just knew that this is what was going to be.

My grandfather didn't go to college. He moved from Europe to Cuba and eventually the United States, and then joined the Army Air Corps. His brother, Uncle Bill, was born in Cuba and moved to the United States with nothing in his pocket and is now worth many millions of dollars.

## Tell me what "Million by 30" means.

I really didn't want to go to college. I went because my parents forced me and I only went for one year because I wanted to get out and start making money like my grandfather and Uncle Bill. Uncle Bill had nine dry cleaning stores and my grandfather had two.

My examples [in life] were not people that were in college or college educated. Aunt Hela had a business with her husband. Aunt Tola had a belt business in Havana, Cuba, with Uncle Jaime. Aunt Eva and Uncle Morris had a leather business in Utica, New York. Aunt Guta and Uncle Issac had an ice cream shop and they were also in the dry cleaning business.

People in business: that was my example, that's what I knew. On the weekends my grandfather would take me to his dry cleaning store and I would help him do things. When I was younger it was to clean the basement of one of the stores. When I got a little older I would earn money by making hangers. I would help him do what we would call "man's work." I don't remember what it was. It was a little hammering of this, a little screwing of that – just being with him.

I saw my Uncle Bill and my grandfather and I didn't know what my grandfather had, I didn't know if he was worth a million dollars, but for some reason, by the time I was 30 I wanted to be worth a million dollars. I don't know where I got the crazy idea; I don't know how it happened, or where it came from or any of it.

**You went to a year of college because your parents forced you and then you dropped out?**

Yes. I went to run the dry cleaning store. I would work from 1:00 p.m. to 7:00 p.m.

In the mornings I would cut the grass and I'd clean my parents' pool. I taught myself to play golf. Sometimes I'd get up really early and play 18 or 27 holes of golf before 9:00 or 10:00 a.m.

Then I got a job in a bar so I'd work from 8:00 p.m. until 1:00 a.m. bartending, working the door, being the short order late-night chef, being the bar back; whatever they needed me to do. I'd go home and sleep from 2:00 a.m. until 7:00 a.m. or 10:00 a.m., depending on how late I stayed out. I had a pretty good life.

**You were running the store so you were making O.K. money?**

No, I was making horrible money and was living at my parents' home. Maybe I was earning $10,000 a year. But life was good.

## What took you out of that?

Like all good stories, it involves a woman. I went to work in Los Angeles for the great uncle of my girlfriend at the time.

I took a picture of a letter that's on my wall from this guy Leonard. The last line in the letter reads: "Regarding salary, we've worked it out at $8 an hour to start for a 40-hour week, plus a monthly bonus of $280 which will bring you to a yearly salary of $20,000."

That was August of 1995. Not that long ago, living in L.A., I was earning $20,000 a year. Every person who comes into my office sees this letter. I pay my people $10 to start, and that's if you can walk and talk and maybe chew gum at the same time. So when people complain or say how hard it is...

I've had temp workers work for me. I was driving around with a couple of them one day in my car and they said, "Come on, Bill, your dad gave you this business."

I said, "No, I started it. I started it myself and you can do whatever you want to do. You're limited by absolutely nothing."

I look at all my grandfather's siblings who literally had nothing and worked hard and helped each other out in a typical old country or European way of life. They busted their [tails] and they did something with it; they made it work. There was a lot of failure, it wasn't easy, but they worked.

Why am I willing to make a phone call with you late at night? It's what you do, you make it work. I sacrifice and work hard now with the hope that I won't have to later.

I don't want to work more than another five or 10 years. It's to the point now that I'm trying to run my business via a Blackberry or a remote computer from Miami a couple of times a month and enjoy, to an extent, some of the fruit of my labor because you always hear the epitaph, "Here lies Joe, never missed a day of work, worked hard, was a miserable man"; that's no way to live, that's no fun, that's not the way I want to be.

When I'm done talking with you, if it's 11:00 p.m. or 12:00 a.m., I promised myself I have to run tonight. There's a treadmill in my office. I'm probably going to run for 20 or 30 minutes. I don't want to break a promise to myself.

**Would you say that integrity of following through on a promise to yourself is one of the reasons you've been successful?**

Possibly, but not the absolute reason why.

I've been asked before, "Can entrepreneurship be learned or does it have to be God-given or innate?"

I think to a certain extent, it's got to be in you. I don't know if it can be learned.

Very rarely will I give advice. Instead I'll speak from experiences because an entrepreneur is more likely to listen to somebody's positive or negative experience, while any idiot can tell you what to do.

Based on my experiences, my examples, my mentors, and the generation of people that I saw: they weren't the smartest people, they weren't the dumbest, but they had integrity and they worked hard and there was desire, there was drive. They were in new countries time and time again.

There was desire to strive and do something, to really make life better for themselves, but especially the next generation. My examples, my grandfather and his siblings, had something inherent; it was in them.

I look at my Jewish ancestry and my Jewish roots and I see a lot of what other Jews, regardless of their observance level, have contributed to society. Between 1901 and 2008, there were 750 Nobel Prizes handed out. Of those, 160 were to people of Jewish decent.[1] For a population that is 0.02 percent of the world's population to have [over 20] percent of Nobel Laureates; what does that say about the desire to live, to desire to prosper, the desire to be better than the generation before you?

I'm not saying that's everything. There are two books, one of them is called *The Biological Jew* and the other one is *The Anti-Semite and Jew,* or maybe it was *The Jewish Mystic.* One thing that's fascinating in the very beginning of one of these books is why Jews were smarter or better in business, so to speak. It's a very simple explanation when you think about it.

Years ago in the non-Jewish world, what happened to the priest or the leaders of the community? They were celibate and their seed did not reproduce. So that brilliance, that opportunity, that bloodline, did not continue, it ended. Whereas in the small communities, the learned person was the rabbi and his child was typically set up through a matchmaker with the butcher's kid. So you have someone with some smarts marrying someone with a different type of smarts. Those seeds continued to reproduce.

I'm not saying that's all of it, but that makes me think a little. You have one series of bloodlines that continues to prosper, and another bloodline, no matter how brilliant and learned and responsive and receptive, that didn't continue. It's not my original thought, but I think it's worth considering and pondering. So that's a little bit more about why I think the way I think.

**Do you know how old you were when started to think about Million by 30?**

In my late teens, early 20s.

Remember, in 1995 I was earning $20,000 living in L.A. – I didn't hit a million dollars by the time I was 30, but by the end of my thirtieth year, I was pretty close.

Then I realized a million dollars isn't that much money. Now I realize maybe if I get $2 million, $3 million, or $5 million put away, then I can really retire.

I'll give you a great money quote: "Mo' money, mo' problems," from Puff Daddy.

It's so true. Sometimes I wish for my more simplified life in L.A. on $20,000 a year. I had great friends who were of considerable wealth.

Some of those friends from L.A. I'm still really good friends with. One of those friend's father has a seat on the New York Stock Exchange and he's produced Broadway plays that have won Tony awards. This person doesn't want for anything. I got to hang out in their house, swim in their pool, use their gym, and eat their food.

Another friend's parents are developers and didn't want for anything. Another friend was struggling at the time, but he's now a successful movie writer. I was great friends with these people and I had nothing. We would go out to dinner and I would order soup and eat lots of bread, because I could afford the $5 soup and throw in a couple of bucks for tip. That was 15 years ago, not that long ago.

**What are the problems you have now that you didn't then?**

They're almost self-inflicted or self-desired. I want to be more successful. As society defines it, as I define it, as my wife defines. When is enough money enough money?

**How do you define success?**

I fight with it all the time because sometimes I think I'm very successful and other times I think I'm not really successful.

I've got a business, I've got property, and I'm able to go to Argentina for a week in the middle of the year. I'm successful because I was able to start a non-profit group with two friends. I'm successful because I have great friends.

**Take me from 1995 making $20,000 a year to 2008 and making...?**

I don't know how much I'm going to run this year. It depends on if I get to bonus myself out if there's anything left at the end of the year.

My salary is modest. I think my wife and I earn each $100,000 a year.

My first year in business, 1999, I generated $400,000 in revenue. I don't remember what I took home, but it was enough money that I gave myself a little bit of a bonus and I could buy my wife an engagement ring. Maybe I made $50,000, maybe $100,000; I don't remember.

In year two or three I generated just over $1 million and was able to pay myself significantly more than the prior year. I reinvested the balance back into the company as the down payment on the warehouse that I now occupy.

**What happened to take you from that level to the next level?**

We got a very large job and we did it; we made it happen.

**What made you decide on the business you went in to?**

The girl in L.A., it's what her great uncle did. Uncle Leonard taught me. I was in the dry cleaning business [prior to that].

I always treated the dry cleaning stores like it was a restaurant and I was the maître d'. I got to know my customers really well. [Then] I figured if I could clean shirts and deal with a suit, a shirt, or a wardrobe, why couldn't I clean the whole house? You've got a fire or flood? I can clean your furniture; I can pack and move it. I can clean it, I can store it.

Years ago I told my parents I wanted to rent out a 10' x 10' storage space, talk to insurance adjusters, and follow fire trucks to get smoke damaged clothes to dry clean to generate some extra business. My parents said, "That's not going to work, that's not really a smart use of your time."

I could have had a 10-year head start on myself.

**You had this idea even before you met Uncle Leonard?**

Yep.

He was a piece of work. He taught me how not to be a boss. He taught me how not to treat people.

**B:** *By the way he treated them?*

And the way he treated me.

In 1995, earning $20,000 a year, those were difficult lessons to learn. They sure did save me a lot of money later on in life.

When we got back from Argentina, the car wouldn't start because the battery was dead. I went to the Lexus dealer to have it replaced. I said, "I don't mind waiting an hour if it's an hour. If it's going to be more than an hour, let me know. I've got a bunch of stuff to do today. It's my first day back in the county–that's not your problem–just let me know."

They got me a rental car and the guy who gave me a ride back said, "What did you think of the rental car? It was a piece of [garbage] wasn't it?"

I said, "It got me from point A to point B and back. I'm happy I had a car today. I didn't care that it wasn't a Lexus. It would have been nice if I had had one, but I was just grateful that they could deal with my issue today."

I can talk to anybody. I don't care if you're the janitor or the president. More importantly, I've taken the motto I like to be nice to the people on the way up the ladder, because I'm going to see them on my way back down the ladder. Why upset somebody, why make a fool of yourself?

**Tell me about the formula for success. You said it can't be learned.**

From my experience, from the examples of the people that I've seen–my grandmother and my grandfather worked together, all of his siblings, the husbands, the wives all worked together–there was no Entrepreneur 101 or Business 101.

None of those people were college educated yet they were all really successful. They escaped Nazi Germany. They took month-long trips on boats from one country to another. They raised families.

That's success. That's real success. I've been lucky to make some money.

**What would you say is your passion in life?**

I love to help others. www.mitzvahheroesfund.org is the website of the non-profit I started. I also do work with the Gift of Life, a bone marrow foundation where I'm now the chairman of the board. Long story short, a friend of mine needed a bone marrow donor 15 years ago. I went to Russia for six weeks looking for his donor. Jay is now alive and well.

I courier marrow all over the world. I took bone marrow to Israel this year. I was there for 36 hours. I went to Turkey twice in six weeks. I've taken bone marrow to Italy. I took bone marrow to Israel three days after they declared no more flying with liquids, and I flew through London.

I like to help people. In my business I also get to help people.

**B:** *But you wouldn't say cleaning and restoring, in and of itself, is a passion?*

No, not so much. For me the passion is getting the work, the hunt.

**B:** *Sales is a passion of yours?*

I wouldn't say sales, [I would say] challenges.

**Do you have written down goals, or did you as you were building your business, of what you wanted to accomplish in life?**

No. Regrettably, I'm not the most disciplined paper work person.

I think part of my success was some of my gutsy decisions. Kind of like a kid on skis when they're young: boom, down the slope. They don't know any better.

I think some of the early decisions and gambles I made helped me to get to where I am today. Now with my business partner, my wife, some of those decisions I made then she would never let me make today.

**B:** *But that's what it took to get it going?*

I think that's part of it.

**B:** *The only real goal in terms of finance or career that you had is the Million by 30?*

Yeah, I wanted to have a million dollars, not just be worth it on paper.

**B:** *To this day do you have concrete goals or visualization that you use?*

More visualization.

After some of things I've shared, this is going to sound a little shallow, but I'd like to be able to fly private, as silly as that sounds.

[Additionally,] it's not enough that I have my own pending 501(c)(3), but I also want to create an annuity so that when I pass on, I can continue to impact and help people.

**B:** *How do you visualize these things: Do you have a conscious process of that or you just think about it now and again?*

Think about it.

**Would you say your journey to success, or the point where you are now, was relatively easy or hard?**

After there's a hurricane, I go. I was in New Orleans two or three days after the levies broke. Within a week I had a hundred people working.

Was that easy? Was it hard? It's what I did. I made it happen.

It wasn't an option for me not to do it. I had to seize the moment, take that opportunity, *carpe diem*. I took advantage of an opportunity.

My financial planner said he could never do it. That's my ability that I can make that happen, I can do that. The woman that I speak to, Annette—my therapist, business mentor, coach—is also not that type of person. She could never do that.

That skill set for me is easy. For me, it's what I do.

**Have you ever tried to boil it down and codify what it is that's made you successful? Hard work, entrepreneurship, what else?**

Family, religion, something within that you can't touch or control, examples from past generations, and desire.

My wife sometimes thinks that we're not successful because the business hasn't grown to X or Y dollar amount, we're still having to be involved in it, or we're not doing what X person or Y person in her YEO group has done.

As much as we've achieved, there's always somebody else that's done a little bit more, who's a little bit better. It's just stuff, it's just things. You can't take them with you. It's impossible to. So why are we working so hard? It's just stuff.

I'm going to try to answer your question.

I don't know if I have the grail, I don't know if I have that formula. It just kind of works for me.

I have ADHD [attention deficit hyperactivity disorder]. I didn't want to take medicine, I didn't want to go see a doctor; I thought I'd be a failure, I thought that the meds would change my personality. I think I'm a pretty funny guy, I'm liked by my friends, I'm not always the life of the party but I like to have a good time.

I think part of my success is my ability to multi-task or to use my ADHD. The founder of JetBlue has ADHD. There was an interview with him one day and he was very outward about his ADHD. He said, "Yes, I have it, and it's my success and I'm not going to hide it."

I used to hide it. I was very ashamed of it. Once he came out with that, I realized I don't have to be ashamed of it anymore. That's who I am so for me that's part of my formula.

I don't know how people put up with me before I started taking meds quite frankly. I used to interrupt people's sentences and not be aware of it and it all had to be about me and my thought. [Now] I try really hard to use my mouth and my ears in the ratio in which they were given to me.

**What do you wish someone would ask you?**

I guess it's kind of presumptuous that I would think anybody would want to ask me anything. I don't know that I have so much to offer.

I would love to be known as the "Master of Disaster." I'd love to be the "Preparedness Expert."

**How did you make the bridge from being an employee to being self-employed? Did you raise money, did you borrow money?**

I moved back from L.A. and came to work for Uncle Bill's son, David, in the dry cleaning business. That was December of 1996. About a year-and-a-half later he said, "Let's talk about that fire and water thing you were doing."

We started grassroots marketing out of one of the dry cleaning stores. I started chasing business, going after fire trucks, listening to scanners, and aggressively getting work.

At the end of that year he said, "This is all well and good," he also owns property, "but I don't want this any more. I'll give you a couple of months to run it and figure out if you want it or not. If you do, great. If not, I'm going to bring someone in to run it."

March 1, 1999, I took over Draiman Enterprises and it became Begal Enterprises. I borrowed $25,000 at 10 percent interest from my cousin and uncle. I had three years to pay off the debt.

At the end of 2000, I wrote my cousin a check for around $18,000. With that payment I paid the note off a year-and-a-half early. The reason why I was able to be successful, one of the main reasons, is that he let me keep the profit from the jobs that we had in progress.

**B:** *He financed it, which allowed you to keep the profit and keep reinvesting in the business and grow?*

Yes, absolutely. That's one of the main reasons I was successful. It allowed me to avoid having to fool with cash flow at a very early stage. I still had the issue, but it wasn't as big of an issue because I was able to make a little bit of money from the very beginning.

It allowed me to create a buffer and the buffer just kept getting a little bit bigger and a little bit bigger. Now I'm to the point where I have this multi-million dollar receivable for two years that I'm still able to keep and buffer.

**Is there anything else you would like people to know that we didn't cover?**

Believe in yourself. Surround yourself with good people. Listen to the naysayers, but don't always believe them. Listen to them because there might be something you can improve.

My experience is you could always be better. I give my father credit with this little ditty he used to tell me years ago, which I thought was stupid, and it's still stupid, but I started to repeat it, so it's stupid but useful. "Good, better, best, never let it rest until your good is better, and your better is best."

The other thing is be careful what you wish for.

**B:** *Say more about that.*

I wanted to be worth a million dollars by the time I was 30. Well, is it all it's cracked up to be? The kid who goes on American Idol has no idea what fame and success is all about – you lose your privacy. Is it really what you want?

The grass, quite often, appears greener on the other side of the fence. Maybe take a look over that fence before you jump over there.

As good as my life is now, and it really is, don't get me wrong, my life was equally good but in a different way when I was living in Los Angeles earning $20,000 a year.

I'm no more of a person now than I was then. I'm no better of a human being now than I was then. I've got some more things, I've got some more stuff. I have more worldly and life experiences because of what money has afforded me, but I'm also able to give away more money now and do better things.

OK, so I can eat better food, which is why I've got to go run now, but I'm no better of a person now than I was back then. My lifestyle was still pretty neat. I had great friends. The parents of the girl I wanted to marry treated me well. Life was good. I don't know if I'd go to back to those days in Los Angeles, but I'm certainly no worse off for them.

I'm appreciative of the opportunity that I had and that was presented to me at the time. Very appreciative. I'm absolutely a better person for it now. I don't forget where I came from because I can be right back there again. It doesn't take that much. All that people think that they had or have now, look how quickly it goes. So that's why I firmly believe you've got to be nice to everyone.

From a biblical point of view, or a Christian point of view, you never know who the Messiah could be so you've got to treat everyone as if they could be the next person. Or even just the adage of do unto others as you would want them to do to you.

From where I am now to where I could be or was, I don't think in the relative scheme of life or the world that there's that big of a difference. I'm happier to be where I am, don't get me wrong, but I'm very fortunate. I'm very appreciative and part of my doing good or helping people is one of my ways of staying connected to those that are maybe not as capable, or not as fortunate.

I don't think that there's one thing. I think it's a perfect storm of things that, at least in my experience, have made me who and what I am to make me successful.

I think part of it is that my parents didn't have much, so I had a desire; I had a yearning, a hunger. If I had the silver spoon would I be as successful or as driven? I don't think so. I would like to think so, but the reality is I don't think so.

****

# Millionaire 14 Doug Krug

Author, *The Missing Piece in Leadership: How to create the future you want*; *Enlightened Leadership: Getting to the Heart of Change*; and *Leadership Made Simple*

Founder, elsolutions

www.elsolutions.com

Married, two children

*I worked for Doug at Enlightened Leadership, a company he co-founded.*

## What did you want to do when you grew up?

I wanted to be a cop. I liked what they did; they made a difference and helped people.

The resource officer at my high school greatly influenced that because he was a class act. He was there for three or four years and I spent a lot of time talking with him at dances, football games, basketball games, and other sporting events.

## When you graduated high school, you went right to the police academy?

No. You can't be a police officer until you're 21, so I went into the Air Force. College wasn't an option in my family financially; there weren't junior colleges and community colleges at that time. Your parents either had the tuition to send you to a university or you didn't go, so I went into the Air Force.

## As a means of gaining some education, some training, or biding your time?

Getting away from the house I was raised in was really the drive. I just wanted to get off on my own, not having had what I would describe at the time a happy childhood. It was an escape.

## You got honorably discharged after a couple of years and then what did you do?

I had gotten involved in a business in Europe when I was there, a bar business.

I kind of owned it. American military personnel weren't supposed to own businesses. I was living with a young lady and technically she bought the bar because the owner was going into the hospital and he didn't know when or if he was coming out.

I was a customer of his and he liked me and the lady that I was living with. He sold us the bar for a dollar and we agreed to sell it back to him for a dollar if he ever got out.

**Did you ever plan on being a business owner?**

No.

I ran the business for close to a year. We had a foosball table and I used to hustle on the foosball table. It was my table and my bar; I was good.

After I got discharged I went home for two weeks, then came back to Europe. During the day I would work in the BX [Base Exchange] selling cars to the GIs. One day when I went into the finance office there was a guy working there that I used to be stationed with; he had left a year-and-a-half before.

I said, "What you are doing here, Barry?"

He said, "I was hitchhiking around the world. The guy I was travelling with had to return to the States so I came here to figure out what I was going to do."

I asked, "What does it take to do this hitchhike around the world thing?"

"Well not much. Just a backpack. Why don't we have a beer after work, let's catch up."

The next morning I shipped everything I owned back to the States. At 4:00 a.m. the following morning a buddy took us out to the autobahn and we started hitchhiking around the world with nothing but a backpack.

**B:** *So you left your interest in the bar?*

Yeah, $0.50 worth.

**So you start hitchhiking around the world because it sounded like a good idea at the time?**

Yeah, exactly.

We did it for 18 months, I believe. We hitchhiked all over Europe, crisscrossed for a long time all through the British Isles and up into Scandinavia.

One of Barry's goals was Israel. We hitchhiked down through the Arab countries and there were numerous adventures in there. We went to Israel and worked on a kibbutz. We were there a few weeks when Barry came in one day after lunch and said, "Let's go home."

From Israel we hitchhiked on a ship to Brindisi, Italy, then took a train to Luxembourg and caught a flight home.

When I first got back, I filled out an application at the police department. They turned me down because you couldn't be a cop at that time if you had any corrective vision. Even though I wore contact lenses, it didn't matter; I didn't have 20/20. I think they could let you have 20/30, but I had 20/1600. I still do.

Meanwhile, I put in an application for this other place and got hired. After a couple of weeks I went back to see my resource officer friend, Bob Laws, to tell him what had happened with my police department application. He said, "That's a crock."

The next day he took me in his captain's office and told him the story. He got me into a program they were starting [in Dade County] at the time where citizens would be backups [to the police]. I worked vice narcotics in the organized crime bureau with a partner. I still kept my daytime job at the insurance company doing claims.

One day I invited another claims guy to lunch. He said, "I got something I've got to do. But why don't you meet me."

I met him in the parking lot of an office building. I said, "This isn't lunch."

He said, "No, I'm actually interviewing for a job. You remember Manny?" Manny had worked with us and had left about two or three months before. "His company has grown fast and they have openings. He just called the office to see who was there and wanted me to come interview for a job. I'm going to interview. Since you know Manny why don't you come in?"

Manny interviewed Greg and then came out and said, "Why don't you come in and interview?"

I got hired and worked there for a little over a year. I was scouting franchise restaurant sites all across the country. The company exploded for about six months and then started a downturn. I lasted through two rounds of cuts.

Then on maybe a Tuesday I got a phone call from a buddy of mine from high school who said he was back in Miami for a business meeting and wanted to know if I wanted to go to dinner. At dinner I said, "You live in Denver? I was just there a few months ago and really liked it. I'd move there in a heartbeat."

He said, "If you ever decide to move there you've got a place to live until you get settled."

That Friday I got let go. I called him and asked, "Is that offer good?"

Saturday morning I put a trailer hitch on the car and loaded up everything I owned that would fit and Monday I drove to Denver.

**All of these experiences were just make the decision and run?**

Every one of them.

I had no job, but the first chief of Lakewood Police Department was the guy who ran the Organized Crime Bureau from Dade County and a number of guys from Miami left to go to Lakewood. So the first thing I did was called him, but I failed the hiring process because Lakewood was the first police department in the country that required a four-year degree to be hired. I had no college.

The insurance company I had previously worked for in Florida had a regional office in the Denver Tech Center. After getting turned down by Lakewood P.D., I applied at the insurance company. I got turned down there, but I didn't like the guy that interviewed me.

I went home and mulled about it for a few hours. I really just didn't like the guy. So the next day I put on a different suit, went back like

I'd never been there before, and filled out another application. I got interviewed by someone else and got hired on the spot.

After about three-and-a-half years of that it was just getting painful, the bureaucracy and stuff; it was a big corporation. The lady upstairs, Lisa, and I were friends and we would cook meals for each other. It was her turn to cook. I was up there and said, "I just have to get out of there."

She said, "You're always saying you can do anything you want to do. What would you do if you could do anything?"

I said, "Open a record store," because I liked music and had bought a lot of records.

She said, "OK, go open a record store."

Five weeks later the doors opened with no retail experience, no money, no record business experience, and never having been in business for myself.

**How did you get the inventory?**

I didn't have much at all; that was the issue.

I kept my job at the insurance company for my first nine months of having the store. I would work daytime and then go down and run the store in the evening hours until closing.

A week after I [had talked to Lisa and] decided to open the record store, a guy I had previously worked with, Marty, and I went to lunch and he asked what I was doing.

I said, "I'm going to open a record store."

"How are you going to do that?"

"I don't know yet."

He said, "Do you have a business plan?"

"A what?"

"Do you have a business plan?"

I said, "No."

"Well I've got one that somebody else did, I'll give you."

I gave my business plan to an attorney that I had negotiated with a lot as a claims adjustor. After looking at it he said, "I value our friendship too much to give you any money because you're going to be working your [tail] off and I'm going to be taking all your money. So I'm not going to give you anything, but I will represent you for free. Anything you need, I'll give you the legal support."

The banker, a friend of mine, said, "I can give you a $1500 signature loan if that helps, but that's my limit, that's the only authority I have."

We had no money to buy anything, so my brother and I built all the fixtures, the counter, and the bins. We had to buy a used cash register.

About the time the store opened, I had dinner with Lisa upstairs and she said, "Friends of mine are coming into town soon and I'd like you to meet them."

Her friends were the managers for the group Earth, Wind, and Fire. During dinner they said, "The band is coming back for their homecoming concert in the Denver Coliseum. Would you like to be a ticket outlet and we can bring the band out to do an autograph party in your store?"

The autograph event brought so many fans that they closed all four lanes of Colfax Avenue in front of the store. The story was on the evening news for all three TV channels. We had to bust out our bathroom window for these guys to sneak out the back. We couldn't convince the crowd for hours that they weren't there [anymore]. The police had the riot squad out controlling traffic. That put the store on the map.

**B:** *You ran the record store for how many years?*

10 years.

I had three of them at one point and a hotel.

I also had other businesses and they all just flowed. That is the key to it: being in the flow and trusting and listening.

**To what did you listen and what did you trust?**

Spiritual guidance. The belief that everything was there for the opportunity in it and that the question to run on is, "What is the opportunity here?"

And not all of the answers are to move forward.

Not all of the decisions, just because an idea comes into your head, are to move forward with it. Sometimes the answer is "this is not a fit," like my heart situation.

A year-and-a-half ago in February, I got picked up at 6:00 a.m. to go to the airport. I was less than a mile from the house when something wasn't right and I knew it. I asked, "Where should I be going right now?"

The answer was "hospital!" not airport.

I had a big thing going. I had something I really needed to go do that I was heading on a plane for. I told the driver, "Take me to the hospital."

After I got there they ran their tests with me on oxygen and said, "We don't see anything wrong with you. Why don't you just go get your flight?"

I said, "No, something's not right."

They asked, "Well, where do you hurt?"

"I don't hurt. I just know that something isn't right."

They said, "We can't keep you here in ER, so we're going to move you into a regular room and we'll do some comparative tests in a couple of hours."

They took the oxygen off. I got about 10 steps down the hall and said, "That feeling is back."

They put me in an ambulance and took me to the big hospital and found a 90 percent blocked artery with virtually no symptoms.

It's about awareness, listening and knowing.

It was little things, like a week earlier I was running to catch a flight in Chicago O'Hare Airport. I couldn't make it all the way running; I got winded. I don't get winded, but I didn't think much of it. I made my flight and that next morning I had a little bit of indigestion. I don't get indigestion. So indigestion showed up plus getting winded. That little piece wasn't enough for them, but it was for me to know something wasn't right.

It has been an incredible journey of listening and a big piece of it is, and this is the hardest part to articulate, the thing about having goals.

It is important to be clear what we want. It is equally important to not be attached to it.

We need the beacon of clarity as to what we want, but as we move toward what we want, we have to listen to everything else, all the other messages on the way to getting there. Because it may turn out that what we thought we wanted wasn't really what we wanted.

But to the degree that we aren't clear as to what we want, what we're going to get is where we are putting our attention. The alternative to clarity on what we want is far too often a focus on what's wrong with the way it is, or a focus on what we don't want or what we don't like about how it is.

That is so insidiously profoundly powerful of a force that most people aren't aware of that distinction and I would be willing to bet that a huge percent, maybe as many as 90 percent of people, are moving toward what they don't want because that's where all their attention is, that's where their clarity is, and because they're asking the wrong questions.

## What's your passion?

Life. The game. Love. Seeing the spirit come alive in people.

Seeing people's eyes light up. Seeing people like grandkids, kids, and family the way it was intended, with abundance and joy.

We come about it in lots of different ways. One of the vital seven habits of Stephen Covey's is "begin with the end in mind", but the way many people have been conditioned to translate that is "after I fix everything that's wrong with the way it is," instead of asking, "What do I want and how do I get it?"

## Tell me more about that distinction.

To me it is one of the key distinctions in this whole thing that we call life, the distinction between fixing what's wrong with the way it is, or creating the way we want it.

The piece that is very often missing for people is they created it the way it is and if they keep doing the same things the same way over and over again they will keep getting the same result.

This is such a simple idiom. So many people have said it. Mark Twain is credited with saying that, "insanity is doing the same thing over and over again and expecting a different result." Dr. Al [Albert Einstein] said, "The significant problems we face today can't be solved at the same level of thinking we were at when we created them."

The way it is now is the way we created it with the same level of thinking that we brought to it. It's not good, it's not bad, it's just that A plus B equals C and if you keep approaching situation B with the same thinking of A, you're going to keep getting C. Period.

Far too many people have learned through conditioning that a big part of the game is identifying everything that's wrong with the way it is so we can fix it.

What if we didn't have to fix it? What if we aren't even supposed to? What if it was all about simply getting clarity as to what we want and then the next question is, "What do we need to do to get it?" That may or may not include fixing problems on that path.

And the degree that we're not clear, we will keep getting more of what we're clear about. We have no choice but that. We're going to get more of what we're clear about. Our choice is deciding what we want.

The quality of the outcomes we produce is directly related to the decisions we make. It's all about decisions. Probably 99.9 percent of the decisions we make are unconscious.

My father was a very harsh man, nasty man, and one of the places he was nastiest was about money. One day it hit me, the memory of the day that I made the decision that if having money means you have to be [a jerk], then I don't want any money.

Once I remembered making that decision, I could change that decision to it's OK having money. It's not whether or not you have it. It isn't that people who have money are [jerks]. You can be a good person and have money also.

From that point forward, it's been a pretty incredible journey as a money magnet.

**When you opened the record store, other than the business plan, did you have a written goal?**

No.

**B:** *When you started Enlightened Leadership, did you have a goal for how many books you wanted to sell?*

No.

**Did you have an idea that you were going to build your first book into a business?**

We had an idea that the ideas we had would work. That's probably as close as it could get.

I'd be interested as you interview more millionaires to hear your feedback about this thing on goals. I believe that goals are very often obstacles to achieving them.

**B:** *Why?*

One reason is the degree to which we get too attached to the definition of what success is. To the degree that we decide what it is, then nothing else that fits that picture fits. So that can be a limitation.

One of the other reasons is that the goal will always be out there instead of recognizing what you've already got. An example: if I had a goal to be happy, what would I be reinforcing every time I expressed the goal? That I was not happy. Who else would have a goal to be happy except someone that saw themselves as unhappy. You can't get there from here. An alternative is to start looking for all of the things you *can* be happy about. The goal "to be happy" is the very obstacle to the goal.

**Did you ever come up against obstacles that made you want to quit?**

Yes, often.

**B:** *With the record business, for instance, you owned it for 10 years; if there were challenges, why did you keep going?*

Love of it would be the first [reason] that comes up. I loved the music business and I loved having people walk out with something that they would listen to and enjoy. People would come in and say, "Last time I was here you turned me on to this and this and this. What else is there?"

I don't see much difference now in the work I'm currently doing, except that now it's helping others with different ways of thinking than they had become accustomed to. It was the same with the record business.

**When did you know in your life you were going to be successful?**

I certainly didn't get any encouragement for it as a kid.

I think the shift wasn't knowing that I was going to be successful, it was knowing that I [already] was. I don't know if there was a moment that I could point to when that happened, but at some point I reframed what success is and then constantly looked at the evidence that there was success.

Every given day any one of us could probably make a case that they were successful and that they were not successful. There is most likely evidence to make a case either way every day. We get to choose where we want to put our attention – which case we want to make. It is the same as with happiness.

**What is success for you? How do you define it?**

Joy and satisfaction from what you're doing.

I went to the doctor yesterday. The receptionist in the office was an amazing woman; absolutely amazing, very successful woman. I don't know if she realizes it, but she reframes what walking into the doctor's office for the first time is like, and the nurse was the same.

That woman is a receptionist at a doctor's office and I'd say she's very successful. That's part of this [garbage] that gets attached to goals. If you don't consider yourself successful until you make a million dollars, guess what? Good chance you're not going to be happy when you do.

There's enough evidence of people who have substantial bank accounts who do not see themselves as being successful and they certainly aren't happy with what they've got.

**What did you learn from your failures?**

That it's no big deal. I've done it. Last count I've started from nothing five times, so it's no big deal.

**B:** *Were some of those new beginnings while you had a family to support?*

Yes.

**B:** *How did you make it through those times?*

You just keep doing what you've got to do; it's not very complex. You keep showing up and you keep going. There have been many times in life when the reasons why things shouldn't work have far outweighed what it would take to get it to work. It all depends on where you put your attention.

Obstacles aren't reasons you don't do things, they're just things you have to get by on the path to getting there. Obstacles are no big deal. The clearer they are the easier it is to figure out how to get past them.

Some people get really clear on the obstacle and see all the reasons it won't work. The difference is being clear on the obstacle and looking for what it takes to get past that one.

The first Sunday the record store was open, a guy walked in, looked around, and said, "When are you going to get your inventory?"

I said, "This is my inventory."

He laughed and said, "You've got to be kidding me. You don't have a chance." He introduced himself as Phil Lasky. He was the founder of a 200 record store chain that was headquartered in Denver – Budget Tapes and Records.

He said, "Anytime a new store opens close to one of mine I like to check them out. I don't know who recommended you get into this business, son, but you won't be around in six months."

The obstacle was no inventory. That night as I was listening to music I thought, "I take good care of my records. Why don't I just take these in and see if I can sell them as used? At least there will be some records there when people come in."

I brought my records in and people started coming in and saying, "I've got records at home that I don't listen to, would you sell mine?"

It would cost me $4.70 to buy a new record and I could sell it for $5.99. I could buy a used record for $1 and sell it $3. So I was paying less to get more inventory and I was making more profit on every one of them.

Up to that point nobody was selling used records. I started used records in Denver. I don't know about anybody else in the country, but I was told many times over the years, that I started the idea in Denver.

The other piece was that when people would start walking out the door without buying anything I would say, "Were you looking for something you couldn't find?"

I knew I would get a "Yes," especially since my inventory was so slim.

Then I would ask, "If I can get it for you tomorrow and I gave you a dollar off, would you pay me for it now?" I had the money in the register before I ever had the record. I would call the warehouses and find what the customer was looking for and have them set it aside for me.

Everybody else opened their store at 10:00 a.m., and they would probably get up at 9:15 a.m. I was up at 7:00 a.m. driving all over town picking up records from warehouses. I would pick up two of the same record because if one person came in for it, there was a good chance someone else would, too. That's what told me what I needed to carry in my inventory.

So there's an example of an obstacle. In many ways that obstacle was turned into a success. Most of what I sold, I sold before I ever had the merchandise and because I did it once, they said, "Here's a couple more things I'm looking for. Can you get these for me?" The next day they'd come back and I'd have it. Then word started to spread and that's what built the stores.

**So you worked incredibly hard, were creative in finding answers, and you went the extra mile?**

Yes. And always look.

**B:** *Always look for the solution?*

Yes – not the solution per se, it was more looking for what's possible.

The problem or obstacle was there wasn't much inventory. When people walked in the door it didn't look very good. So how do I fill the bins? When I brought my used records in it started filling the bins. It looked different when people walked in the door.

**What do you say to somebody who in their eyes is struggling to make it; they want to make a difference, they want to break through, they want to make money?**

The first thought that came up is what are you willing to do to make it happen? What are you willing to give up?

There are people who wait for it to happen, people who complain that it didn't happen, people who blame somebody else for how it happened, and then there are those who make it happen.

What's it going to take and what are you willing to do, what are you willing to pay? And it's not money. Nolan Ryan and Tiger Woods are seen as some of the best ever in their fields. Even when they would win they would still go out and practice afterward.

And the biggest suggestion is celebrate even the smallest successes, the smallest improvements.

Ask outcome-based questions; questions based on where we're going, how we're going to get there. "What's one thing I learned today?" "What's one obstacle I overcame, how did I overcome it?" "What's next?"

I struggle with this consulting project [I'm currently on] because they want agendas – minute by minute accounting of what will be done when. I don't do agendas. I produce outcomes.

I said, "I have no idea what I'm going to do at 11:00 a.m. It depends on what comes out of what I did at 8:00 a.m. I know where you'll be when we're done."

I can't always tell you what we're going to do to get there until we start the journey. When I stand up in front of a room the question is, "What's next?" And the answer is always there and it's seldom anything I've thought of.

If I had a dollar for every time I've said the following statement I'd have a whole lot more money: "What's coming up for me right now, I'm not even sure how this fits, is…"

I'll put it out and somebody will say, "I know how that fits. Here's what that just brought up for me," and it was the perfect thing that needed to be said for the time and place.

Or, I've said something like, "This has come up three times now, so this must be the time."

Einstein said, "All of life's answers are available if we just knew which questions to ask." I sure don't claim to be any brighter than Einstein, but after spending over 20 years learning about questions, it's getting pretty clear as to what the questions are.

**That's a talent of yours that you didn't really implement until you hit your 40s, is that fair to say?**

Yes it is.

**B:** *You implemented other gifts that you have along the way. Sometimes we have to go as far as we can see and then the next piece is manifest.*

I've done lots of things, you've only gotten the tip of the iceberg of the jobs I've had. I've started to capture some of these stories for myself. They were just stepping-stones. Every one of them added a piece to the next level.

**Is there anything else you'd like people to know?**

Well, here's what comes up. If you knew what God wanted you to do, would you do it?

All God wants is for us is to live our lives full of joy and satisfaction, and the place to start is with what we've already got. To me, that's one of the biggest pieces.

When it is a struggle, that's an indication that we're out of sync with Source, whatever someone defines Source to be. Mine, I say God, but it doesn't matter what the Source is.

When we're out of sync with Source, life sucks. And, when life is sucking it's an indication that we're out of sync with Source/God. We're not one with what's going on.

When there's struggle and effort in something, that's the time to step back and look at, "What do I want, and what are other ways of getting there from here? What haven't I thought of yet?" or "What's next?"; some version of those questions.

It's amazing, the answers that come when we're asking the right questions.

And most of all, be grateful.

\*\*\*\*

# Millionaire 15 Cynthia McKay

Founder, Le Gourmet Gift Baskets

www.legift.com

Married

Bachelor's in Communications, J.D., Master's in Psychology
(earned since interview)

*I found Cynthia through an Internet search.*

*Cynthia hated every minute she spent working as a lawyer. One night, she received a professionally made gift basket that she said was awful. She thought, "I can do better than this," so she quit her job and started Le Gourmet Gift Baskets.*

## Did you have written goals?

No, no written goals at all.

As I went to get my business license someone in passing said, "Do you have a business plan?"

I thought, "Oh, no, I don't have that." I said, "I should, right?"

She said, "Oh yeah, everybody has a business plan."

I wrote one on the back of a cocktail napkin that just said, "I'll be the best I can be."

That's a very cliché thing to say, but it worked for me because the second line said, "I hate my job and I have to get out of here."

I had no creative ability, no interest in any of this until I saw a need for it [when I received the gift basket]. Then I thought, "I can do that, I can do it better."

I think sometimes when you have an entrepreneurial spirit you also develop these delusions of grandeur. Overnight I was like, "I am so good. What a great idea. I'm going to do better than everybody else."

I was failing to recognize that I totally lacked the basics of everything related to the business. It was really interesting.

## Is that perhaps why you succeeded; you didn't know what to fear?

Exactly.

I'm in school full-time again–I go to school as a hobby–and people continually tell me that I don't have the credentials, the basics, to pursue any kind of degree in this area.

They'll say, "What makes you think that you'll make a living at this type of thing?"

You get to the point where it's like, "I don't know, but I seem to be going in the right direction because it feels right to me."

I think at that point in time you need to dispense with everybody's opinion and just go with your own instincts. That was really not a problem when I started Le Gourmet, because I had more of a drive not to succeed in the area, but to get out of law.

**When you got that gift basket, there wasn't something that went off in your head and you said, "Ah, this is the opportunity I'm looking for. I've been open to opportunities and this is a good one." It was more naïve than that, right? It was, "This basket is terrible and I can do it better and I don't like my job"?**

Oh, I'd say it was naivety with a capital N.

The basket I received was a creation from a professional company, but I looked at that and thought, "I know nothing about retail, but this is horrific. I can do better than that."

That's how much naivety was involved. I really didn't recognize that I had no ability, talent, or knowledge. Those are the essentials I think a lot of successful people have and they believe on what they have. On the opposite end of the spectrum there's somebody like me that's so obnoxious when it comes to saying, "Oh yeah, I could do better than that."

That's not how you should run a business, but I think with that certain instinct and drive it can be done. You might shortchange yourself and say, "I don't have the business degree from Wharton, I don't have experience." But if you've got that drive, you can really make things happen. That's the dichotomy people face. They just don't know what to do with an opportunity when it's right in front of them.

**Did you ever think before that point that you would be a business owner?**

Oh no, oh my goodness.

My parents told me early on that it was about education, that I would be an attorney or a doctor. I couldn't pass the math to get through medical school, but law school doesn't care what kind of calculation abilities you've got or whether you can pass Algebra, which I could not, [so] I chose law school.

You can certainly do extremely well with or without those specifics [of calculation abilities and mathematical aptitude] in your educational background.

I decided on a whim to take the law school admissions test and I made a deal with myself that any law school that would take me I would move there, I would go there, whatever I had to do.

**How did your education or the process of your education help prepare you for business ownership?**

None of it did.

I was a communications major and that has no bearing on anything I've done, except I've learned how to listen to people well. There is a lot to communication that will indicate other things and you can watch for that.

The only thing that prepared me for the business was survival. Having survived law school, which was single-handedly the worst experience I've ever been through, I realized that beginning a business, even if I failed, would be minuscule compared to that three-and-a-half year experience that I went through.

Life's experiences prepared me for this business in that I have had a lot of challenges in a variety of ways. So starting this business just seemed like, "So what. Of course it's going to work, but so what."

Everyone else when you talk to them about beginning a business will say, "What if it fails? What if this happens?"

There are just four million excuses for not doing it, but if you look at it in the proper perspective, like, "At this moment I'm going to pursue a business compared to the previous life I had," then really the business is no big deal. If it fails, you are out the money and you can make money again.

**After you started the business you put out a contest to your first distributor. Other than that, did you have goals? Did you write down, "I want to have this much in sales by this point," all that kind of stuff?**

No concept, in fact. That's not something I would have done.

**Did you visualize where you wanted the business to go or were you just living day-by-day taking the opportunities?**

I did have the idea of the franchising early on. When I went to the bank to start up this business they literally laughed me out of the facility because there was such a conflict for them.

"Where has she come from? What's she trying to do?" and it was more like I had a mental illness as opposed to no entrepreneurial experience. People thought that I was unstable and definitely not worth the risk. I understand that completely, I really do.

I would get over those obstacles one at a time because I didn't visualize the big picture so I wasn't going to let that bother me.

But the experience at the bank is what gave me the idea of franchising. I thought, "Here I am with a bachelor's degree and a law degree and it's been difficult for me, so what does that mean for other people?"; specifically focusing on women at that point because I thought they must be having a devil of a time. [I saw franchising as a way of helping women get into business.]

I'm not a big feminist, but it was really demeaning when I would go into the bank. The men were particularly caustic. They were very difficult, saying things like, "Stay home." It was borderline insulting. When I went into the bank the first time for a loan, they asked, "Are you married and what does your husband do?" Would a guy have gotten that line of questioning?

When I started it, people thought that this would be like owning a little flower shop. There was no intent in their mind for me to get beyond that little mom and pop organization.

**As I was listening to a previous interview you did, I thought, "Quitting her job would have been a big thing, but she was married. Paul was there making income so she knew she had something to fall back on." Then you followed it right up with, "and we were $200,000 in debt from law school, had the mortgage on the house, two brand new cars, and were just recently married."**

That is correct. We took the bar exam the Monday after we were married.

You could look at all that and ask, "Could you make your life any more difficult?" It was one thing after the next and it was all brought on by me and the circumstances. I look back and go, "Wow, that was pretty risky." It's amazing when you make decisions like that.

**B:** *You look back and say it was risky, but at the time you knew you were going to succeed. You knew it.*

Oh, yeah, because I would not have done that and jeopardized my family life had I not felt very secure about this decision. It's funny because I never listened to those voices before. I've always been a pretty cautious individual.

When you do something like this it really is a sink or swim kind of thing because I was putting a lot out there. I couldn't get funding so I put everything on a credit card and with that kind of debt…it's not the most intelligent thing people can do.

**B:** *You knew you were going to be successful from the bottom of your heart and that was the only option, but at the same time you understood, "If I do fail, it's not the end of the world."*

Yeah, because one thing I was trying to avoid was talking myself out of it. I didn't want to have the chance to do that. You can't put yourself in a position to say, "It's probably not going to happen."

I've heard so many people say that they have talked themselves out of what could have been a great idea. You cannot allow yourself to have those ideas infiltrate your mind because anybody can second-guess anything. There are times that you just have to forge ahead.

I look back now and shudder and think it's pretty risky what I did. But you've got to look at that and say, "I can stay here and remain this way for the rest of my life, or it will take a change to get out of this."

That's where I think people make the mistake; they get accustomed to comfort levels, especially in this economy. In this economy, people think it's extremely irresponsible to jump out on a ledge and do something that's categorically crazy, that the economy just won't allow for that right now. That's where you have to make those informed decisions without informing yourself too much.

It goes to over-analyzing. If you open up a coffee shop right now, is that smart because Starbucks is laying off? Well it might be if you've got some differentiation between yourself and the five million Starbucks that are around the world. What is it that makes what you're doing special?

I think that's where people undercut their own thoughts. They undermine themselves and they go, "I can't do better than Starbucks." But you could, and you just don't want to, I guess.

That's where a lot of people differ. People with bona fide business degrees really know how to look at things and do demographic searches and compare their product and that kind of thing, but I think so much of it is from the heart and it's instinctive. You're the only one that's going to know your own abilities.

**Do you have a restless spirit?**

Yes.

**B:** *You like to have options and you're never satisfied.*

Yes. That is exactly right.

**B:** *You're doing your [master's] in psychology, is that right?*

That is correct.

I don't know if anyone else has mentioned this, but you're almost sometimes uncomfortable in your own skin. There's always another opportunity around the corner. It's what keeps you awake at night.

**B:** *Are you comfortable with who you are?*

Sometimes, but with your circumstances that changes on a daily basis; sometimes you change with it. You're influenced by things: the people you meet, the challenges you're faced with and that can amend your personality. So there's no definitive answer for me on that one.

**Did you have a mentor?**

No.

If you have a mentor it's not your idea anymore.

If a mentor is going to give you their way, their concept, then that degrades your whole idea. It becomes something else because it's been influenced. It's not something raw, it's not something that's untested, and it's somebody else's influence. Then you're falling into that genre of a businessperson [not an entrepreneur and then it becomes], "Here's how you have to do it."

If I did my business the way I was supposed to do it, it wouldn't be the unique entity that it is today. That's what I'm most proud of because it's something nobody thought of and they didn't conceptualize it the way I did. Had I had a mentor then it would totally be back to them and their idea. That's why I hate the idea of mentors.

I think that it's a way to shirk your responsibility. If you fail, you can go back and say, "Well that's what my mentor told me to do." It could be an excuse for failure.

## Did you have people that inspired you?

My father. He was a corporate executive. Both my parents told me in no uncertain terms, "You can do anything you want to do, as long as it's become a doctor or a lawyer."

They gave the instruction I needed, but with that came restrictions.

## Is there a belief system that guides your life as far as religion or thinking patterns?

That changes for me.

I'm influenced by listening to other people, hearing experiences, and living life. My belief system is sometimes challenged or altered.

I haven't had a stern or particularly vivid upbringing concerning religion. I think I'm not very well versed. I'm challenged in some areas because I just don't have the information to fall back on, so I'm open to ideas.

**B:** *It sounds like your mother and your father were very supportive; it sounds like they were probably successful. Your father was successful in the workforce, I'm imagining your mom was a stay-at-home mom who nurtured and loved?*

Right.

**B:** *So you had that stable foundation. Now that you've been successful, you're continually advancing yourself and looking back and helping others.*

That's a big thing for me. I may not be well versed in life or the afterlife or superior beings, but I think if you treat people well and you're living life appropriately and giving back–the people that constantly take concern me. If you're taking but you're giving back and each year you try to do more–and if you learn as you go along, I think that's a pretty reasonable way of getting by.

## How did you balance spending time with Paul as you were building this business?

I asked him for his patience.

When I quit my job, he came home the next day and I said, "By the way, I opened up a business today."

When you do that to a man that you've been married to not very long and he doesn't condemn you, challenge you, or question you, you've got a very special person. Need I say more? He has been just a rock. He's been wonderful, he's been patient, he's allowed me to indulge these ideas and never criticized me or questioned how it would affect him.

I did the same thing to him again when I went back to school. That takes time away from us. The way that I rationalize the whole thing is that when we are together, we're really together. That time is really precious time and nothing gets compromised there.

Your spouse, when you're an entrepreneur, just has to know that you're with them and no matter what the extenuating circumstances are or anything else that happens, the marriage is first and foremost, although it doesn't appear that way all the time. So you're offering caveats.

**B:** *You're saying the family has to know and understand they are first and foremost, but there will be times that the business is pressing?*

Yeah, and when I hear people say, "My family comes first no matter what," that's not true because it [depends] in the moment what's going on. If something happens and you have to get a root canal, that's where you are at the moment.

You just have to allow for that and realize in your heart that you've made certain arrangements and agreements to people and have certain responsibilities. Sometimes it will be the job, sometimes it will be the family, and people that say it's never like that, the reality of it has not set in because you've got to prioritize at that moment.

It's not a constant priority that you can rely on because things change and people have to be open to change.

**What makes you in particular successful?**

Probably ignorance. I don't do a post-mortem on everything I've done. I forge ahead because I know some ideas are going to work and some are not.

The way you can portray yourself and what you're offering has a lot to do with ignorance because you don't have to fall into this format that somebody else set up for you in order to be successful.

**How would you describe your passion?**

First we have to define passion because I have numerous passions.

My life, my dog, my husband, my job, my school, charity work, going to Starbucks, splurging; a million different things. The other day I had the best day of my life. I took off an hour and I got a Pepsi and wandered around Target. I didn't need anything; I just wandered around, looking at people, seeing what was going on there. It was so amazingly fulfilling and I didn't spend a dime.

People that are known as entrepreneurs will say, "Oh, my passion is my work and what I've accomplished," and that's not it [for me]. My passion is having a well-rounded life, but being a little obsessive compulsive about work has given me different opportunities other than what I would have normally had.

You have to realize that your passion might be one thing one day and something the next day, if you're honest with yourself. Variety is a great part about life and variety is my passion. This idea of Le Gourmet is great, but then when I came up with this other idea a couple of days ago, that's my passion today because I've been thinking about it today. It's ever changing is my passion.

**If you were to go back, what would you do differently?**

Nothing. Absolutely nothing.

One thing I would say, though, I would buy a building sooner than I did. I rented space for a while and that was just money going out the window. I think I would have bought more property early on if I was able to.

## How do you define success?

That's a tough one. I don't know if I can define success because there's so much more out there. A lot of people equate making money with success and I don't.

True success is when I sit down someday and go, "I've done it all. I've done everything in my life. Happy as a clam, I have no more ideas and that's it for me." That's probably success and it's never going to happen.

## Did you ever set out to be a millionaire, or along the process did you ever say, "I want to hit that million-dollar mark?"

No, not at all. I've never been motivated by money.

I was brought up in a very comfortable environment. I never needed anything, so I wasn't out for this fortune. Actually, it was very unexpected for me. I was looking for a job. I wanted my own job and I wanted to be comfortable. I liked the concept, but I never developed this whole thing with the idea of making millions, driving a nice company car or anything like that. I was looking for peace of mind and knew I wouldn't find in a paycheck.

**B:** *You were looking for peace of mind and what you got with it was international acclaim, magazines, articles, media coverage, you're mentoring and coaching several women, you've helped 510 women and men own their own distributorship, on and on, and on.*

Yeah, that wasn't on the menu at all.

I was looking for a comfortable thing. I thought maybe I'd do well with being self-employed because I wouldn't have to get up early, I could wear jeans to work, and I could bring my dog. I was looking at other things that weren't financially affiliated with the concept; life's comforts. I think you'll find a lot of people that are entrepreneurs are encouraged by things other than financial.

I've only had a few people say, "I want to make a million dollars," and those are the people I won't coach or sell a franchise to. They've got the whole concept of entrepreneurism wrong. It's not about that. It's not about implementing something and making a million dollars.

You've got to be propelled by an idea, or the concept or the business, but not about a paycheck. These people that come right out and say, "I want to do it because of the money," that is a recipe for failure if you ask me.

**What would you tell someone who is looking for their break or looking to be successful?**

I hate the concept of breaks.

If you're going to pigeonhole yourself in something and be satisfied with that, there's no such thing as a break; you're just going to stay there. To use the word "break" would mean opening yourself up to a lot of different opportunities.

I was talking to somebody the other day and she said, "I never get asked out."

She's looking for another husband and she never leaves the house.

I said, "You're missing opportunities."

That concept [applies to] business and [to] life. It's about opportunities. If you're not out there doing something, you're not going to see other things and think, "I can improve upon that concept." You just have to be there, but more than there. You're present, but you're still open to ideas.

**If three months before you started Le Gourmet, someone said, "You need to be open to opportunities, you need to look for them," would that have even impacted you?**

Until you're in the middle of an opportunity, I don't think you're looking for one. I had no idea. I wasn't out there looking for anything.

**Is there anything else you want people to know about you, about life, about anything?**

No. I'm happy as a clam, wouldn't change anything.

Striving for new accomplishments is a good thing, but I'm not doing it for anybody else, I'm doing it for me. I think that's what people ought to do: quit worrying about what people want you to be, what people think you should be, just go for it.

If you're happy doing what you're doing on a day-to-day basis, great. If you're not, change it. That's the problem in this economy, for example. People have been told, "It's going to be mediocre, you're going to suffer," and that turns into reality for some people. It doesn't have to be that way.

For people to completely rely on day-to-day Dow Jones and media reports, you're sealing your own destiny on that. People need to be open to the possibility that things can and should be different for them, whatever that may be.

Sometimes there are ways to amend your life; some people are spending too much and they could get brand B instead of A, or they could get a cheaper car, or whatever the case may be, but those are individual decisions. I don't want to do that because a financial expert got on TV and told me to do that. It all goes back to instincts and using your brain.

We should all quit second guessing ourselves and see what happens; give things a chance and it if it doesn't work out, it's like one of the other millionaires you interviewed who said, "I'll just go back to $5 an hour."

When I hear people say, "I was born to do this" – really? Really? When you were six-weeks-old was your whole destiny written in stone? I just don't know that for a fact. You're given options and a lot of us have to make choices and take certain forks in the road and we end up somewhere.

You've got to be open to the fact that you've been given a good set of brains and use them. Go with what's right for you at the moment and go back and keep revisiting it.

That post-mortem drives me crazy. Learn from the experience and move on.

****

# Millionaire 16 Lane Nemeth

CEO, Co-Founder, The Ultimate Sparkle

Founder, former CEO, Discovery Toys; Co-Founder, Petlane

Married, one daughter

Bachelor's in English Literature, Master's in Education

*I met Lane through a series of people, the last being Laura Udall[1].*

*After obtaining her education, Lane was managing multiple day care units and therefore had experience with educational toys.*

**You wanted to buy some great educational products for your daughter Tara and you couldn't find them anywhere?**

They were only available if you were a teacher and could go through a teacher supply house with a purchase order. I couldn't do that so it became very complicated.

**B:** *You asked them if you could pay with a personal check and they still said no?*

Yes, that's when I got mad. They said they couldn't sell it to me. It was a state funded institution through California and the state said I couldn't piggyback on the purchase order with my own check. I lost my temper.

**B:** *You're an emotional and passionate person, is that right?*

Correct.

**B:** *You got mad and that anger caused you to find a solution.*

Correct. I wasn't just not going to take care of Tara. She was way too important to me.

**B:** *You said in a previous interview the only thing an entrepreneur hates to hear is "no."*

Yes.

**B:** *So you just went to work?*

Yes.

**B:** *You scraped together $5,000 from friends and family?*

My grandmother gave me $5,000.

**B:** *Where did you go to buy the toys?*

The first thing I did was write every toy manufacturer I could learn about through Thomas Register [a list of all the manufacturers in the U.S.], thinking that they were going to be so excited to hear my great idea.

I got three responses; one was for basketball nets. It was a joke. I didn't know what to do. It wasn't where I needed to go. Then I found out about a wholesale toy show in Los Angeles. I don't know how I heard about it; I absolutely cannot remember that.

[Prior to hearing about the show] I taught in Pittsburgh, an inner-city environment. Their philosophies and my philosophies were extraordinarily different and I began to think I was going a little crazy, so I went back to the junior college to take some early childhood classes to reassure myself that I knew what I was doing.

One of the teachers [there] became my best friend and mentor. When I thought about going to this meeting in Los Angeles, I couldn't in my wildest dreams visualize going by myself. I asked her if she wanted to come with me and have some fun. She said yes; otherwise I don't know that I would be in business because I don't think I would have gone by myself.

**B:** *Doesn't it seem that there are small decision points that turn big levers?*

Yes, and you wonder whether they're coincidence or meant to be. Who knows these things?

**B:** *With the benefit of hindsight they worked out, but in the moment you just don't recognize it, right?*

Oh, no, of course not. I just was thrilled that she said yes, because I didn't really have any big plan in mind. I was just kind of exploring the whole thought process. I didn't know how to run a business. I was thinking I would open an educational toy store, but I hadn't really gone that far yet. I was looking at properties and learning about signing leases; I didn't know what I was doing at all. I knew if I was going to do any of it I had to get product.

We went down to this show and as is typical of the toy world, most of it was nothing that I was interested in. There were a couple of manufacturers from Europe that were exactly what I was looking for and gave me hope that this idea wasn't completely stupid and that maybe I could find enough products to put a line together.

[Before going to the show] I was in the process of thinking about signing this lease and I was telling my dad all about my great idea. I was going to open a store and every half hour I was going to run different seminars, because all I really know how to do is teach. I was going to teach parents how to use educational toys because I understood they didn't know.

My father is the most positive man ever and was my guiding light in my life. He was always very encouraging with things like, "You can do anything you want," but when I told him my idea he said, "That's the worst idea I ever heard."

I was so devastated because he never said "no" to me.

He said, "You've got too much energy to sit in a store and wait for people to come to you. Think how to market it."

I'm looking at him like, "What do you mean market it?" My husband was sitting in the same meeting and said, "Honey, why don't you try it like Tupperware?"

Well, when you know nothing about nothing, you're not scared. I had absolutely no preconceived notions of anything so that seemed as good a way to do it as any. What did I know? I had never been to a Tupperware party, but I did know what their thought process was; I thought I did anyway.

I called a bunch of friends and said, "I have this great idea for educational toys. Would you be willing to host a party so you could show your friends?" Everybody was very receptive and very willing to be helpful. I did a bunch of parties and a lot of people liked what I had to offer. We had some real sales.

Then I couldn't deliver anything because it was late in the season. By then it was almost December and the educational supply houses don't keep a lot of inventory on hand. They don't need to because schools are willing to wait a reasonably long time to get stuff.

I wasn't off to the best start in the world, but it didn't really bother me that much because the whole thing was just one big experiment. It wasn't a joke, but I wasn't terribly serious. I was just playing with this whole thing. I did think that there was enough interest and response that it sounded like a really good idea.

I decided to see if I could get serious. After that is when I went down to the toy show and then I realized if I'm going to buy stuff at wholesale, surprise, surprise, I have to pay for it. How am I going to do that? That's when I borrowed money from my grandmother, the $5,000, to get just a little bit of stuff I could put in my garage.

I was very lucky because my grandmother believed in me. We started with $5,000 and very quickly started selling way more than that and the $5,000 wasn't going to keep me. I was extraordinarily lucky that I had a brother-in-law who made his own money and was willing to lend me $50,000.

I had to make some projections about how much inventory I should buy. How do you know that? I stuck a finger in the air and said, "What's the biggest amount of money I could possibly sell and be very successful?" I came up with the figure $100,000. I have no idea why. That just sounded to me like huge success if I could do that.

There is a thing in the industry called "dating." If you buy X amount by say, June, you don't have to pay until December, so the $50,000 was able to stretch. We ended up our first year having sold $250,000.

It was a nightmare. I had absolutely no idea how to project inventory. I kept running out of everything. I was delivering a quarter of what was ordered. It was not fun. It was just hard.

I spent December writing letters to people who had ordered stuff apologizing that I couldn't send it to them and I understood this was a Christmas gift and I was really sorry and I won't let it happen again next year. I sent them a little something as an apology gift. Most people were pretty cooperative. I didn't get a lot of hostility back.

Then I had to get through my second year and I thought, "How much should I project? How do you do this?" We didn't have computers in those days; we didn't have anything. It was a nightmare. Being the crazed human being that I am, I said, "I think next year I can sell a million dollars."

Most businesses don't quadruple in a year, but that's what I thought I should be able to do.

Between the little bit of profit that we were making and the dating, I was able to buy enough inventory to not be in quite such a mess that time. We sold almost a million dollars that year – $900,000.

It was a very successful idea because nobody had heard of educational toys before. It was still the era of the stay-at-home mom who had time to play with her kids, so it was just the right time and the right place.

The end of that year I was so proud of myself because I was so successful. A friend of mine walked into my warehouse in January and said, "It strikes me that you have too much inventory on your shelf for a toy company in January."

I said, "Oh, don't be ridiculous. I did so well, I'm so successful."

He said, "I don't know, just a gut feeling."

What I hadn't done yet was pay all those dating bills. I had no way of understanding what my cash flow was; I wouldn't have known how to make that judgment. I just didn't know anything.

Once I paid all my bills, I was $100,000 short. I couldn't pay my manufacturers. That was really scary. I called everyone who I owed money to and said, "I'm in a horrible position. We sold almost a million dollars this year, but I ran out of cash without realizing it. I will find a way to pay you, just please stick with me, don't throw me into bankruptcy. Just let me see what I can figure out."

Pretty much everybody said, "Because you called, we really appreciate that, and we'll hang in with you for a while."

Then I found out about a factoring outfit–I don't even know if those guys still exist–where I could borrow money at 27 percent interest. This was the days when interest was probably 18 percent or so.

I borrowed this money, not having the foggiest notion that there was no way that I could pay that kind of interest. On top of that, they charged me $500 a month to secure my warehouse, which meant they put a notice on it that said my inventory belonged to them.

It was very rapidly deteriorating to the point where I was going to go out of business. I didn't see any other options; the banks wouldn't talk to me, they just laughed. It was very scary and very tough. Then the phone rang. The voice at the other end said, "My name is Phil. I'm a venture capitalist," which I didn't know what the heck that was, "we're interested in investing in your business. Are you looking for an investor?"

I practically dropped the phone. I was virtually going out of business. I had no way of keeping myself alive and here's this guy saying he wants to invest and it was like, "Yes." It wasn't very hard to figure that one out.

I was so incredibly naïve. This guy came out to meet me. His wife had gone to a toy party and told him that this was the hottest thing going and he had to invest in it. That's how he found out about me. He asked for my financial statements. I had turned all my books over to an accountant because I was incompetent. I didn't know what the financial statements said. I couldn't read them, I just got them.

I gave them to him and he was very readily able to see that I was out of business. He saw it more clearly than I saw it. He danced around with me for a couple of months until the point where we were down to zero cash. He had said during those couple of months that traditionally they give businesses like mine $100,000–magic figure, because that's what I needed to pay back these factoring guys–for 10 percent of the business. I was thinking maybe I could talk him into eight percent or something.

The day came when I was flat out bankrupt and he said, "Here's the proposal. We will give you $100,000 for 20 percent of the business and we will take a management fee of $10,000," so in effect I was only getting $90,000.

I said, "Wait a minute, you said all along that it was going to be 10 percent."

He responded, "If you were naïve enough to believe that, it's not my problem."

I said, "Naïve enough to believe that? If you're that much of a liar and a cheat, you'd be the last person on earth I would want to do anything with," and I stalked out of his office. The problem was I could stalk out all I wanted, I was out of business.

I thought about it for a couple days and decided which was worse, going out of business or working with him? So I called him up and said, "Phil, I really don't like you and I don't trust you, but you and I both know that I'm in real trouble and I have no choice but to take your offer. But I don't want you to be on my board." Why I thought I had alternatives around this, I don't know.

He said, "OK. We'll put somebody on your board that I think you'll really like."

He wrote a contract, but instead of the typical warrants and demands and all that stuff that they usually ask for, he wrote a very simple one page, "We'll give her $100,000 for 20 percent of the company." That was basically it; no out, no nothing. His thought process was, "In two seconds she's going to need more money and then we'll own the company so I don't have to go through this enormous contractual procedure with this angry lady now because we're going to own her anyway."

My thought process was, "I will never take another dime from this man as long as live, I'd rather go out of business." I was so mad.

[Phil's company] helped us go through the SBA [Small Business Administration] process to get a line of credit, which the SBA had not done to that point; they'd only done long-term loans. They also introduced me to Bank of America.

Six months went by and we were literally out of business again. I didn't have another dime to meet payroll. The SBA line of credit still hadn't come through. I went to the bank with my board member and said, "You can't do this. You're putting me out of business."

He said, "I'm really sorry, but the SBA is really slow and there's nothing I can do without their permission. I cannot give you this loan."

I said, "I'm not leaving your bank. I will sit here and call the media and you can call the police and the media can show you taking a woman entrepreneur out of your business in handcuffs because I'm not leaving without this loan. If I do, I'm out of business."

The guy thought I was just being silly, but I meant it. I did not leave his conference room.

It wasn't fair. We had done really well. It was our third year and we were around $2.5 million in sales and I knew I had a really big success on my hands. I just flat out wasn't going to let it go under because of bureaucracy. At the end of the day, he came into the conference room and said, "Are you a Catholic?"

I said, "No, I'm Jewish, why?"

He said, "I'm going to light a candle and say a prayer because I'm going to give you this loan and if the auditors come in before SBA does, I could lose my job. I really believe in what you're doing and I believe the SBA will approve this loan, so I'm going to go ahead and give it to you."

It was a miracle. I've had a lot of miracles happen in the time I was in business; this was one of them. We were able to keep going without having to get more venture money. From then on, I lived the entire 20 years underfunded because I never took another penny from anybody except bank loans, which is no way to survive because you're under-capitalized.

We lived on retained earnings, which were never that high, but I meant that I would rather go out of business than deal with a venture capitalist again.

Our next major tragedy came at the end of 1982. We hit $10 million. Phil and I had made peace and he said, "Ten million dollars is where entrepreneurs fail because they don't know how to take it from that to the next level. You're a typical entrepreneur, you have had no business experience, you really need a CEO. You should continue to work with the product and the field."

I was so exhausted. You can imagine what it's been like, and I had a young child. Plus, it was very obvious the massive changes that were happening in the business. We were going from a non-professional to a professional organization that needed a warehouse manager that knew what he was doing, it needed a CFO; it needed a lot. It was obvious to me that I was in over my head as well.

I let my entire executive team go and got a new one. It was a very painful thing to do because these were people who had started with me.

We hired a CEO who turned out to be an alcoholic, among other things. Our October financial statements, which by then I understood how to read, showed a $400,000 loss, which there shouldn't have been. He had a really good story for everything. I chose to believe him. I just didn't want to know anything different. The thought of having more trouble was more than I could handle.

November 11th I got my financial statements and we were $800,000 in the hole. Bank of America called on the 12th and said, "We're pulling out. We're not going to fund you anymore." I was virtually bankrupt and at the same time our computer system crashed; it could not handle the volume we were putting through it and the company wouldn't come out and fix it.

I went home and it felt like I had been in a severe car accident. I just went to sleep. I didn't even take care of my child. I woke up the next morning and lay there thinking, "If Tara was in intensive care in the hospital, I wouldn't be sitting here feeling sorry for myself and worrying about what to do. I'd be in the hospital yelling at doctors and finding a way to make sure she could stay alive. So what am I doing in bed?"

I put on my one business suit and put in my contact lenses – I decided I had to look as professional as I could look. I pulled my executive team together and said, "Here's the reality of the situation: I don't know if we're going to be here in January, but between now and then let's see what we can cut in the way of expenses. I'm going to fire our CEO. I'm going to get a CFO in here from our accounting firm to get some temporary help and figure out what happened and where we go."

I got a temporary CFO in and at the same time I threatened the computer company with a $40 million lawsuit. They came out and helped us limp through the rest of the year, but by then we were so far behind that we didn't deliver any December toys. It was a nightmare.

Jim, the new CFO said, "I'll see you through until the next couple weeks. We'll see if we can figure out what's going on and maybe we can talk to a bank."

He found fraud and helped us get bank financing. After getting the financing, Jim was planning to quit. I said, "You absolutely can't quit. I will be lost. You're like my white knight."

He said, "Alright, I'll see you through until tax time." [He ended up staying longer.]

We overcame the computer challenges, including someone having a nervous breakdown, by building a new system. Jim headed up that project and literally turned the company around with it.

Then came December the next year. Everything was up and running, we had a great year, and Jim had a heart attack and died. At that moment I almost gave up. I was very close to saying, "I can't do this anymore."

The good news was that in 1984 I had hired a new operations vice president, Mike, who became my partner, and COO, for the next 10 years.

Mike was an absolute genius and we were a marriage made in heaven. I'm the creative/sales/marketing side, he was the operations/finance side and we did brilliantly together. We had a great CFO from then on. The company hummed along and then Mike developed cancer and died at the age of 45.

That was a blow I no longer could tolerate. I went into a mild clinical depression and didn't know it. I felt so tired and frustrated and lonely.

AVON had tried a number of times over the years to buy the company and in 1997 they re-approached me. They said, "You'll run the United States and Canada, all we need is your product and your understanding of party planning because we don't know anything about that, and we'll take over the international business and you'll make money on it."

It was the right time because I was so exhausted and it was so exciting to think that I could do all this international business without having to be the one who did it. They bought Discovery Toys and we had a really good relationship for about 15 months.

We were in the process of doing all the legal work for Brazil and I was going to New York because Jim, the CEO of Avon whom I loved, wanted to meet some new regional managers I had hired. We met in the afternoon and he was going to have dinner with us [that night]. He said to me, "I can't meet you for dinner."

The hair stood up on the back of my neck and I thought something's wrong; it's just not his style.

I said, "What's the problem?"

He said, "I have a conflict, but I'll join you guys for a drink."

He asked me to come by the office the next morning. I had a flight out, but you don't say no, so I changed my flight. I had that same feeling that night that a truck was about to run me over. Everything in my body said something massively wrong was about to happen. I had no idea what it was; I just knew I was in big trouble.

I walked into his office the next morning and he said, "Lane, I don't know how to say this to you, but we had a board meeting last night and I'm no longer with AVON. The new CEO is from Duracell Batteries and he doesn't think that AVON should have a toy company so we're going to sell Discovery Toys."

I just looked at him. I had no response. Me, who talks, just sat there. I cried the whole way home on the plane. I thought, "This is one too many. I cannot do this anymore."

They asked me if I was interested in buying it back. I didn't have it in me; I couldn't take another blow.

They sold it to a private investment firm and I consulted with them for a little while. It was not a good relationship so I ended up leaving the company completely.

At that point I had a nervous breakdown, literally. A complete breakdown and went into a massive clinical depression where I couldn't leave the house for a year. I was really black; I was suicidal. It was just awful. One day I was the head of Discovery Toys and we were going international and the next day I'm not part of it? I didn't know who I was, I didn't know what happened to me. My second-born child had been taken away. It was a very bad nightmare and it took me years to recover.

One day during this time Tara came home with a little three-pound King Charles Cavalier Spaniel and I thought, "He's so cute." My dogs were 110 pounds and 50 pounds, big guys, and here's this little, tiny, stuffed animal thing. I said, "Oh, honey, we've got to go shopping for the puppy."

I didn't remember what puppies needed because my guys were 10 and 12-years-old. We went to all the big box stores and one of the local boutiques and came home with nothing because nobody could tell us what puppies needed; nobody cared. I came home very discouraged, very upset, and very sad.

Tara brought home the puppy again and I was re-motivated. I happened to be back with Discovery Toys on a very part-time basis and was flying over to Hong Kong with my long-time friend and toy developer in Discovery Toys.

On the plane we had nothing but time and I said, "I have this notion that dogs have about the intelligence of a two-year-old. Everything goes in their mouths. They learn everything by touching, by tasting, they have very short attention spans, they need a tremendous amount of attention, and they need training. They just strike me as two-year-olds. I wonder if we could do educational toys for dogs."

We started laughing, but we thought maybe it's not so stupid after all. We started designing stuff on the airplane, just fooling around with ideas. I asked my toy developing people over in Hong Kong, "Do you think I've lost my mind or is any of this sensible?"

It was the beginning of an uplift for me because everybody was like, "Lane, if you're going to do it, we'll back you. Anything you want, we're here to help."

It was incredible. It was such an affirmation for me. I was really excited about that.

On the plane home I said, "I can't do this because that means I have to sell to Walmart and PETCO and PetSmart and I know what that's like. I've watched the Toys R Us buyers for years and I can't be on the other end of that. It's not who I am." So I dropped it.

About three months later I woke up at midnight, woke up my husband, and said, "Honey, I know what I'm going to do for the rest of my life. I'm going to go back into direct sales, the [heck] with Walmart and PetSmart."

The other thing that had happened is Tara, when she brought home the puppy the second time, said, "Mom, you're killing our dogs by feeding them Science Diet," which I thought was top-of-the-line food.

I said, "What do you mean I'm killing them?"

She said, "Have you read the label?"

I said, "What would I know if I read the label?"

She explained to me what was actually in the food. I almost passed out. She explained what I should be feeding them.

I started doing a whole bunch of research in the pet world and pet industry. I thought, "There's a huge need for education because most pet parents know very little, way less than we think we know, and there's terrible product. I think I can go back in direct sales and teach people about pet parenting." That's how Petlane was born.

**As I interview people I ask, "Did you ever have written down goals?" "Did you use visualization techniques?" Folks are telling me no.**

I agree.

**B:** *You didn't go into this saying, "I'm going to be a multi-millionaire. I'm going to create fantastic success for other people."*

My thought was that if I could teach every parent in the United States how important it was to play with their children and how important it was to use some of the right tools when you did that, you could change the child's self-image and increase it dramatically.

If I could raise a generation of more secure kids then Tara would have all these wonderful people around that she could be friends with and could want to marry and it would be a better generation.

I was just a maniac mom so I wanted to change the whole world for my daughter. It had nothing to do with money. I was making $5 an hour and my husband was out of business, what did I know about living like a wealthy person? It was a foreign concept to me. That wasn't what it was about.

**If you were to go back, what would you change?**

Everything.

I would get more funding because it was just too fragile. I would have gotten more professional staffing earlier. When Mike died, this is all hindsight, I would have sold the business. I lost my passion and once that's gone, you need a partner.

**You're getting out of Petlane what you originally wanted out of Discovery Toys because you wanted Tara to take over Discovery.**

Yes I did. I wanted to work with her in the worst way.

She wouldn't do that because she always felt she would be in my shadow. But since we started Petlane together, she feels like a partner.

**Are you having some of the same frustrations that you had with Discovery Toys?**

Different. Things like computers for example. There's software out there that has been built for multi-level companies so I just had to buy one, I didn't have to invent it.

I hired Laurie from Discovery Toys so we've created 30 of our own products already. Creating catalogs is easy, I know how to do it.

The hard part is figuring out how to recruit people and help them succeed. But that's probably always the hard part. Discovery Toys spread virally. Petlane is slower. There's a whole Internet component that I am not of that generation. I'm learning quickly.

Once I decided it wasn't going to be a mystery and I stopped being scared of it, it's not hard to learn.

**You have some strong opinions. How has that helped you and or hurt you?**

It's helped me far more than it's hurt me. I have very strong opinions, but I like to hear everybody else's opinion and have lots of dialogue. I'm very verbal so I find that the most exhilarating thing is to debate an issue.

I'm always willing to change my opinion. You give me a better reason than I have and I'm there. I'm never afraid to say I'm sorry. I'm never afraid to say I'm wrong because I don't think there's anything wrong with being wrong. I'm wrong a lot. Strong opinioned is just good backbone for a CEO. It's leadership, but it's good leadership because I'm not a dictator at all.

**What was your passion 30 years ago? What is your passion today?**

My passion 30 years ago was to make the world a better place for Tara.

As Tara grew up and out, my pets became my new kids so I put that same love and desire and cherishing into them. I'm really passionate now about helping other people who love their pets as much as I do become really good pet parents.

**When you were 10-years-old, what did you think you would accomplish in life? At 15 or 20-years-old, did things take on a different shape?**

It depended what day you talked to me. One day I wanted to be a theater critic. Another day I wanted to be a writer. Another day I wanted to be an actress. It just depended on the moment. I had no preconceived notion.

After I graduated from college, I was very drawn to and stayed in the human services. I had one experience in business and hated every minute of it. I really loved being out with people in human services. That's where I thought I'd end up, and really I did. It's astonishing to watch in direct sales what happens to people's personal lives and their confidence. That's the part that exhilarates me.

**You mentioned that you were Jewish. Is that still the belief system that guides your life?**

I'm almost an epicurean Jew. We eat a lot of good food. We get together on all the holidays as families around the dinner table.

I was never religious. I never went to temple. I would say that the strong family principles and strong education principles that Jewish families hold are very much my guiding principles, but I wouldn't say there's a religious background to it.

## Did you have any mentors along the way?

My best mentors were Mike Clark, my COO, and Jim, my one-year CFO. Employees really were my mentors.

**B:** *You didn't have a formal mentor relationship?*

No.

## Were there people that inspired you?

My dad. He was always a sales/marketing executive. I think I developed his personality.

He's an exceptional human being. He was very tall and handsome, very skilled athletically, very skilled with people, and very successful. He supported me and gave me unequivocal love, which not too many of us get.

When I was little and would spill my milk, he would congratulate me on trying to hold the cup. He was amazing and a very optimistic man.

## How did you balance time with your husband, Ed, and Tara as you were building Discovery Toys?

Tara wasn't hard for me because I would get home by 5:00 or 5:30 p.m. every day–I was never one who stayed at work until 9:00 p.m.–and then I would be with her until 8:00 p.m. About 8:15 p.m., I kind of collapsed and my husband, who's a night person, would take over.

On weekends, usually I was exhausted, so Saturday my husband would take Tara on an adventure and then Sunday was family day.

It was wonderful. We're a very close family, but if anybody lost in the battle, my poor husband came third. That was very tough. It was some real rough times that we came out of, thank God. He didn't like being last and I don't blame him.

He's a very special human being. I don't think most men could have put up with it.

We got married at 21. I fell in love with him at 17, and I never fell out of love with him, so despite whatever hardships we went through, there was such a close bonded love that we were willing to fight through it, with marriage counseling at times, if necessary; whatever it took.

**What is your greatest joy in life?**

Working. When Tara was younger, being a mom was number one and then working came number two. I don't have a lot of hobbies. I don't really have a lot of time.

**Do you have a restless spirit?**

Yes, extremely. If I'm home on a weekend for more than a couple hours, I'm like, "What am I going to do now?"

**Are there opportunities presented to everyone in life?**

I think so. I think there are constant opportunities. It's just a matter of if you can see them.

**B:** *How do you see them? The success books tell you to keep an eye out for opportunity or to create opportunity; is that possible?*

Anybody can create opportunity. It's a matter of how driven you are and how much you want it. One of my father's famous statements is, "Anything that's worth doing is hard to do or everybody would be doing it and there'd be no opportunity."

I used to complain, "This is so hard," and he would say, "That's why you're going to be successful, because other people can't imitate you."

The level of passion and commitment that you have to have if you're going to be successful at something is really striking. I don't care what it is: a relationship, a mother, a businesswoman, an Olympic athlete, or whatever. You have to have so much passion and drive that all the things that come your way–here's the secret–you look at them as challenges not problems. I almost get excited when things go wrong because it's a new opportunity for me to stretch my brain and figure out what to do.

When things are too smooth, I get bored.

Most people tend to look at problems as problems and then you're dead because we all have loads of them. If you get beaten down by a problem it's finished. You're done.

**Other than that perspective, what has made you successful?**

Sheer drive.

I had a mission. I was going to change the world so my daughter could grow up not bullied in this wonderful, magic place called the world.

That mission was so overwhelmingly strong that I had to do it. There wasn't a matter of "nice to do" or "I could do" or "I wanted to"; I *had* to, so everything that came along that was trying to prevent me I thought, "Get out of my way, you're not going to stop me."

**Was the journey relatively easy or hard?**

It was extremely hard, but it was a lot of fun. The high times, the fun times, were so exciting that they made up for the really difficult times. Some of the high points were convention and incentive trips and the recognition; people whose bosses or husbands or friends never said, "Good job" were queens on stage. That's worth a lot. What I got from my dad I reproduced for others.

And by the way, the self-help books are good. Putting that kind of positive energy in your mind is a good thing. I don't think any of them have "the" answer because there is no "the" answer, but a lot of them say the right stuff and at least keep your mind taking those problems and making them into challenges.

**How many books a year do you read?**

I don't read any of those. I fully support them and I recommend them to other people, but I don't read them. I read a lot of novels.

**How would you define success?**

Accomplishing something that you set out to do. That can be tomorrow's idea, it could be running a $100 million business. There's a million, trillion steps along the way so really it's a matter of waking up in the morning and saying, "I'm going to accomplish X today" and then doing it.

It makes you feel good when you accomplish what you say you're going to do.

**Is there advice that you would give to people who are looking to be successful?**

Don't beat yourself up. If you set a goal and don't achieve it, don't beat yourself up about it. If you have come further than you would have by not setting it, then you're successful.

Most people are afraid to set a goal because they're afraid they can't meet it, so they never set it to begin with. A goal is just a thing to aim at. Mike used to say, "We're going to head north. We're going to go a little south, and a little west, a little east, but we are constantly heading north."

If you want to be successful, head north and know that you're going to detour all over the place, but ultimately you keep getting closer to north.

**What do you wish someone would ask you?**

I wish people would be able to achieve their dreams more than they do. I don't know what stops us. I see so many people start Petlane and so many start Discovery Toys with these great intentions and then they never go anywhere.

I always wish I could wave a magic wand and help them get to where they really want to go. I guess they really don't want to go there badly enough, but they think they do. The first couple of challenges they're done.

I feel very sad because whatever they thought that goal or dream was they're not going to get there.

If you keep saying, "I want something," and you keep not getting it, all you do is feel bad. You need to look at your own behavior because your behavior tells you what you really want, not your words. Decide whether that behavior is what you're happy with and go for it or change your behavior.

In this country, maybe around the world, there are people who believe that somewhere there's a get rich quick easy scheme that they just haven't found yet. It's kind of a lottery theory. I'm here to tell you, it isn't going to happen. Anybody who promises you you'll get rich quick, run from them as far as you can because all they're going to do is take your money.

**Bonus Information**:

*Lane's discussion about depression is so valuable that although I didn't include it within the context of the questions, I've included it here below.*

That depression as horrible as it was, and there are still moments where I have to fight it, really gave me a depth of understanding. I always thought that you could do anything and if you didn't do something, you chose not to do it. I had very little compassion or empathy.

I have a tremendous amount of empathy now for human beings, realizing that an awful lot of life we create ourselves, but not all of it. Sometimes there are things you can't avoid. However, I think even with the depression, antidepressants only do a very small amount and the rest of it is up to you to fight like a steer to get out of it. There's no magic medicine that will do it.

You have to get the exercise, food, and sunshine, and you have to wake up every morning and say, "Today I'm going to try to not allow myself to get depressed," and fight it. To a point you can and to a point you can't, but medication is only a small part of the answer.

I couldn't control so much of what happened to me, but I could control if I got out of bed and put on my business suit or if I quit.

*An update on Lane:*

*Between the time of interview and the time of publishing, the economy forced her to shut down Petlane. She and Tara started a new venture.*

****

# Millionaire 17 Bryan Willis

Executive Vice President, Investor, and Owner of ET Investments

www.etinv.com

Married, six children

Bachelor's in Business Administration, MBA

*A millionaire who had to back out of the project referred me to Bryan.*

**When you were 10-years old what did you want to do when you grew up?**

I wanted to be a professional baseball player.

I didn't give meaningful consideration to a real career until after I returned from my church mission in Alberta, Canada. I knew I wanted to be able to make a living and support a family, but I had no idea what or how that may happen.

I was a pretty poor student in high school; I wasn't very motivated. My first year of college, I played baseball and continued to be a pretty poor student. I knew education would be a way to be able to make a good living, so I thought I would do some kind of advanced education, as inconsistent as that may seem with the actions I took as a student.

While I was a missionary, I decided that when I got back into school I would try to get straight A's just one time to prove to myself that I was not stupid. I found out that if you go to class and pay attention, take notes, and read the materials, it's not as hard to do well in school.

I had always told people, "I'll be a corporate lawyer"–although I had no idea what that meant and still don't know exactly what it means– because I thought it sounded like a prestigious career. Instead of pursuing law I changed my mind and thought I would go to medical school so I started to take biology and chemistry courses. As I got into the classes with students who were likely going to medical school, I realized that peer group isn't what I wanted for my career. I changed my mind again and went to business school.

**B:** *Where did you grow up and where did you go to school?*

I grew up in Reno, NV, and I graduated from Southern Utah University.

## You finished school and then what?

It wasn't a good time to finish school. I finished in 1992, which was the last recession we had before this one. About half of my class didn't have jobs when we graduated. I had a couple of offers and once I got the first one I found that it was a lot easier to interview because I wasn't so worried.

I went to work for Chrysler as a financial analyst in Detroit for a couple of years and then went to work for Armco, a steel manufacturer. I was there a little less than a year before they asked me to be a controller at one of their divisions in Tennessee with an eye toward shutting that division down. They wanted me to figure out how we could shut it down without costing us too much.

After being there a little while, it became apparent to me what the issue was. The primary goal had been to keep that facility busy at full capacity. To do that, they were bidding on work at a price that made no sense.

Instead of recommending that we shut it down, I came back with a plan to shrink it, stabilize it, and then sell it. That's what we did.

In the meantime, the people that I was close to at Armco had left, so I really didn't have a lot of motivation to stay there. I participated in the purchase of that division from Armco as an investor. It was mostly sweat equity. I didn't pay much, but I put in the work and got equity as a result.

**B:** *Did you plant the seed with the buyer that you would like to stay on or they saw you were valuable and asked you to stay?*

They asked me to stay.

The partner we had taken on was out of Hong Kong and he seemed like a very good guy, but I knew that business is done differently in Asia; I worried about ethical issues. As I explained things to him he always seemed to come around though. I talked to him about bribes and how it's illegal for an American company.

We built that company and were in the process of taking it public. We were under the pressure of an initial public offering and some of the Asian projects that we were working on were not progressing. The partner was talking to me about what we could do to improve our earnings and to move these projects along because we weren't able to have as much revenue as we were expecting with these projects delayed.

All we could do was actually move them along and he seemed to be looking for gimmicks as to how we might move them along. Construction accounting is very simple, but if you want to game that process it's easy to do. I spent all of an afternoon in Hong Kong, probably eight hours, talking with him and going over why we couldn't do many of his suggestions. We had a factory in China that was doing some work for us and we drove up there the next day. The conversation during the car ride was similar.

That night in the hotel I was sitting there thinking, "How did a nice guy like me end up in a place like this? What am I going to do?"

About two months before that I had gotten a call from Pete Leemputte, my former boss at Armco. He had gone to work for Chicago Title and asked me if I was interested in coming to work with him there. I told him, "No, I'm an owner here. I'm committed; things are moving along, we're doing pretty well."

That night in China I decided I should explore some things because I was worried. I wasn't worried that I couldn't keep things under control because I thought I could, but I was worried that to be able to do that I was going to have to be in Asia for two weeks every month. I was unwilling to do that and I worried about having to be the policeman instead of [us] being on the same page.

As I considered my options, one of the things I talked with my wife about was if my career was too much and I needed to find work that was less challenging. I had been working 80- to 100-hour weeks. There are a lot of people who talk about working that much, especially when you get into a corporate arena, but I've never worked with them. I did and it's a lot. If you work 80 hours and you don't work on Sunday that gives you six days to get in 80 hours.

My wife, who is very supportive, ultimately said, "You'll go nuts if you're not challenged, so let's find something challenging."

I called Pete and asked if he would consider talking to me again.

He said, "I haven't been able to find the right person, I'd love to talk to you."

I left Flour City, the construction company, and went to Chicago Title as their corporate controller. It was more than I was ready for probably, and because of that I had to work a lot to be able to move things ahead at the pace that I wanted to move them ahead. With my lack of experience and lack of know-how it required lots of work.

**B:** *Lack of know-how in that industry?*

I had somewhere around 50 to 60 employees in Chicago when I got there, which we cut back to 43 or 44 by streamlining processes, reducing staffing, and reducing costs. But we changed the reporting structure so that a field organization of 500 accounting and finance people reported to me as well.

It was a lot for a young guy that hadn't managed large staffs. At Flour City, I started with 20 employees and that was down to 10 or 11 when I left. Chicago Title was like trying to turn an aircraft carrier instead of a battleship, so it required a lot of work. I like work, though, so that wasn't a problem.

Pete is a very smart guy and I really enjoyed working with him, trying to do things that would take some of the load off his plate. If he can see 10 things that can be done, he's going to be doing 15. He's always trying to move things forward at a very brisk pace. It was challenging; I enjoyed that and was happy.

In August of 1999, we became involved in due diligence for the company Chicago Title was being acquired by. I had a chance to talk to and work with the people that were acquiring us and decided that staying there was not for me. Around Christmas I decided to start to work on a resume.

My wife and I talked about what we wanted to do and I decided I wanted to slow down a little bit in terms of the workload. One of the primary reasons was that our family was growing and our kids were starting school so they wouldn't be able to continue to stay up late [which is when I would see them]. I wanted to be challenged, but I didn't want to have to work 80 or 90 hours a week. We [also] decided that we'd like to come back West.

In January, I got a call from a headhunter that was interviewing for a CFO position at United General Title Insurance Company in Denver. They were doing a little over $100 million in revenue and were not profitable, but I really liked the people who were in control of the company.

In the meantime, my former boss, Pete, was looking for work. He and I were hoping to be able to work together, but he's a Chicago native and that's where he was going to live and my wife and I had already talked about coming back West, so those two paths were in conflict.

[After talking with United General] I had decided I was going to work there, but we had not finalized any terms. Right after that, Pete called and said, "I've got great news. I've landed a job and I want you to come over with me."

I called John, the President and CEO at United General, and said, "I need you to make me an offer quickly because I got a voicemail from my former boss. I want to tell him I've already gotten and accepted an offer."

John said, "I can appreciate that's what you would want to do, but I think you need to talk to him. When you're finished talking with him and deciding what you want to do, call me. If you want to come here, we'll work it out, but you need to talk to him first."

I'm still angry at him for making me do that. I called Pete and told him my wife and I wanted to go West. He was very understanding.

As part of my compensation at United General, I got options for a chunk of the company. After I had been there about a year, the largest shareholder, a separate investor, wanted out. Two of the other managers at United General and I bought his interest in the company and that put John, the president and CEO, in control of the company as the majority shareholder.

Between 2000 and 2004 we grew the revenues from $110 million to $260 million. The economy was a big factor in our growth, even though I like to think our success was driven by us doing several things well.

There were companies calling us and asking if we were interested in being acquired. In the past we had always said, "We're not interested," but in 2004 we were worried about some of the trends in the industry so we decided to consider selling.

We had no idea that the economic meltdown would come as soon as it did or be as severe as it was. If we had, we probably would not have sold the company because the trend we were worried about was the big companies in the industry, fueled by an intense drive for market share, were doing unsustainable and, in my opinion, unwise things. If we had known there was going to be such a quick market correction that would cause them to quit doing those things, we would have liked our chances for continued success a lot better. We thought by the time they recognized what they were doing, though, we would be collateral damage of their activities.

We were approached by a company that we thought would make a really good marriage. They were outside the industry and had relationships we didn't have and our network was something that they didn't have. We were a couple of weeks away from the scheduled close of that deal and the buyer backed out. It was disappointing because we thought there were some exciting things that could happen with the merger of those companies.

A week after the time we were supposed to close we got a call from one of the regular companies that called every year to see if we were interested in being sold. We met with them and sold United General in early 2005.

There were several people that did not want to or did not receive an offer to stay with the acquiring company, First American, so we brought many of them over with us to ET Investments, a company we had formed while we were still running United General. We had formed it to purchase title insurance agencies that sold policies for us. Although we had purchased a couple of agencies, we weren't active in building ET Investments until we sold United General.

When we sold, we decided that we would build ET Investments into a platform where the former employees of United General that didn't want to stay with the acquiring company could work and we would build something together. Our controller at United General is our CFO at ET Investments. The head of IT at United General is the head of IT here. Our corporate counsel at United General is our general counsel here. We had a manager of financial analysis at United General, he's our controller here.

We brought just about everybody that would be disaffected by the sale of United General. We also brought any of our field people that didn't want to work for First American and started agencies around them. Now our goal is in every case to have a local partner who owns part of the business and to help them build some financial stability and a financial future for themselves.

Our hope is to help the people that work with us get what they want out of life. For some people what they want is a paycheck and not really anything else. That's OK, we can take those kinds of people. For some people it might be to make a fair amount of money. We can take those people and help them, too. Hopefully all the people that we work with want a place where they can work on being a better person.

One of the reasons I really like the people I came to work with at United General was we talked about development of the whole person, not just the workplace. One of the really valuable things John mentioned to me and that we talked about a lot was the notion that there aren't two people, the one of you that comes to work and the one of you that goes home. There's only you, you can't separate and compartmentalize.

## What have you learned from your mistakes?

I learned with the job interviews after business school that you shouldn't try to do something that you don't want to do. I don't know very many things that I couldn't be passionate about, but there are a few. One of them is being an HR manager [which is one of the jobs for which I interviewed after business school]. Dealing with employee problems is my least favorite thing.

I had a lawn service when I was in high school and helped pay for college with it. I've joked with people, but it's really only a half joke, that if things ever get rough I can do the lawn service; I had a good time. We'd mow a lawn, maybe it was a 15-minute lawn, and we'd spend a half-hour drinking a glass of lemonade, talking with the customers, and changing a light bulb in their closet. I enjoyed that, I enjoyed those people, I enjoyed that when I showed up the lawn looked ragged and when I left it looked good.

I think you can have fun doing a lot of things. I think I could have been a successful and happy lawyer. I think I could have been a successful and happy doctor. Maybe I'm wrong because I haven't tried those things, but I enjoyed working with Chrysler, even though there were things I didn't like about it, I enjoyed working with Armco, I enjoyed the time with Flour City, and I enjoyed Chicago Title.

## What is your passion?

There are two reasons that I didn't stop working when we sold United General.

One, my wife said I was too young to retire and I listen to her. Two, I want to help create for other people the kinds of opportunities that have happened for me.

I like work. I could count on one hand and still have fingers left over the times I haven't been excited about coming into work; I enjoy it. In life, you might as well be doing something productive along the way.

**B:** *Why do you enjoy work?*

I like trying to solve problems. I like analyzing situations. We're looking at a potential spin off business; I'm excited about that. I think we might be able to build a pretty substantial business.

My oldest son has worked here this summer. Last night I started to have him build a spreadsheet model that will be the basis for the financial projections for this potential venture. It was really fun to go through with him some of the things you think about when you're figuring out if something's going to make sense or not.

I enjoy analyzing and trying to figure out how to make something better; the process of business analysis, I really enjoy that. I like the idea of trying to help others to be able to see success.

As you can tell, there's been nothing spectacular about my career. It's been things that have come my way. I've done nothing to find those things. If not for Pete Leemputte…

I learned a ton from him; I really enjoyed working with him. I'll never be as smart as he is, but I can work as hard as anybody. So hopefully I can use what I do know and help some other people in a way similar to what's been done for me.

### Where does that work ethic come from?

Growing up, probably.

I'm the youngest of 12 children. My dad left shortly after I was born. At that time, my mom had never worked outside the home. She started going to nursing school during the day and did in-home care at nights for an elderly lady. Once she became a nurse, she got a job working at the hospital during the day and still did in-home care on weekend nights and on her days off during the week. She definitely showed us how to work.

We had about eight acres. We had horses, a cow or two, chickens, and that kind of stuff, so we had fields to irrigate and ditches to dig. There was no shortage of things to be done, even though I tried my best to get out of them.

When I got older, I wanted to be able to support a family. That's what drove me to finally decide to do OK in school and to work hard in a career. I grew up relatively poor–maybe it wasn't so poor, we didn't ever starve, but we didn't ever have lots; my mom did a fantastic job with what she had–but I was hopeful that I'd be able to support a family with a little more resources than what I grew up with.

I like work, too. It's not hard to work if you like it.

**How did you balance time with your family while you were building your business?**

My wife is amazing.

When I worked at Chrysler I would generally go to work at 7:00 a.m. and get home at 7:30 or 8:00 p.m. At the beginning, my wife worked so she would drop me off in the morning and in the afternoon she would go home after work, do a couple of things, and then pick me up. We'd do our grocery shopping together, cook dinner together, and that kind of stuff.

[An interesting side story:] The headhunter that called me about Armco said, "We're looking for somebody with 7-10 years of experience." I told him, "I've only been working for a year-and-a-half; I'm not what you're looking for." He said, "Well, I'll talk to you anyway."

When I went to Armco, I typically got in the office by 6:00 or 6:30 a.m. and didn't get home until 9:00 p.m. My first project was to go to a steel mill in Mansfield, Ohio. I would drive out Monday morning and come back Thursday or Friday night. At the time we only had one small child and my wife and he would often come with on those trips.

At Flour City, I worked even more. When I was in the office, quite often my wife would bring dinner to the office and we'd eat together. Our son stayed up until 1:00 or 2:00 a.m. so I could come home and play with him then go to bed.

In Chicago I worked a lot. I would leave home by 5:00 or 5:30 a.m., and I was always sitting at my desk by 6:30 a.m., often by 6:00 a.m. I was usually not home until 11:00 p.m. Our daughter was a baby and she didn't always stay up, but both my sons did. I could eat and play with them for a little while and then go to bed.

I don't know that it's balanced, but that's what I did.

**B:** *How's the balance now? Much different?*

Yeah, I don't work nearly like I used to.

**Did you have mentors in this process?**

Certainly Pete. Any success I've had in my career, any of the things I do pretty well, are because he taught me.

**B:** *He wasn't a formal mentor, was he?*

No, it's not like he signed up and said, "I'll be your mentor." But he was a great boss.

**Did you have written down goals?**

Most of my goals as far as a career were pipe dreams. I wanted to make $100,000 a year by the time I was 30.

I have no idea where I came up with that or why I did, but I wanted to.

**B:** *You made that.*

I did.

And I hoped to have a million dollars by the time I was 40.

But I didn't write any goals down. I just wanted to be able to support a family. I don't know why I even had those other goals in mind. I don't know that they were really goals; they probably weren't.

**Did you use visualization to see what you wanted and then go after it?**

No.

**Did you have a system for success in your mind that you followed?**

I knew work. I've never considered myself to be super smart. I think I'm adequately smart, but I'm not like Pete, I'm not like John. But I can work.

**Was the journey relatively easy or hard?**

I hope it's not done.

I'd say relatively easy.

**B:** *On account of?*

I really haven't had to do much other than show up. The opportunities have presented themselves for my whole career. I got a call to go to Armco; I didn't have to look for that. I was asked to go to Tennessee with Armco; I didn't have to look for that. Flour City asked me to stay when they bought that division; I didn't have to look for that. My former boss called me; I didn't have to look for that. I went to Chicago Title and when the company was sold, a headhunter called me; I didn't have to look for that. We had ET Investments; I didn't have to look for that.

It just sort of happened.

**B:** *As you read the book you'll probably enjoy that perspective as shown through others.*

I think other people probably have more of a plan.

**B:** *No. Some of the folks I interviewed mentioned, "I was just fortunate enough to be in the right place at the right time."*

That's probably the case for me.

## What would you say are your greatest successes?

Marrying my wife was the first real success and everything else follows.

I never could have worked the way I worked without a supportive wife. I value that support probably more than anything in terms of not just in my career, but in my life.

And then our kids, I'm exceptionally proud. We've got great kids. My oldest is headed off to college and my youngest started kindergarten this year, so bad times, they're all going away. I think they ought to be 30 before they leave home because I love spending time with them. We have a great time together.

They are still little so who knows how they'll turn out, but I'm very proud of the way they are. They're on a great path so far, each of them.

**B:** *How rewarding is that?*

It's not a reward for something I've accomplished, but I sure enjoy being a spectator watching them with all they're becoming. It sure is satisfying to be able to be associated with them.

## What would you say makes you successful?

I don't think of myself as successful. I don't even know that I've ever tried to define success.

I know that I want to be a good father, I want to be a good husband, and I want to support my family. I guess to that extent I'm successful. Except don't ask my wife about being a good husband or my kids about being a good father because they may not agree, but those are the things that are important to me.

In terms of a career, I've certainly been able to support our family. We can do the things that we want to do. That's a two-edged sword. The biggest concern I have for our kids other than just the world and the challenges they face is that they may have it too easy. They may start to think somewhere along the way that we have more than this guy, so therefore we're better. My wife and I have tried pretty hard to make sure that doesn't creep in.

## Success for you is?

Being able to do meaningful work and enjoy what you're doing. I would never want to spend even a day at a job that I didn't like. If there were something I did not like, I would try really hard not to do it. Having said that, I'm not sure there is such a job. I think I could have enjoyed lots and lots of things.

Being able to do something that you enjoy, that hopefully is meaningful, where you add value to others along the way, where you're able to learn and grow, and where you're able to fulfill your family obligations and interact and associate with your family in meaningful ways, doing things that help you grow together, I guess that's what I would say is success.

Certainly a relationship with God and serving in the church is important to me. I don't know what your audience is and if they'll care about that, but I consider that to be a pretty important thing, too.

## What is the belief system that guides your life?

I'm a member of the Church of Jesus Christ of Latter-day Saints. I have an absolute commitment to and faith in the gospel and I spend time learning and growing in that.

I think of it in three parts. The first part is that we need to know there's a God; that's the key and the foundation for everything. Then we need to discover what it is He wants for us. Then we need to bring our life into harmony with what we discover. We never really need to go back to the first step of knowing that there's a God, but we can continually discover more about His nature, more about what He wants and then continually adapt our lives to be in better harmony with that.

## What should people who want to be successful know?

They should talk to someone who knows.

I don't know. I'm not qualified to say what anybody else would need to know.

**How did you get where you are?**

I've described it.

I don't know why I've been as lucky as I've been. The only thing I can say is that I have worked hard and as opportunities have presented themselves, where it felt like a good thing to do, where it seemed to make sense, it's like the plate has been put on the table and I've gotten to eat. It's not that hard to stick a fork in the food and pick it up.

**If you were to go back, what would you do differently?**

I'd probably be a better student early on. I would have spent more time earlier trying to be more helpful to others.

Early on in my career, it's not like I tried to be bad to other people, but my focus was to do as well as I could. I probably had some amount of drive or greed or whatever the right word is; my behaviors were to help me get ahead, not so much to help others. It wasn't like I was trying to trample on other people to get ahead, but I was not really interested in lifting anybody else up along my path of advancement. It would have been nice to learn the importance of lifting others earlier.

John helped me to understand that I can't compartmentalize. Being a better person, working on this discovery and harmonizing process that I talk about, doesn't just happen at home in the evenings. It's got to be happening while you're at work, too. If you don't have that in mind, you're probably not going to get where you want to, certainly not as quickly as you want to get there.

Also, I wouldn't have had to work as much early on if I knew then what I know now, but I don't know how that happens. I don't know how you get the knowledge without going through at least some of the experiences.

## What advice would you give someone who's looking for a break, an opportunity?

In my experience, both as a person working and as a person hiring and managing people at work, when someone does everything you give them and does it well, you're going to give them more.

So work hard and do the things in front of you. Whether you're vacuuming the floor or doing accounts payable, if you do those things really well and show a capacity to do more, you're going to get more, and the more is a break. It may not come in the time you want it; I would probably tell people to be patient, but that's a little disingenuous because I haven't had to be.

Do what's in front of you and do it really well and everybody notices and you're going to get more opportunities.

## What's your greatest joy?

The times when I feel like I'm on the path I ought to be on and my family is on the path with me. And when we have occasion to have other people who I can somehow be a part of helping them get on the path, too.

## What is money to you?

A burden. A responsibility.

I should clarify: to have enough has been a driving force for me. I didn't like feeling like we had no money. I grew up in an area where I was, at least in my mind, the poorest of all the kids at my school. I wanted cool shoes and I never had cool shoes. I used to have the leather work boots that laced up and went all the way to my calf. I would ride my bike and get going as fast as I could and drag them hoping I could wear them out so I could get a pair of tennis shoes that were cool.

I didn't want not having enough money be what my kids would have to experience.

But beyond being able to support your family–and again, that's a little bit disingenuous for me because we've always been able to support a family, we've always had enough–it's a burden.

Is it OK for me to live in a house that costs twice as much as a house that I could be comfortable living in or should I give that money to somebody else? Should I be using that to help somebody else have a job? Is it OK for me to learn to fly? What if I want a plane when I become a pilot? Are those kinds of things OK? Am I doing the things with the money that I'm supposed to?

There are two different levels: To have what you need is important. Beyond that, it's a burden and it's a responsibility.

**\*\*\*\***

# Millionaire 18 Shawn Kane

Owner, Kane Consulting

www.kaneconsultinginc.net

Married, five children

Associate's Degree

*I met Shawn through a speaking organization, Making it Count, which presents informational seminars to high school and college students. Shawn speaks for them part-time for fun.*

**When you were a kid, what did you want to do when you grew up?**

I don't recall. I just wanted to be successful. I never really had the thought of, "I want to be a doctor, or a fireman, or a police officer."

**B:** *What did it mean to you to be successful?*

I saw my parents and they were successful. They worked extremely hard.

We were not deprived of material things and pretty much had everything we wanted. We weren't spoiled, but we knew that if you worked hard, you can pretty much have whatever you want in this world.

That was my concept of success: if you work hard and continue to work hard, you can attain the things that you want in this life.

**B:** *When you were 15 to 20, what did you want to do with your life?*

At this point, at 38, I still don't know what I want to do with my life.

After college, around 23-years-old I was traveling all over the country and in some parts of world. I really didn't know what I wanted to do. I fell into the profession that I'm in now and it became my passion.

**Tell me how your life progressed from the time you graduated high school up to the point where you are now.**

I graduated and started modeling and doing part-time acting and commercials. I did that for a couple of years.

My dad called me up one day and said he needed my help. I came out to Utah and I helped him with his businesses for two or three years.

While I was helping him, I was asked to be chairman for an organization called Riverdale Crime Solvers, which was a citizen-based organization. It was a way to get businesses together to work with the police to help solve crimes that were perpetrated against businesses. I worked with the local police officers and did public relations work with the businesses.

That's where this actually all started. I received a lot of training from Riverdale P.D. [Police Department] and different organizations on check fraud, credit card fraud, and went through different classes.

I was a liaison working with P.D. as a civilian for businesses, but I was doing it for free. I thought to myself, "There's got to be a business in this. If I'm doing it for free and getting such good response, there really has to be a business aspect of it where someone can make money."

I continued on the path to get more education, to be more knowledgeable about the security industry, on everything that my clients ask [for] so that when they need something to do with security–cameras, consulting, training, education, investigations–I and or my staff can provide that.

**You said this grew into your passion; tell me about that.**

At that time [in my life], I still didn't know what I wanted to do. I was traveling the world, enjoying life, modeling, and making bank. It was fun, but during the time I started modeling it was a false front, a façade, industry and I didn't like that. It wasn't real.

When I got into Riverdale Crime Solvers, I enjoyed it. I realized there's money to be made in this industry. It became my passion because one, I enjoyed it. Two, as I learned more, as my clients asked for more from me, I had to learn more, get more involved and be knowledgeable so that my clients could turn to me for anything they needed to do with security and investigations. So it really became my passion.

Could I have gone into another industry, into retail [for example], and done something else and that have become my passion? Sure. But I fell into this industry and started to really enjoy it, so it became my passion.

**B:** *Is security your passion, or is it something else? Is it growing something? Is it being knowledgeable and being the go to guy that is your passion? Is it all the same to you?*

It's all the same…every part of what I do has its rewards. Each day for me is different, which I think is part of the excitement for me. My passion stays heightened because I'm always doing something different.

## Did you have a formal mentor?

No, other than watching my parents work as hard as they did. Watching my dad get up at 6:00 a.m. and going to work, I'd say that was my mentoring. He worked a long day.

## Did you ever have written down goals?

I wouldn't necessarily say written down goals. It was more personal targets I wanted to hit. For instance, "Within three months, I want to have five new clients. Within six months, I want to have those clients referring me to other clients."

It wasn't that I wrote the goals down. I'm not necessarily a writing-goals-down-oriented person. It's more like, "This is the way I see it, that's what I want to do, I'm going to do it and get it done." And it gets done. I give myself a certain timeframe–[I don't] necessarily write it down–and check it every month.

## Did you have a system for success in mind that you followed, or just followed heart and you took it step by step?

A little bit of both.

One, I followed my heart and I always wanted to take care of my staff. In order for me to be successful and grow to the point where I am, my staff became priority.

Whether it's pay them more, take them to lunch, take them to dinner, thank them, or give them the perks that they deserve. Without a good staff you can't get the job done. That was the first thing: I can have a name, I can have a company, but if I don't have a staff, I'm not going to go anywhere.

The second thing to me was taking care of my clients. I'm always making sure my clients are taken care of, that my staff or I have met their needs with a personal touch.

The third part is that human touch – keeping it real. If I don't have to email a client and I can go to them in person, I'd rather do that than just email back and forth.

So those three things became my direction for success.

**How did you balance time with your family while you've been building and as you continue to work your business?**

Family comes first. No matter what, family is first.

If I work three weeks straight out of state, I'll take a week off and just oversee the business, [so] I'm there for my family. I try to do that as best as I can throughout the year because family is first.

**Has the journey to get to this point been relatively easy or hard?**

It's been easy as far as I knew where I wanted to go and the direction I wanted to take, but there have been times that have been difficult.

I would love to say it was easy all the way through, but there are times that I missed a mortgage payment because business wasn't as busy or I was growing. I had to put money into the company because I had to get equipment and missed a car payment here and there.

It's not that it's been an uphill struggle all the way, but it's been uphill. I'm at a good plateau in life now [such that] I can afford the things I want. I don't have to go without; my family is taken care of.

Now, though, with the way the economy is, I have to rethink structuring because people don't want to spend as much money and one of the first things to go is security and people don't want to pay money on investigations.

**Did you at any point want to quit, pack up the business, and say, "Forget it?"**

No.

If somebody came to me today and said, "I'll give you this much money for the company, do you want to sell it?" I'd sell it.

I'm still young; I'm 38. I don't know what else is out there that I'd want to do. I love the public speaking; it's a blast.

Could I walk away tomorrow from this? Yes, if I knew that what I built up would continue and if my staff was taken care of and my clients were taken care of because I look at this as my baby. It's something that I started from scratch [with] my sweat and tears and this is what I built.

Could I walk away from it? Sure. Why? Knowing what I know now and being able to build what I built, I have confidence that I could take an idea and continue to build it and make it a success. It's a determination thing in me.

**Where did you have the confidence to start your business?**

With my first contracts I was scared to death.

In the environment that I grew up in, watching my parents work as hard as they did and learning at a young age that if you work hard, sure, you're going to struggle and there's going to be obstacles you have to overcome, but it came down to my desire, my know-how. The desire for me was there in the sense I watched my parents be successful but they worked hard. So I learned that even if I get knocked down or didn't get a contract, it's OK. [The question to ask is,] "What can I do differently next time?"

I have the know-how, I'm continually getting the know-how.

**Do you think you have a restless spirit?**

I don't think that it's a restless spirit, I think it's an active spirit. I'm always going. My doctor said that I've got high blood pressure. He said, "You ought to reduce your stress."

300

I said, "Doc, I don't get stressed. This is my life, this is what I do, it's not stress."

Sure, I have a hundred and fifty billion things going on, but I don't get stressed. It's part of life; you've got to do it. If I have a job to get done, it's got to be done.

**Outside of work, what's your greatest joy?**

My children.

Hanging out with my son, watching my son play football, being there to be the cool dad taking my son and his friends to lunch during the day, watching my girls do a play, being with my wife. I golf, play football and basketball, hang out with friends, go shooting, and do all that stuff. It's all meaningless if you're family's not there and you're not enjoying it with your family.

**What's the belief system that guides your life?**

I grew up Catholic. I have been fortunate enough to study all of the other religions. My children go to a private Christian school. I don't go to church on Sunday.

My mom asked, "Why don't you go to church on Sunday?"

I said, "My belief system in life is every day I try and do good. Every day I try and make sure my family's taken care of. Make sure that I'm honest, ethical, and professional with my job, and make sure I do what I can for my family."

Do I need to go to church and profess that to God? No, I don't believe that I do. I believe that if I'm genuinely a good person then I'm living a Christian life. Whether I'm going to be judged for that at the end, I can't say, but at this point in time, it's worked so far.

**What have you learned from some of your failures?**

[Laughing] Frustration.

There's always another way to do something, there's different perspective. A failure to me is not a failure. It's a challenge to learn a better way to do something.

**Why do you think you were elected or appointed at 21 to head up Riverdale Crime [Solvers]?**

I really don't know. I had a good rapport with the police.

I think it was, "Hey, Shawn, you want to do it? Great, you're in." We had an official election, but I can't remember if anybody ran against me or not.

**That in combination with your dad asking you to come back and help him shaped where you are today, but at the moment you wouldn't have known anything about it, would you?**

No, not at all. I wouldn't have even thought twice that I'd be where I was based on 14 years ago.

**B:** *Did you know you were taking advantage of opportunities? You had no idea, right?*

No. I didn't. At the time when I was doing Riverdale Crime Solvers I was thinking, "This sounds like fun."

**B:** *And that was probably as deep as it went, right?*

Yeah, pretty much. I never thought that it would be a career, that this could be what I'd be doing 14 years from that point.

**Who or what inspired you along your path?**

I'd say my basic desire to succeed is what inspired me.

Growing up in northern California, every other house had a BMW. I was fortunate enough to go to private schools and I grew up learning about success and being successful. I watched my parents work and they were a success.

I didn't have any specific person I constantly looked up to.

You hear stories about listening to Anthony Robbins at 3:00 a.m. I was too busy trying to be successful and failing, succeeding and learning, and trying to advance my career to listen to somebody motivate me on how to be successful.

It's not that they're not good, don't get me wrong, it's not that they haven't made a life for themselves. I was too busy working to be successful to listen to audiotapes on how to be successful.

**What would you say are some of your greatest successes in life or with your business?**

As far as the business goes, the overall respect that I have gained in my industry is my biggest success.

And it's not one thing. It's everything that I have tried to do with reference to if someone says Kane Consulting, if somebody hears Kane Consulting, or somebody looks back on what I've done and sees that I'm the security director for major events in Salt Lake, major events in Ogden and across the country. I have a client list that's longer than I am tall. I think all those little things [add up] to I've created a successful business. Everything I've done has gotten me to this point in life that I'm successful.

Outside of business: my children. I like to brag. I love them. They're great.

**If you were to go back, what would you do differently?**

In the early stages I would have probably gotten more like-minded people involved because I did a lot of the work. I probably could have built it a lot quicker than where it is.

Am I disappointed? No. I think instead of it being 14 years and really considering myself a success, though, maybe it would have been eight or 10 years.

**What should people who want to be successful know?**

It's hard work.

Unless you're one of those lucky ones that comes up with some idea like the pet rock or you create something that takes off immediately, success takes work.

And you have to define what you believe is successful. People say to me, "You must be rich."

What do you define as being rich? Do you define it as your family is taken care of and you're happy? Or do you define it as you're dirt poor and your family is taken care of and you're happy?

Being successful takes time, but if you have the desire, you can learn the know-how off the Internet on anything nowadays and you can get a degree anywhere. If you have the desire to be successful and it's something that you want, you just have to define what you believe is success.

But it is hard work. We don't accept the nine to five thing.

**What is success to you?**

One, is my family taken care of, am I taken care of, am I happy?

Two, looking at the respect of the industry that I am in; do I have the respect of my peers? I could be a billionaire and people hate me. If I were to die today, would people remember Shawn Kane? I hope so.

Success is the respect that people have hopefully for me and for what I've built. I think it is demonstrated by my clients constantly calling me back. They utilize me, they utilize my company, they utilize my staff, so I've done something right.

**Bonus Question**: What do you wish someone would ask you?

Am I happy?

I've got a great life. I've set my life up that I've got a great family, great kids, my company is doing phenomenal, I'm happy. I can't complain. There's not a lot I'd do different in the sense of where my life is right now.

I don't want to say I'm content because that means I'm stagnant. I can always grow in all kinds of ways, but I am happy.

****

## Millionaire 19 Judith Briggs

Franchise Owner, 1-800-GOT-JUNK

www.1800gotjunk.com/boston

www.1800gotjunk.com/worcester

Four sons

Associate's, Bachelor's in Business, MBA


*I found Judith through an Internet search for female entrepreneurial millionaires.*

## When you were a kid what did you want to do when you grew up?

When I was a young girl growing up I wanted to do two things with my life. I wanted to be a professional figure skater and then as I got older I wanted to be a pediatrician.

I figure skated until my first year in college, but I wasn't competitive like the Olympic competitors, so that was out. Then when I realized how much college was–I grew up in a single parent household–I realized I couldn't afford to go to school to become a doctor. Nor did I think I had the energy to do that many years of schooling.

I got my accounting degree. Right out of college I got my first job working for one of the larger insurance carriers in Massachusetts and I loved the working world. I loved the daily challenges of it, meeting people. I was putting puzzles together with the financial work that I was doing for the carrier; it was a lot of fun.

**B:** *What took you to accounting?*

In high school I had a phenomenal accounting teacher and she made it fun; as fun as finances can be. I really enjoyed the numbers and I need to know how everything fits into one piece and where all the numbers come from and how things tie out. I'm very methodical so I guess it was a perfect fit to follow the accounting field.

**B:** *You grew up in a single parent home?*

I did. It was just my mother, who was a single mom. She had an older sister whose husband had unfortunately passed away, so my mother and my aunt raised me. They say only children are spoiled; I wasn't really spoiled. I got a lot of love and my mother taught me the value of hard work. She provided. She didn't have a lot, but she worked hard to give me everything that I wanted, so I appreciated that. That's how I realized you have to work hard for what you have.

I've worked since I was ten years old. I had a cousin who owned an electronics store. School vacations and weekends when my mother was working, his mother would babysit me. I spent a lot of time at his store. He paid me so I was able to buy things for myself at an earlier age and I thought it was great to have money.

For the longest time I had two jobs, especially when I became a single parent myself. I had four small children and I knew I had to provide a roof over their heads and food on the table so I had to do what I had to do to get by.

**How did the transition go from the accounting world to being a vice president of human resources?**

That's when my kids were a little bit older and I was starting to miss out on a lot of their sports activities because I was about 45 minutes away from the home. I needed something closer [to home] that fit into my schedule.

I found the HR position, five minutes from my house, so I could literally take my lunch at 3:00 p.m., spend an hour at the game, go back to work and still be back at the game before it was over.

When the kids headed off for school, I could leave for work five minutes before I had to be there. I could go home at lunchtime. I was able to spend a lot more time with my kids at that time.

**What was it that caused you to think, "I've got the skills to be an HR vice president"? What caused you to jump into that with both feet?**

It was funny. When I originally applied for the job, probably six months beforehand, I applied for an executive administrative position because I needed to be closer to home to be near my kids.

The guy that I interviewed with said, "You're far too qualified for this position," so I was rejected. Six months later they were working with an outside consulting firm who said, "You need to get your act together."

They called me back and because of my management skills and people skills–I had worked in management for quite some time–they said, "We'd like you to come back. How do you feel about human resources?"

I can do anything I put my mind to so I said, "Sure."

## How did 1-800-GOT-JUNK come into the picture?

I had just gotten remarried and my husband at the time had always wanted to go into business for himself, but never found the right business until he saw an article in the newspaper about 1-800-GOT-JUNK.

It was the fall of 2002. He showed me the article and said, "Take a look at this and tell me what you think." [I didn't] realize where he was going with it. I thought it was very interesting because we were homeowners so we knew what it was like to try to get rid of large bulky items.

The next thing you know he's investigating the company and came to me and said, "What do you think about us looking into buying a franchise?"

I said, "OK." You know, naïve.

The next thing you know we went for an interview up to Vancouver. They really liked us and what I really like about the company is they don't just hand out franchises. If you hand them $50,000 it doesn't mean you're going to get a franchise. They are very picky in terms of who they bring into the franchise system. They want to make sure it's a right fit for not only you and long-term growth but their growth as well.

We were awarded a franchise and for about three months I worked two jobs; the HR job and the JUNK job, which I did part-time. After about three months I said, "I can't do this," so I quit my HR job and I went to work for 1-800-GOT-JUNK full-time. I've been running it pretty much since day one.

I still consider myself the chief, cook, and bottle washer. I do it all.

**I read a quote where you said you never had this goal of becoming a millionaire, you just wanted the business to be successful.[1] Tell me about that.**

You always have those people, family and friends, the doubting Thomases, who joke: "You got into what kind of business?" and they laugh.

I just looked at it in terms of allowing me the flexibility to spend more time with my family. I never really thought about being a millionaire. I knew at that point that there were a few [1-800-GOT-JUNK] franchises reaching a million dollars in revenue per year, but I never really thought about it. I just honestly wanted to go to work everyday, earn a good living, provide for my family, and drive the business and make it successful. The next thing you know, I made a million dollars in revenue. It kind of all of a sudden hit me.

Starting off I never had the goal of being a business owner.

**In year two or three you didn't say to yourself, "I want to hit a million dollars this year"?**

No, no. We just wanted to continue to grow.

We were growing in the first couple of years at 30-35 percent.

**What were the toughest parts along this journey?**

I would say the most difficult time was going into business with partners. The original partners that my husband and I had didn't work out, so within the first year we severed our ties. Then in the last year-and-a-half, the relationship with my husband, now my ex-husband, that partnership was severed obviously in more than one way. That was difficult as well.

Other than the partnerships, there's never a dull moment. One day you can have an HR nightmare and then the next day you have an equipment nightmare.

We do have lots of days that are great. You just never know what's going to be thrown your way every morning when you get up.

**Even back when you graduated college, did you have specific goals of money you wanted to make or places you wanted to live? Did you write goals down?**

Up until about a couple of years ago I did not, but I'm a member of Entrepreneurs Organization (EO Boston).

I'm part of a forum group, which is in essence like a board of advisors. We meet on a monthly basis outside of the chapter event. About two years ago–we do an annual retreat–we worked on our lifetime goals.

I had business goals, my top three for the year, but in terms of both personal and professional [goals] I really never sat down to write an extensive list. We challenged each other two years ago to write our hundred lifetime goals. I thought it would be a piece of cake.

I got to about 30 and said, "This is hard." I put it away for a little bit and then as I would be talking to somebody they would say, "I went to Florida and swam with the dolphins," and I would think, "What a cool idea. I'd love to do that." So I added that to my lifetime goals.

Over the course of about two months I got my hundred and then some. I'm at 143 lifetime goals right now. I make it a point at least once a month to read them to see where I'm at because a goal is not a goal unless you write it down; it's just a dream. I look at them once a month to make sure that I'm staying on track with where I want to be in life.

**B:** *Up until a few years ago you had some ideas of what you wanted to accomplish and most of what drove you was an internal sense of being successful. Then recently you've started to put goals on paper. Is that fair to say?*

My mantra has always been–and this stems back to when I was divorced in 1993–"Failure is not an option for me. I am a survivor."

When I got divorced in 1993, I had four small children and an OK paycheck. I said, "I need to provide for my family." I will do whatever I have to do to survive.

**You also had another quote that I read: "By having education, drive and passion for business, any woman can succeed at anything regardless of the industry."**[1]

Oh absolutely. I am a female in a male-dominated industry.

A couple of years ago when I first hit a million dollars I was invited into the Top Performance Club. Once a year they go on a four-day retreat. I went to the first one and I was the only female out of about 22 of us. I thought, "This is amazing. I'm in a male-dominated industry and I can do the same things these guys are doing, if not better."

I thought about it and said, "It's because I love what I'm doing. I have the passion. I have the drive and it doesn't matter that I'm a female." As long as you have the passion and the drive, you can do anything you set your mind to.

**B:** *It sounds like even though you have your revenue goals and you're always trying to improve it, you're still not driven by the revenue. You're driven by creating something successful and making it better.*

I would say that that's an accurate statement.

**You mentioned your high school teacher; that wasn't necessarily a former mentor relationship. Did you have any other relationships like that or formal mentor relationships?**

No, I didn't. I've had a lot of teachers and professors along the way, but nobody with whom to have a once a month sit down, heart to heart discussion.

I've done a lot of reading. I try to attend a lot of conferences and listen to different people speak. I recently was in Arizona and heard Jim Collins speak. He talked about his book *Good to Great* and how now those companies have gone from good to great to good to extinct and how they got there. A lot of it hit home.

## What have you learned from your failures?

I'm glad you asked that question because sometimes people will ask, "What have you failed at?"

I don't look at failures as failures. I look at failures as learning experiences. I guess you [could] say that my two marriages failed; I don't look at them as failures. I look at them as they each offered me an opportunity. If I hadn't gotten married the second time, I wouldn't be in the business that I'm in today.

In both of them I learned to be a lot more independent. I've learned how to do things around the house myself. I've learned that I can run the business by myself. I don't need that business partner. I just work a little bit harder. I don't necessarily have somebody to spring ideas on, but that's where my forum comes in.

So you learn from failures. You can't look at it as, "I've failed." You can't dwell on it. You always have to make lemonade out of lemons. I know that's so cliché, but it's so true.

## As you started to build the business how did you balance time with your family and how do you still balance time with your family?

Now it's a little bit more challenging because my kids are older and they've got jobs, they've got things that they're doing. Obviously teenagers like to spend more time with their friends than they do with their parents, but family is important to me.

In today's day and age families don't sit down and have dinner anymore, so it's a requirement at my house. Every Sunday we have dinner at my house. Yeah, the boys argue sometimes, but we sit together as a family.

Then one of my goals that I've written down is each month to have a date night with one of my boys. Each boy has a date night, one-on-one, with mom and then once a week I try to have dinner with my kids outside of the Sunday dinner. And working with them helps, but that's a little difficult when you don't see eye to eye.

It's important to do things with your kids because when you don't that's when kids tend to get into a lot of trouble.

**Did you ever have a success system that you followed or did you just follow your heart?**

Success system in terms of business?

**B:** *Business or personal.*

I think being a woman it's just been intuition with me. Like I said before, failure's not an option. In terms of getting to where I am today, a lot of hard work and intuition.

**What's your greatest joy? What do you enjoy doing in life?**

Besides making my kids happy, putting smiles on people's faces. I grew up in a lower income household and I know the smile my mother put on my face when I was growing up, [I] know that she had to work a lot of hours to put me through ice skating lessons; it wasn't cheap. I like to give back to people in one way or another.

**How would you describe your passion?**

It's hard to explain. For me, it's a twinkle in my eye. I thrive on it.

I know it's crazy, but I love going to work everyday. The people that I work with have become family.

**What's your belief system? Do you follow an organized religion? Do you have your own variation?**

I was raised Catholic. I go periodically, but I'm not your type of person that only goes on Christmas and Easter because I used to complain about those people all the time.

I pray a lot; every night. I pray for my family, my friends, etc. I try to get to church on a regular basis, not every week, but on a regular basis.

## What should people who want to be successful know?

I did a radio interview and the same question was asked of me. It was basically for women who wanted to start over and get into business.

Unless you're passionate about what you do, don't do it. You have to have the passion for what you're doing to be successful at it. If you just go to a job everyday, you're not going to put the effort into it. If you don't have faith in yourself, you're not going to be successful. You have to believe in yourself as well as be passionate about the job that you're taking on.

**B:** *When did your passion for 1-800-GOT-JUNK develop?*

It was in the interview stages. I think it was April of 2003 when I went up to Vancouver and interviewed. I was blown away by the company, the culture, and the vision. I thought, "I really want to be a part of this organization." I was amazed.

I knew at that point it wasn't a done deal. We went back home that weekend and I thought, "I can't wait until the phone call on Monday. I'm going to be disappointed if they don't offer us a franchise." I prayed all week and I'm like, "Please let this work out." I really love the organization.

## What is success in your mind?

Success is being happy. You don't have to have a lot of money to be successful. I wish I had a million dollars in the bank. Yeah, I do a million plus in revenue every year, but money doesn't make people happy. Material things don't make you happy.

I'm happy with myself. I love my kids. I love my work. To me that's happy. Plus my feet hit the floor every morning, which is a great thing.

**You said you have an entrepreneurial spirit and you're always looking for a challenge; would you say you have a restless spirit?**

If you want to call it that, yeah. In my experience, the entrepreneurs that I have known always have that next pan in the fire in the back of their minds.

I have three business ventures in the back of my mind that I could possibly be working on for the next few years.

**What would you say are your greatest successes?**

I've got four, well-behaved, well-mannered children. My children are four of my successes.

Obviously, my business.

It's hard to say. I think my entire life has been a success. I've faced a lot of challenges over the last 45 years, but I guess the success has been overcoming those challenges. I can't pinpoint one success.

**What else would you like people to know?**

You can be successful at anything you want to be as long as you have the passion and the drive for it. Life isn't easy. Business isn't easy. It's just what you make of it.

I don't know if you've ever seen the movie *The Secret*. You have to get it. It's very powerful. It's all about the power of positive thinking and the law of attraction. If you tend to think bad thoughts and bad things, you're going to attract bad things. If you think about good things all the time, you're going to attract good things.

I highly recommend watching the video or getting the CD. I have the CD's in my car and I put them on every day.

**Bonus Question**: Why do you do what you do?

Oh, lots of reasons. It's fun. Flexibility. I never want to go back to corporate America. Yes, the pay was good. It wasn't fun.

I love going to work every day. You make your day, you make the most of it.

You can either make someone rich or you can make yourself rich. I don't mean rich in terms of money, rich in everything, the important things.

****

## Millionaire 20 Rob Emrich

Serial Entrepreneur: Founder, Road of Life; Founder, Boundaryless Brands; Co-Founder BULX.com; Co-Founder, Speakersite.com

www.BULX.com, www.Speakersite.com

Engaged

Bachelor's of Arts in Innovation, Entrepreneurship, Science and Reason

*Peter Galvin, a friend and former co-worker, referred me to Rob.*

*Rob had a successful career at a young age as a social entrepreneur founding and running a non-profit that generated $70M in social return on investment. In the intervening years he turned to business, creating several companies worth seven figures.*

## What did you want to do when you grew up?

I loved politics. I still do. I probably wanted to be a politician.

## As you got into college you decided to study what and why?

I was pre-med in college and my major was philosophy. I thought about becoming a doctor. I took philosophy because I loved it and I could pretty much major in anything I wanted to and be pre-med.

I ended up not going into medicine. The further along in college I got, the more I realized it wasn't the lifestyle I wanted to lead and I didn't think I'd be able to make as much of a difference as a professional practitioner as I would with a little bit more freedom.

I realized if I don't go into medicine, somebody else will. If I don't create a non-profit organization, it's not necessarily true that somebody else will. If I don't create a business, it's not necessarily true that somebody else will. [So that road] was a little bit more appealing.

## Did you ever have thoughts of going into business before you entered college?

No, I was pretty against it actually. It was something that I reticently later accepted about myself and my personality, that it was something I was good at and if I could harness the talents I have for that to do it in the right way, then it could still bring me happiness. That's my goal now.

*Note: Rob's sister Karen was three-years-old when she passed away from neuroblastoma, a non-preventable form of cancer.*

## How big of a part did your sister's cancer play in all of this?

A lot I think. When I was growing up, my parents had a yearly event for her at our synagogue. That was a really important event in my life. I learned a lot from my parents about the way that they handled that.

I always wanted to do something in memory of my sister for the rest of my life. I assumed it would be a lot later in life once I had the means to do it.

I started it in college when I certainly did not have the financial means to do it. I did it more through will than anything else.

My original idea was to start a non-profit organization to fund cancer research in my sister's memory. Around that same time, my mom had an issue with breast cancer, which turned out to be fine. I also had a cousin who died from a brain tumor. He was a young Rabbi and I saw his family going through a lot of the same things my family did. I thought, "I don't want to see this happen again. I want to do something that makes a difference in this particular issue and makes a substantive difference. Not just to create an organization to create an organization."

I sold my car and some of the stocks I was given from my grandparents when I was a kid. I hired a really good friend of mine and got to work on trying to make a difference in that fight. We moved into cancer prevention for children, specifically because there was absolutely no one doing it well and we knew there was a really big need. There was a lot of opportunity for us to do well.

**You were as busy as can be with classes and working in the cancer research lab and you started a company. You contacted the National Institutes of Health, hired somebody, and away you went?**

More or less. We didn't contact National Institute of Health to begin with, but we did contact other entities.

After years of work we came up with a program that solved a lot of the problems we were presented with, which was how to get to kids.

We chose to go through the classroom. We made our cancer prevention program relevant to math. The kids would count when they exercised. They would use math to figure out servings of vegetables and fruits per day. We integrated our program into history, science, math, and reading. Teachers had a way that they could accomplish what they were supposed to for their state academic content standards and also keep kids healthier in their classrooms. Those two things are much more closely aligned than people realize. Kids that are healthy learn better and perform better academically.

**What made you think that you would be successful and that this would be viable?**

I didn't think of it in terms of, "Could I do this?" I actually felt the opposite; it didn't feel like I had very much of a choice. At no point in that venture did I consider the question, "Can I?" I just knew that I had to. So that was the attitude that I took, that I had no other choice but to make this work.

That experience was much more difficult than starting the companies I've started since then.

Since I was a kid I've put myself in a position where I have to succeed. Once I told people what I was going to do, once I sold my car and stocks and didn't have anything else, I wasn't really in a position to let this fail. That wasn't an option. So I worked a tremendous amount, and everybody on our staff worked a tremendous amount, for those first years just getting it to work and getting it viable.

There were times we had major setbacks and I thought to myself, "That didn't work out. Let me think about why it didn't work out. What lessons can I learn from this?" Through that process we were usually able to reorganize, maybe change gears a little bit, and make things work.

**As you started moving along this path and building the non-profit, did you have people that you looked to and said, "They've done X, Y, or Z successfully, I should pattern a little bit of what I do after them"?**

I really wish that I had had more people like that because there are not very many. One of the biggest issues in the world of [social] entrepreneurship–and it's getting better–is there are not very many people to pattern off of.

I'm still supportive of that field because I think more people would do it if they understood how, if there were more of a road map for them or even more of a community where there was some camaraderie and a place to commiserate about some of the difficulties.

It's a difficult thing and there's not a lot of precedence for it. People have done it, but there wasn't something like that for me and I wish that there was.

**B:** *Because it was non-profit or do you mean in the entrepreneurial world?*

Because it was non-profit.

When we were seeking funding, the first place I went wasn't foundations. I went to for-profit angel investor groups to explain what we were trying to do. I wasn't trying to prove a point, I just figured that that was the easiest place to go and most realistic place to get funding. They had absolutely no interest.

In retrospect it seems absurd, but that's where we went originally. We made our way towards more traditional non-profit entities like community foundations and government grants.

I always just approached it from a perspective of how can we get from here to where we want to be? And I didn't really care so much how we got there.

**Did you set forth a plan? Did you write down specifics of what you wanted the foundation to accomplish?**

Yes, for sure. Everything I start, I start with a plan.

**Do you have written down goals at the start?**

Yes.

**B:** *Do you still work off of goals?*

You got it. I write down goals for myself for the year, for five years, or ten years.

**B:** *Every project you're involved in, you have specific goals?*

Yes and a plan on how to get there. It changes frequently, but I always have a plan.

**B:** *The plan changes or the goals change?*

Sometimes both.

**B:** *What do they change based on?*

The circumstances, they're unique. Adaptability is a huge asset when you're working on a project. If it's a business, a specific project of a business, or a non-profit, you need to be willing to change.

That's a difficult line to walk because you have to be cognizant of what your original goals were, but at the same time it takes some courage to say, "This isn't working. Why? Can I modify this to make it work better?"

Sometimes people get so caught up in not changing. Some people don't change what their plan is or what their intended goal was based on the circumstances.

It's this hole that people experience, wanting a defined set of activities to get to a certain goal, which, in my experience, is not the way that the world works. I'd like to have a defined set of activities: "If I do this, then this result will happen," but in business, in social entrepreneurship, I don't think it's like that.

I think that's why not everybody gets into business. It's difficult to deal with that uncertainty. It's really difficult to change. It's difficult to process a lot of that.

**You started Road to Life trying to think about, "What's going to make an impact here? What can we start with?"**

Right.

**B:** *You figured it out as you went along.*

Exactly.

**B:** *How did you know what to present to angel investors and foundations? How did you know what they were looking for?*

We certainly didn't know what they were looking for or else I never would have gone in front of a for-profit angel investor.

I read a lot. Whenever there's something I don't know, I read about it.

The way that I learned about programming and web marketing, which is what I do now professionally, is by having to do it for Road of Life. At the time it was really expensive to hire those types of people and we didn't have the budget for it so I learned about it. I went to a coffee shop and read a 600 page book on how to set up a mail server and then came back into the office within the next two days and did it.

We live in a period of time where people are happy to share the secrets of their success or how they did something. That information is out there; almost all the information you could possibly ever want is available in books or online now.

**When you were putting together your curriculum, did you hire professional curriculum developers, or did you just hire people you knew who you thought would be great for it?**

At the beginning it was a mix.

Now it's professionals that have a background in it. We didn't do that originally because we didn't have the budget. We needed to get to the point where we had something that was workable, that we could distribute, which then allowed us to eventually hire professionals to do it.

**What kind of heartaches and disappointments have you experienced?**

There are a couple of big ones that I can think of, at least for Road of Life.

We were working with a large, national non-profit on a partnership to do our program in all of the schools that they were in. We got far into the process and they ended up not doing our program because they got a grant to do another program.

Every single setback has turned into an opportunity for us. We expanded beyond just that one partner and we went toward a much broader approach. That certainly led to greater success for us.

Another setback was with a local professional sports team. We had a large fundraiser scheduled at their arena and we lost a significant amount of money because they went on strike. We did some press about it, which wasn't the best idea because they got pretty upset with us. But that experience forced us to diversify our funding, which we did, and we learned from it as well.

I don't regret making any of those mistakes. I think we're better off for it.

Bad things happen to everybody and my philosophy is that in a lot of ways those are gifts that you're given; they are an opportunity to learn. I know that sounds hokey, but I believe when bad things happen it's a gift that you're being presented if you look at it in the right way.

That's the way that I look at my sister's death. I look at it in terms of her giving me a gift. I was able to start a non-profit organization that I learned a tremendous amount from and met amazing people through and have a deep sense of meaning in my life because of.

When I was 18-years-old, I lived in Israel for six months. I survived a terrorist attack in downtown Jerusalem, which is a pretty terrible thing to go through. It took a while to get over it, but once I finally did, that experience made me stronger. It made me appreciate the political situation in the Middle East in a much different way. It made everything a lot more real for me in ways that I didn't anticipate. It gave me more of an edge as a person.

I really push myself hard. That experience pushed me to start every day thinking, "What can I do today?" because I thought that I could've died. I wake up and I feel anxious–antsy–to get something done right away.

**Did you, anywhere along the process and up to today, have a mentor or a role model?**

Maybe by committee.

I've learned a lot of different things from a lot of different people. There have been a lot of people who have helped me get to where I am, but I don't have one clear mentor, which I wish I did.

**Now that I'm at the end of the interviews one of the clear themes is that each of you has done things your own way; you've taken your own path.**

**You knew you were at point A and you wanted to be at point B and you just did something. You didn't seek others' advice. You didn't wait for them to tell you it was OK or how they would do it. None of you had the one individual mentor. If you did, you would have gone in much different directions. You wouldn't have followed your heart, which has led you to exactly what you've got today.**

I think you're right.

One of the reasons I've been successful is I'm not afraid of anything. I don't wait for somebody to give me permission to do something, ever. If I see an opportunity, think it through, come up with a plan, and it looks like it's something that's worthwhile, I start it.

There are things I start and it's like starting a book. If I read 50 pages of a book, I make sure to finish it. If I read 40 pages and think to myself, "This isn't a very good book," I put it down and won't hold it against myself. That's how I feel about a lot of the potential businesses and projects I start. The only way to really know if something might work is get it started.

I know a lot of people who wait to start. They think they have to have everything figured out in their mind before they get going. They plan and they plan and they plan. Then they start working on it and immediately something changes and it's not in their plans they worked out so intricately in their mind or on paper and that stops them.

I look at opportunities a little bit differently now. I look at it from a visual perspective; how much space is there? Whenever I'm looking at an opportunity, I know everything is going to change, probably dramatically, so I think to myself, "Is there room for me to go in a different direction in this opportunity? Is there a lot of space here? Is there a big market here? If and when we end up doing something that's different than what the original concept was, is there still room for us to make mistakes?" Then I ultimately come up with something that's workable and successful.

No one likes giving up; I think you just have to change your frame to realize you're not giving it up. It's just that priorities change. If you're not flexible enough to deal with that, you're going to miss a lot more things, a lot more opportunities. Life's too short to not take advantage of the best opportunities in front of you.

**What is your passion?**

I have a real desire not just for change, but also to see things done better.

What gets me going is fixing things and in the process building something that has a life of its own. I like that feeling a lot, that really gets me going.

**What's the belief system that guides your life religiously and or philosophically?**

I don't really have one. I was raised in a very religious Jewish household. That's a major part of my family and extended family and culturally that's something that continues to be important to me, but from a spirituality perspective it's not relevant to me.

A lot of [my belief system] goes back to the point that what people perceive as hardship is actually in a lot of ways a gift for them. That in a lot of ways has to do with maybe why we're here and why we're alive; that through that mechanism of coping, you have a much richer life experience.

Every venture that I start is, for lack of a better word, a process of learning how to cope and deal and adjust to that challenge. That's what makes my life more invigorating.

**If you were to go back to any part along your journey, what would you do differently?**

There are a couple of things.

One, I think I would have made less specific promises at the beginning of starting Road of Life knowing what I know now.

Also, when you have your head down and you're working on something, which is the way I feel when I'm working on something intently, you can alienate people who are close to you, whether they're co-workers or friends.

I've lost friends–not a lot, but a few–in the process of creating Road of Life and some of these companies. It's impossible to please everybody, but I think there are some things I could have done differently to please some people more.

**What part of what you do is most enjoyable?**

I feel like my life is really cyclical because of the way I've reached out and accomplished, reached out and accomplished.

There are a couple of exciting moments in that process. One is when you feel like you've figured out a way that you can get to that goal. It's not usually the final plan, it doesn't usually work out that way, but when you start to see a clear path about how you can get there, that is a really exciting time for me.

Then the afterglow once you've accomplished something, for a short period of time, is really fun as well. And it's back to work laying out another goal and moving towards the next step.

Those are the most exciting points.

The third one is right at the beginning, when you're first laying out a new game plan. I really like those times as well.

I take time once a year to reflect on the year. For a long time I've gone to Mexico for a few weeks in December to think about what I've been able to do that year, what my plan is for the next year, and what's important to me. There are times of reflecting, especially when I've been able to do something that's relevant and important to me during that year. I really enjoy those times as well.

**What have been your greatest successes?**

Road of Life is the first in my mind. If I died tomorrow I would feel good about my life. I'd feel like I had done something that has meaning to me and other people, and built something that was beyond me. It's one of my biggest accomplishments so far.

I'm involved with the next one right now with the businesses that I'm building and creating value [in].

I honestly don't care so much about money—I'm not the type of guy to go out and buy big things—but I feel like it's a resource that allows you to accomplish so much more with whatever you're trying to do philanthropically, politically, or influence in business. The material value of the money is absolutely worthless. It's just not something I care about. The other things that come along with it are.

**It was never your goal to become a millionaire?**

It's never been my goal to become a millionaire so I can drive a nice car and have a nice house. It's my goal to have resources to affect the change that I want to see, to put myself in a position to work on philanthropic causes that are really important to me, and to work on political causes. When I talk about being wealthy or being a millionaire, that's what I think of.

**How do you define success?**

Success has to be a relative idea of what you can do, how much meaning you can provide for other people based on your capabilities and your capacity.

*An update on Rob:*

*He has sold some of his companies and was last seen taking a great vacation...*

****

# Millionaire 21 Richard Zuschlag

Founder, Acadian Companies. Currently serves as CEO and Chairman of the Board.

www.acadian.com

Married, three children

Bachelor's in Electrical Engineering

*Colleen Andrus, wife of Millionaire 7 Vance Andrus, put me in touch with Richard. They had known each other for several years through the Lafayette, LA, community.*

# Tell me about your growing up years.

I was raised 60 miles north of Pittsburgh in the small community of Greenville, Pennsylvania. I'm the oldest of four children. My mom and dad were very hard workers. My dad delivered milk for a dairy. I used to help him in the summer time. My parents taught me the value of work. I used to bag groceries, weed shrubbery, paint, and take care of people's yards.

I was 17-years-old painting the outdoors of a radio station when the announcer walked off the job. The boss man came outside and asked me if I would play records because there was no one in the station who could do it. I got started in a broadcasting career.

I learned how to do news, be a disc jockey, do classical music, rock-n-roll, country-western, and broadcast live remotes. My great grandfather was an auctioneer and I think that it helped me to learn how to be a promoter, somebody who could market or sell something.

In that hometown there was an ambulance crisis when the funeral homes quit doing ambulance rides. A gentleman who had returned from WWII remembered that in Belgium they sold subscriptions to underwrite the cost of parking an ambulance in a small community. They were selling subscriptions in my hometown to underwrite the cost of a good quality ambulance. The radio station was helping promote the sale of the subscriptions. I got involved in talk radio where callers would want to know why they needed to be a member of the ambulance company.

I later left Greenville to travel to Washington D.C., where I attended Capital College and got a bachelor's degree in electrical engineering. I thought I wanted to be a broadcasting engineer. I was somewhat concerned about the Vietnam War when I graduated in 1970 and ended up taking a deferred draft draw with Westinghouse in Baltimore.

After being there for six months they told me they were going to send me on a field assignment to Saudi Arabia to teach them how to operate microwave systems, or to Lafayette, Louisiana, where they were experimenting with re-educating technical engineers like me on how to do social work so the company could receive federal money.

I chose Lafayette, Louisiana, and came down to teach disadvantaged young people who had not completed high school. When I got to Lafayette on July 22, 1970, it was the hottest day of the year. Being from Pennsylvania, I was not used to the humid, hot climate.

For the first several months I thought I made the worst mistake in my life. I thought I'd be better off if I had gone to Saudi Arabia because in Lafayette they all talked funny and had highly seasoned food, [the] mosquitoes [are] as big as houses, and they all went to school in flat-bottomed canoes. I was not really happy and I thought several times about quitting my job.

At the end of the one year assignment, when they got ready to send me back up to Westinghouse, I had fallen so much in love with the way of the Cajun people, the family atmosphere, and attitude of "let the good times roll" that I quit my Westinghouse job and founded Acadian Ambulance patterned after the membership program that I first learned about up in Greenville, Pennsylvania.

I started the company with $2,500 and two partners. We financed two ambulances through GMAC at 18 percent interest and I drove the ambulance for the first couple years in the daytime and dispatched at night.

I had this passion to save every life I could. I hired Vietnam medics. I thought it was a shame the cement truck and a beer truck had better two-way radio systems than the ambulances did with the hospitals. So I built a big part of my company based on a great communication infrastructure so that people could communicate with each other and knew what was going on.

And because I was saving lives, I had to create a sense of urgency. When somebody called and needed help, you had to move quickly.

When professors from the University of Tennessee came to study our company a number of years ago to find out why we had been so successful, one of their points was that we seemed to have taken this sense of urgency on saving lives and put it on the business side of the company, to where everything that we did created a sense of urgency to get everything done today and not let anything wait until tomorrow.

I look at this as an opportunity where a Yankee came south and fell in love with the area and the people and took the opportunity to organize some of these Southerners who had great loyalty and wanted to be able to help others. I just think I was at the right place at the right time.

I had a very hard work ethic. The first year I would sleep in a sleeping bag at the office. It was a lot of hard work. I believe that passion for the work and the sense of urgency helped a lot.

One of my weaknesses was I was not a very good planner. I have been forced in recent years to plan 18-24 months ahead. In the olden days, we were doers. Lots of people sat around and planned and never did anything. We were doers.

The phone rang and somebody was dying, we responded.

That's the same way we ran the business part of it. The next-door county—down here we called them parishes—called and said, "We have a problem. We can't afford our ambulance service anymore and you're doing a good job in Lafayette. Will you come take over our ambulance service?" Rather than planning on what areas we should go to, we just went wherever the phone rang to go.

When you look back on it, it might not have been the best economic way to make money because some of the rural areas didn't have enough patients for them to pay for the cost of the ambulance. The bank kept loaning me money and finally said, "You can't keep breaking even. You have to make a reasonable profit to invest in future capital."

I honestly think that the first 20 years if we had sat down and put a budget together to figure out how much money we could make we would have failed. But because we were so naïve and innocent and were trying to save every life we could and just wanted to break even and provide a reasonable salary for everybody, we actually became successful and made money.

336

I have been criticized as being too much of a micro-manager. That's one of my weaknesses and I'm trying to let go of some of that, but it's the minding of the details that makes the difference. Making sure that you're getting those batteries for the defibrillators charged so you don't have a mishap, acquiring diesel ambulances and not gasoline so you don't break down on an emergency. If we make a mistake, we'll learn from it and not make it over again.

I surrounded myself with some of the most loyal people a person could have working on their team. They may not have all had the formal education, but their work ethic, their loyalty, and their honesty were uppermost in our success.

I came down here as a Presbyterian. After five years of working around the clock, I finally met a nurse when I was driving the ambulance and got married. I converted to Catholicism. Seventy-five percent of the people in this part of the state are French Catholic and I truly believe that part of the success of Acadian is that 80 percent of my management staff graduated from Catholic high schools. Their morals, their forgiveness, their Christian attitude toward each other, and particularly their work ethic, were unbelievable.

You don't find harder working people than down here. I used to admire how hard they would work, but then how much fun they would have when they got off of work. These people know how to live.

I always went out of my way to be very demanding, very much into everybody's business to make sure things were being done right, but also to be a great giving person.

Those qualities of sharing with the employees and not keeping it all for myself helped motivate them to help me create a very successful organization that continues to grow. It's gotten more formalized and there is more strategic planning now, but in those early days, we all stood in each other's weddings, we're Godfathers and Godmothers to each other's kids.

If I were to write down all of the qualities that I had that made me successful, it would be hard to list them all because some of them are intuition, some of them were taught by my parents.

I had a pretty tough mom. When she told you to go make the bed, you'd better be moving in 30 seconds or the broom was coming after you. It's the same way when the 911 phone rings: you better jump into that ambulance and get that patient and not dilly-dally around. She always had that sense of urgency that when she spoke you better move or she's going to get after you. My dad was very hard working. They pretty much gave everything they had to raise the four kids.

I've stayed so busy that I don't kick back, take my shoes off, and say, "Look where I've arrived and look what I've done." I just don't think of that, but I had a doctor say to me after we went duck hunting [one time], "Do you ever sit back and think the spark you started 40 years ago, what that's done in terms of how many people are still walking around today that wouldn't be if it hadn't been for you?"

When I travel around the state people always come up and talk to me about us having done something with one of their relatives, and it just seems to me that almost everywhere I go somebody wants to tell me. I'm pleased to say that most of the stories have very good outcomes, or in the relative's mind or the patient's mind they think we did a good job. That gives you a lot of passion to have that kind of work.

One of my big challenges right now is to get this younger generation to have more responsibility and better attitudes. It's hard to teach them why they have to be at work on time and why they have to have a clean ambulance and why they have to take time to be nice to their patients.

The management team places a lot of emphasis on coaching and encouraging this new generation of workers. It's more difficult with the younger workforce today than it used to be.

## What is your passion?

I don't know how to explain this, but I get excited to come to work every morning. I love what I do. I'm 64-years-old and I just love getting up and coming to work.

I've enjoyed taking young people and nurturing them, training them, seeing them blossom, and getting them to move up in the organization to have a better quality of life for their family and for their children. I like to promote them being civic-minded and trying to help give back to the community that's been so supportive of us.

I enjoy making a positive change in people's lives. Lots of satisfaction comes out of that. As I've matured and grown older, I'm not quite as nit-picky or demanding as I used to be. I used to really push our people hard.

## Your passion is to help improve people's lives, but that was not why you started Acadian, was it?

The reason I started it was for me to stay here in Lafayette. After initially not liking Lafayette, I fell in love with it. I was simply looking for a business that would let me stay down here and work.

When I look back at the pictures of me being 23-years-old I wonder how I could have ever convinced the city of Lafayette to let me do this. One of the other two partners was older, and they both lived here. We were told no twice, that we were too young. The third time I sat in the mayor's office from 4:00 p.m. to 7:00 p.m. I wouldn't leave until I could talk to him. I got him to call the mayor in Greenville, Pennsylvania, to see how that membership program had worked.

I had so much persistence. I loved to finagle things and get things done that nobody else could do. It's hard for people to tell me "no" because I find a way. I'm a very persistent person. I sometimes maybe go a little too far, but if what I'm trying to get is right for the community and it's not self-serving to me, I can usually get it if I work hard enough at it.

## How do you define success?

Creating a better community with better jobs, with happy people, and being able to make a decent living. I don't think it's all about money. I just worked real hard and the moneymaking came by accident.

It's only the last eight or ten years that we tried to put together an annual budget and have a profit and loss statement. Up to that time it was just hard work every year and every cent I got was always spent on making the equipment better, paying the people more, and providing better benefits. I was always satisfied just to break even and make a decent salary.

I loved to have staff meetings with the top vice presidents and say, "It took a Yankee to come south and organize all you Cajuns."

And a couple of them would say, "And us Cajuns made you some money."

They're exactly right. They did make some money for me and for themselves, too.

## Whatever made you think before you started the company that you were going to be successful at it?

I never had any great plan for expansion or being successful. I just wanted to stay in Lafayette and have a little bit.

When I first started I thought if I ever had three or four ambulances and just had Lafayette Parish, I'd be content. I never really thought about trying to do all the other expansion. I just wanted to make sure we got enough money in to pay our bills. That was my success.

I was criticized later on for not having an organized plan for growth. We just answered the phone and when they wanted us to come, that's when we expanded. We probably could have done it in a better, different way.

**B:** *Who criticized you?*

Other business leaders have gone back and said, "You should've done this differently." "You should have done that differently." Or "You should have had more planning" or "You should have been more on the offense and gone out and looked for strategic growth patterns and not just waited for the phone to ring to see where they wanted you."

I tell you one thing, when they called and wanted you, it wasn't too hard to grow because you didn't have to fight any politicians. You just went in, opened up, and started providing service.

I am not perfect and I'm trying to learn some new methods and make minor changes in my behavior in the way I run this place, because I'm trying to be more of a consensus builder and leader rather than a dictator. But I've got a lot of mentors that say, "It's OK for you to make minor tweaks, but all the things that you've done for 40 years can't be all that bad; look at the success you've created."

I did notice as I was running the show how many other people were trying to get started in different kinds of businesses and how much time they spent in planning sessions. They spent all their time planning and never getting anything done.

That was one of my bright spots; I was a doer. When I got up in the morning, I started doing.

I taught my people that you have to have your list of things to do written out early in the morning. You can't go to work and just start rambling around looking for something to do. You have to be organized and know these are my tasks today and I'm not going home until I get them done.

### Did you have a formal mentor?

No. These were elders in the community that I came to rely on when I'd get in a pinch.

I learned pretty early on that no one person was right and it was better for me to talk to three to five of them that I really trusted and then mix it together and formulate my own plan. They all had their weaknesses and strengths and I learned how to sort through those.

I would share concerns or problems I was having and get their informal advice on how they would handle it. That was good for me.

**You were so naïve that you thought you could save every person's life and that naiveté drove innovation and pioneering. You have become one of the world's foremost authorities on delivery of ambulance service. You found your passion of saving lives and helping people. Is that fair to say?**

Yup. That's what happened.

I just have such great excitement to see young people grow with me, to see people who may not have had the chance for a formal education to run this company. The president of this company started out as an 18-year-old ambulance driver.

He is so organized, so fair with his people, so multi-task capable, very innovative; my best friend. It's very hard to have a close friend like that. We work very well together. Better in our older age than our younger age. We used to spar a lot.

The guy that runs my air division is my best friend. He's been with me for 37 years. There are just a lot of things that have happened when you look at the history of what we've done together.

**As you were younger and then as you were building the business, did you ever expect or want to become a millionaire?**

No.

**Did you ever have written down goals, concrete financial goals?**

No.

**Did you ever have a system of success in mind that you followed or did you make it up as you went along?**

Made it up as I went along.

## How did you balance time with your family as you were building your business?

I didn't. I did a very poor job. For the first 15 years of my business I very seldom saw my wife or kids. She raised the kids without me being around. She is a very good Catholic mother who did a great job, but I put my business ahead of my family. I get a little emotional talking about it.

I certainly have made up for it in the last several years. I put my family first now.

I think about me being so busy that I didn't even go with my son for his golf match. When he was a senior he went to the state golf tournament and I did go to that.

My whole attitude changed while they were in college and I've been with them for everything. In fact, I think now they think sometimes I'm too much of a pest because I want to do too much with them.

## If you were to go back, what would you do differently? What have you second-guessed yourself on?

I would've tried to spend more time with my family in the beginning and I would've tried to do a better job delegating responsibility. I tried to be involved in almost every decision that was made concerning the business. I wish I would have done a better job letting go of some of that responsibility and assigning it to others. It would have created a lot less stress for me and the others on my team.

The people who are with me now–like the in-house attorney who I love who has only been here 12 years or the doctor I hired who's only been here 12 years–don't have the same work ethic as the rest of us used to have. They want to spend more time at the ballpark and with their kids and I've learned now how to accept that with grace and not be bitter about it.

## As you were building the business what kind of salary did you pay yourself?

First year, 40 years ago, I paid myself $800 a month. My goal was always to make my grandma's age in salary–she was 96 when she passed–and I did not make it until 1988. I'd been here for almost 16 years before I made $96,000.

I didn't get into the category I'm in now until three or four years ago. I used to not make more than $400,000 or $500,000 a year. In 2004, it started getting up to $750,000 and then the last couple of years it's gone over a million.

## What do you want to accomplish between now and retirement?

I want to help grow the company in an organized manner without going too fast.

I've got some people on my board, some of my younger people that would like to see me be more aggressive in growing. I like to keep my growth around 10 to 12, maybe 15 percent. I believe that growing too much too fast would comprise the high standard of service we provide. I'm trying to balance growth with quality – ensuring that the services we provide are the best they can be is paramount to expansion in my mind.

I want to see if we can make things a little bit more efficient and get through this healthcare crisis we're in right now. I'd like to be creative and see if I couldn't set up some medical taxi cabs that could respond to non-life threatening calls, do some screening, and take these people to the appropriate non-emergent clinic and not pile all these 911 people into the emergency room that are just using the 911 system to get access to healthcare and creating a real barrier for those dealing with life-threatening emergencies. I'd like to try some new models of how we transport patients and differentiate between those that think they're emergent and those that are really life threatening.

I'd like to use tele-health and programs like that to be more technical in the pre-hospital care area. I'm looking at some other technology devices that will give us a better response to the real emergencies.

[I'm also] trying to keep current maps in the ambulances to give us more efficiency. Technology at a cost effective price is also important to me.

**Do you think you would have experienced the growth you did if you hadn't authored the ESOP [Employee Stock Ownership Plan]?**

No. The ESOP drives employees to be more efficient and innovative in what they're doing and I think they like being employee-owners. There is a real sense of pride in ownership and that pride permeates the workplace. And it probably has tempered me to be more conscientious on how the annual budget is determined.

I'm very careful about how we spend our money. I recognize there's an obligation to 3000 employees and all their families, probably 8,000 people. I think about my employees and their families in almost every decision that I make at work. Their welfare is what's most important to me.

**What part of what you do is most enjoyable?**

I've got too many parts that I like. It would be hard for me to put them all together.

I like the Tuesday morning executive committee meetings where we discuss all the major issues and try to build consensus on which direction we're going to go with hospitalization for the employees or salary adjustments or growth or risk management.

I like the art of politics. I like being friends with the Democrats and the Republicans to place myself in the best position to maximize my Medicare and Medicaid reimbursements.

I'm fortunate enough to have a very nice duck lodge on the coast. I get great enjoyment out of entertaining people and bringing them together for camaraderie and fellowship, card playing and hunting. That's a big joy of mine.

I will spend around 35 days at the duck lodge during duck season with employees who get a chance to come hunting because they won a contest; senior management; district attorneys; hospital CEOs; newspaper publishers; TV owners; and state and federal politicians. I get a big kick out of doing all that. That's a lot of fun.

I love solving problems. Because I'm fairly good at it it's helped increase the popularity of my company. Normally, a little ambulance company doesn't get the kind of recognition we get.

**Would you say your journey has been relatively easy or hard?**

In recent years, easier. I was too hard on myself in the beginning. I pushed people too hard and caused relationship problems.

There were some times, not in the last 10 years, but in the first several, where I got discouraged and thought maybe it would be better for me to go back home to Pennsylvania and run that little radio station. That was my dream, to run that radio station. I'm glad I never did that.

I'm glad that I have learned how to have a better attitude. [An employee] taught me it's important to get up in the morning and spend some time in meditation and prayer and to start the day out in a very positive attitude and convey that positive attitude to all the people you come around. Since I've started doing that my life has become a whole lot better.

I used to let things strangle me and didn't handle them in a positive way and took it out on some of my co-workers. I've learned how to handle that in a better way now and I'm proud of that. That was a weakness I had.

I ran the place more on emotions than I did on data and I'm glad I've gotten away from that. I credit some of my co-workers for helping me through some of those difficult times.

**What have you learned from your failures?**

No matter how good you are at what you do, you're always going to fail and I come back to my persistence. When I fail, it's like the mouse in the maze; I turn around and go back the other way until I find my way out. Sometimes I'll fail two or three times, but when I am determined I will stay after it.

Over the last couple years I've developed "Z's Ps." My Z's ["Z" for Zuschlag] Ps are Persistence, Positive Attitude, Passion, Politeness, Practice, Patience, Pride, and Prayer, which all lead to Prosperity.

I love when I speak to talk about Z's Ps because I can expound on each characteristic and how I learned it. While some of that came to me naturally, when I put it in writing I was able to practice some of the ones I was weak in, particularly patience.

**What should people who want to be successful know?**

You have to have a vision or a dream and be passionate about it. You have to go after your dreams more out of passion than financial motivation. Too many people today sit around and try to figure out how much money they can make and how fast they can make it.

You've got to make it the old fashioned way. You've got to get out there and work for it. If you're not greedy and just go out and try to make a decent living and treat your people right in terms of sharing with them, then you can be successful.

Some people think success is all about money. Success is about being happy.

**You say you have to have a vision and a passion to be successful. When you started your business you didn't have either one of those.**

You're right. I wanted to stay here in Lafayette. When I started the company it was more of a job for me than it was for a company that was going to make a lot of money one day.

I did not have a vision – I had a passion to stay here and then I had a passion to do the work once I started it.

I had lots of people tell me, "You were lucky." And I say, "Yes, but I made that luck by hard work."

I was lucky and I had a lot of good breaks, but nothing could take the place of hard work. Washing the ambulances, fixing the ambulances, dispatching, driving, paying the bills – it was a lot of hard work.

## What would you say your greatest success is?

Creating so many jobs for so many people in healthcare and saving so many lives.

When I look at the amount of people that we have saved or that are alive today, many of them wouldn't be there without the capability and the extraordinary heroism of our employees to save their lives. So I think that would be the great accomplishment.

It's probably easier to have passion for saving lives and making a better community than making bolts or cutting widgets. Not everybody can have that kind of a job, but whatever you're doing you can figure out how that's going to improve a situation even if it's just providing good, economic, stable jobs. That's good for our community, too.

**B:** *These other folks I've interviewed have worked hard and have stumbled into their passion as well and have just as much passion for the things they do as you do for what you do. That's the value of hard work.*

Yes. Nothing replaces hard work.

Too many of our young people today are trying to figure out how to make it big without all the hard work.

I have a nephew who came to live with me 15 years ago, then moved to Atlanta. He told me before he left that he was going to find a way to make a lot more money than I had but not have to work so hard for it.

I asked him how he was going to do that. He said, "I hope to be a good investor. I want to sit at a computer and invest other people's money."

I said, "Good luck."

Everybody's looking for the short way out, the easy way out, the fast way out.

\*\*\*\*

# Conclusion

Pretty fascinating yet normal people, huh? That's just it. Now you have the real story of how ordinary people create extraordinary success.

You're probably expecting a big conclusion to pull this all together, a final summary of my findings wrapped neatly together with a pretty bow to send you on your way.

It ain't gonna happen.

The book started with my observations, but the ending is about thoughts and conclusions that are far more valuable than mine – yours.

I hope you've had some thoughts of your own about what made these people successful. More importantly, though, I hope you've come up with some thoughts about your success – whatever that is for you.

Neither I nor the gurus can tell you how to create that success, but what I can tell you with reasonable certitude, because it seems consistent for at least these 21 entrepreneurial millionaires, is that when you work hard, patiently take life as it comes, do the things that work and don't beat yourself up over those that don't, and pay attention to that inner voice guiding you, you may find yourself at the right place at the right time to where you can wake up one day and realize that small, consistent efforts over time have brought you something pretty special.

Keep working hard whatever you do and good things will come.

Thanks for spending part of your success journey with 21 millionaires and me.

Cheers.

****

# Notes

## Chapter 1

1.      Dieter F. Uchtdorf, "The Way of the Disciple," *Ensign*, May 2009, 75–78

2.      Thomas S. Monson, "Seven Steps to Success with Aaronic Priesthood Youth," *Ensign*, Feb 1985, 22

## Chapter 2

1.      The Book of Mormon. 2 Nephi 28:30

2.      As quoted by Todd Goodsell, "Single in a Family-Oriented Church," *Ensign*, June 2011, 50

## Chapter 3

1.      Gina Schreck is a speaker, founder of Synapse 3Di, and a Digital Immigration Officer.    She is also past President of the Colorado Chapter of the National Speakers Association. www.synapse3di.com

2.      Ashley Andrus is President of Zoe Training & Consulting. www.zoetraining.com

## Millionaire 6 Steve Rosdal

1.      Theresa Byrne is 3rd Degree Black Belt in martial arts, a fitness instructor, personal trainer, motivational speaker, life/empowerment coach, and creator of "Finding Your Voice," a self-empowerment program for adults. www.umac.us

## Millionaire 12 John Simcox

1.      1 Timothy 6:10

## Millionaire 13 Bill Begal

1.     www.jewishvirtuallibrary.org/jsource/Judaism/nobels.html

## Millionaire 16 Lane Nemeth

1.     Laura Udall is Founder of ZÜCA and Donte Designs. www.dontedesigns.com

## Millionaire 19 Judith Briggs

1.     Cowen, Kristina. (March 15, 2007). *A Butcher, a Junk Hauler & a Professor - All Women, all Millionaires! Women millionaires tell how they did it.* PayScale. http://blogs.payscale.com/content/2007/03/a_butcher_a_jun.html

A very big THANK YOU to:

The Millionaires, Ashley Andrus, Theresa Byrne, Gina Schreck, Laura Udall, Debbie Miller, Alicia Ahlstrom, Chris Ware, Erik Templin, Peter Galvin, Ed Reynolds, and many friends who read manuscripts, voted on book cover designs, and listened for four years about a book I was writing.

Deborah, for invaluable insights, and our wonderful children.

####

Thank you for reading.

To connect with Brandon about speaking to your organization, visit https://www.brandonpipkin.com

For more personal and organizational development resources, visit https://www.21for21.com

Twitter: @21for21com

Facebook: https://www.facebook.com/21for21

Made in the USA
San Bernardino, CA
15 September 2018